Law, Society, Policy

Series Editor: **Rosie Harding**,
University of Birmingham

Law, Society, Policy offers an outlet for high quality, socio-legal research monographs and edited collections with the potential for policy impact.

Also available in the series

Egalitarian Digital Privacy
Image Based Abuse and Beyond
By **Tsachi Keren-Paz**

Polygamy, Policy and Postcolonialism in English Marriage Law
A Critical Feminist Analysis
By **Zainab Batul Naqvi**

Intersex Embodiment
Legal Frameworks Beyond Identity and Disorder
By **Fae Garland** and **Mitchell Travis**

Unsettling Apologies
Critical Writings on Apology from South Africa
Edited by **Melanie Judge** and **Dee Smythe**

Death, Family and the Law
The Contemporary Inquest in Context
By **Edward Kirton-Darling**

Deprivation of Liberty in the Shadows of the Institution
By **Lucy Series**

Women, Precarious Work and Care
The Failure of Family-friendly Rights
By **Emily Grabham**

Pandemic Legalities
Legal Responses to COVID-19 – Justice and Social Responsibility
Edited by **Dave Cowan** and **Ann Mumford**

Find out more at
bristoluniversitypress.co.uk/law-society-policy

Forthcoming

Observing Justice
Digital Transparency, Openness and Accountability in Criminal Courts
By **Judith Townend** and **Lucy Welsh**

Children's Voices, Family Disputes and Child-Inclusive Mediation
The Right to Be Heard
By **Anne Barlow** and **Jan Ewing**

Adult Social Care Law and Policy
Lessons from the Pandemic
By **Jean McHale** and **Laura Noszlopy**

Sex Worker Rights Activism and the Politics of Rights:
Within and against the Law
By **Katie Cruz**

International advisory board

Find out more at

bristoluniversitypress.co.uk/law-society-policy

FRAGILE RIGHTS

Disability, Public Policy, and Social Change

Anne Revillard

BRISTOL
UNIVERSITY
PRESS

First published in Great Britain in 2023 by

Bristol University Press
University of Bristol
1–9 Old Park Hill
Bristol
BS2 8BB
UK
t: +44 (0)117 374 6645
e: bup-info@bristol.ac.uk

Details of international sales and distribution partners are available at bristoluniversitypress.co.uk

British Library Cataloguing in Publication Data
A catalogue record for this book is available from the British Library

ISBN 978-1-5292-3100-7 hardcover
ISBN 978-1-5292-3101-4 ePub
ISBN 978-1-5292-3102-1 ePdf

Cover design: Andrew Corbett
Front cover image: Shutterstock/MrVander
Bristol University Press uses environmentally responsible print partners.
Printed in Great Britain by CPI Group (UK) Ltd, Croydon, CR0 4YY

FSC
www.fsc.org
MIX
Paper | Supporting responsible forestry
FSC® C013604

Contents

Series Editor's Preface

The Law, Society, Policy series publishes high-quality, socio-legal research monographs and edited collections with the potential for policy impact. Cutting across the traditional divides of legal scholarship, Law, Society, Policy offers an interdisciplinary, policy engaged approach to socio-legal research which explores law in its social and political contexts with a particular focus on the place of law in everyday life.

The series seeks to take an explicitly society-first view of socio-legal studies, with a focus on the ways that law shapes social life, and the constitutive nature of law and society. International in scope, engaging with domestic, international and global legal and regulatory frameworks, texts in the Law, Society, Policy series engage with the full range of socio-legal topics and themes.

List of Figures, Tables, and Boxes

Figure

Tables

Box

List of Abbreviations

AAH	*Allocation aux adultes handicapés* (disabled adult benefit)
ACTP	*Allocation compensatrice pour tierce personne* (third-party compensation benefit)
ADA	Americans with Disabilities Act
Ad'AP	*Agenda d'accessibilité programmée* (programmed accessibility agendas)
AEEH	*Allocation d'éducation de l'enfant handicapé* (disabled child education allowance)
AES	*Allocation d'éducation spéciale* (special education allowance)
Agefiph	*Association de gestion du fonds pour l'insertion professionnelle des personnes handicapées* (association in charge of managing the fund for the professional integration of disabled people)
APF	*Association des paralysés de France* (association of paralysed people)
AVU	*Auxiliares de Vie Universitaire* (university support assistants)
AVS	*Auxiliares de Vie Scolaire* (learning support assistants)
BTS	*Brevet de technicien supérieur* (vocational training certificate)
CAF	*Caisse d'allocations familiales* (family benefit office)
CAP	*Certificat d'aptitude professionnelle* (certificate of professional competence)
CAT	*Centre d'aide par le travail* (sheltered employment centre)
CDAPH	*Commission des droits et de l'autonomie des personnes handicapées* (disabled people's rights and autonomy committee)
CDD	*Contrat à durée déterminée* (fixed-term employment contract)
CDES	*Commission départementale d'éducation spéciale* (local special education commissions)

CDOI	*Commission départementale d'orientation des infirmes* (local commission for the professional orientation of the infirm)
Cotorep	*Commission technique d'orientation et de reclassement professionnel* (technical commissions for vocational guidance and reclassification)
CP	*Cours préparatoire* (preparatory class [for children aged 6–7])
CRPD	UN Convention on the Rights of Persons with Disabilities
EA	*Entreprise adaptée* (adapted enterprise)
ENA	*Ecole nationale d'administration* (national school for the public administration)
ERDV	*École régionale pour déficients visuels* (regional school for the visually impaired)
EREA	*Établissement régional d'enseignement adapté* (regional institution for adapted teaching)
ESAT	*Établissements et services d'aide par le travail* (establishments and services for assistance through work)
EWEPD	European Week for the Employment of People with Disabilities
FIPHFP	*Fonds pour l'insertion des personnes handicapées dans la fonction publique* (Fund for the Integration of Disabled People in the Public Service)
GIAA	*Groupe des Intellectuels Aveugles et Amblyopes* (Group of Blind and Amblyopic Intellectuals)
GIHP	*Groupement des intellectuels handicapés physiques* (group of physically disabled intellectuals)
HALDE	*Haute autorité de lutte contre les discriminations et pour l'égalité* (high authority in charge of the fight against discriminations and for equality)
HR	human resources
IME	*Institut médico-éducatif* (medico-educational institute)
IMP	*Instituts médico-pédagogiques* (medico-educational institutes)
IMPro	*Instituts médico-professionnels* (medico-occupational institutes)
INJA	*Institut national des jeunes aveugles* (national institute for young blind people)
MDPH	*Maison départementale des personnes handicapées* (literally departmental house of disabled people – one-stop shops administering all disability-related provisions at the level of the departments, the 94 French administrative territorial units)

NGO	non-governmental organization
OETH	*Obligation d'emploi des travailleurs handicapés* (obligation to employ disabled workers [quota scheme])
PAM	*Pour aider à la mobilité* (helping with mobility)
PCH	*Prestation de compensation du handicap* (disability compensation benefit)
PMI	*Protection maternelle et infantile* (protection services for mothers and children)
PPS	*Plan personnalisé de scolarisation* (personal education plan)
RQTH	*Reconnaissance de la qualité de travailleur handicapé* (disabled worker administrative status)
RSA	*Revenu de solidarité active* (active solidarity income payment)
S3AIS	*Service aide à l'acquisition de l'autonomie et à l'intégration scolaire* (service for the acquisition of educational independence and integration)
SEGPA	*Sections d'Enseignement Général et Professionnel Adapté* (Specially Adapted Classes for General and Professional Education)
SESSAD	*Services d'éducation spéciale et de soins à domicile* (Special Education and Care at Home Services)
ULIS	*Unités Localisées pour l'Inclusion Scolaire* (Localized Units for School Inclusion)
UN	United Nations
UNESCO	United Nations Educational, Scientific and Cultural Organization

About the Author

Anne Revillard is Associate Professor of Sociology at Sciences Po (Paris). She is the director of the Laboratory for Interdisciplinary Evaluation of Public Policies (LIEPP) and a member of the Centre for Research on Social Inequalities (CRIS). Her research explores the interplay between law, policy/politics, and the contemporary transformations of systems of inequality linked to gender and disability, based on qualitative methods. She has contributed to qualitative policy evaluation through an approach in terms of policy reception, which is illustrated, in this book, by the study of the reception of disability policy in France.

Acknowledgements

I first want to express my deepest gratitude to the people who gave me their trust and time to share their stories with me through biographical interviews. If I have learned a lot in preparing this book, it is above all thanks to them. Several association leaders and a personal assistant were instrumental in helping me to reach these people. I do not name them in order to protect the anonymity of the research participants, but I am deeply thankful for their trust and interest in my project.

This work is based on an original manuscript for a French habilitation to supervise research (HDR), for which I was coached by Virginie Guiraudon: to the kind supervisor, the tireless reviewer, the erudite researcher, the outstanding mentor, but also to the constant friend, I address my sincere thanks. Her unfailing support, her availability and her reviewing helped me considerably in the course of the small and large choices that marked the preparation of the original manuscript. I would also like to thank my first readers, Lilian Mathieu, Jean-François Ravaud, Robin Stryker, Isabelle Ville, and Philippe Warin, who agreed to take time out of their always pressured academic time to read this work and to be part of the HDR committee. Their comments were very useful in the revision of the manuscript for publication.

The research project that gave rise to this manuscript ('The reception of disability policies: a qualitative approach') was financed in 2013 under a call for projects from the Laboratoire interdisciplinaire d'évaluation des politiques publiques (LIEPP). As such, it benefited from a public grant overseen by the French National Research Agency (ANR) as part of the 'Investissements d'Avenir' programme LIEPP (ANR-11-LABX-0091, ANR-11-IDEX-0005–02) and the Université Paris Cité IdEx (ANR-18-IDEX-0001). Beyond the logistical support, the combined scientific contributions of LIEPP and the Observatoire sociologique du changement (OSC – now Research Centre on Social Inequalities [CRIS]) were decisive in the orientation of this research. The regular exchanges at Sciences Po, with my colleagues at LIEPP, OSC, but also at the Centre de sociologie des organisations (CSO) and the Centre d'études européennes et de politique comparée (CEE), have nourished my reflection. For the suggestions and encouragement they gave to this project at different stages of its development, I would like to thank in particular Philippe Bézès, Amélie Corbel, Marta Dominguez-Folgueras, Pierre François, Aden Gaide, Morgane Laouénan, Pierre Lascoumes, Nathalie Morel, Christine Musselin, Étienne Nouguez, Marco Oberti, Bruno Palier, Mirna Safi, Louis-André Vallet, Agnès Van Zanten, Etienne Wasmer, and Cornélia Woll. Discussions with several other researchers have fuelled my thinking on reception processes. I would like to thank Lorenzo Barrault-Stella, Patrice Duran, Pierre Muller, Jean-Pierre Nioche, Héléna Revil, Madina Rival, and Philippe Warin.

This research also extends the work I have been doing for several years in the sociology of law, as part of American (Law and Society Association) and French (Réseau thématique 'sociologie du droit et de la justice' [RT13] of the French Sociological Association) collectives. I wish to thank Katharina Heyer for introducing me to the disability rights movement, and of course, David Engel and Franck Munger for the inspiration – reading *Rights of Inclusion* formed the initial motivation for this research. The advice and encouragement of Jennifer Fredette, Anna-Maria Marshall, Sagit Mor, and Robin Stryker has always been welcome and helpful. Without being able to list all the RT13 faithful members, I warmly thank Vincent-Arnaud Chappe, Jacques Commaille, Claire de Galembert, and Martine Kaluszynski, who gave me their support throughout this work. Thanks to Pierre-Yves Baudot for all the pages written together on the politics of rights, which inspired the following ones.

My thematic conversion towards the sociology of disability was welcomed and accompanied with openness and kindness by several specialists in the field, who contributed to making this turning point an exciting experience. I am particularly grateful to Emmanuelle Fillion, Jean-François Ravaud, and Isabelle Ville, who, thanks to the seminars of the Programme handicap et société (PHS) and ALTER conferences, introduced me to a fulfilling research group in which I am delighted to participate. I would also like to thank Emeline Brulé and Aude Lejeune for our discussions about this project and their insights into different aspects of disability policy implementation. A big thank you to Mark Priestley, Anna Lawson, Angharad Beckett, and all the team of the Centre for Disability Studies in Leeds for their welcome and our exchanges in autumn 2019.

I want to thank Patrick Le Galès and Pierre François for welcoming this proposal for an initial publication in French in the 'Gouvernances' collection at the Presses de Sciences Po, and I am very grateful to Rosie Harding for the enthusiasm with which she received my proposal for a translation as part as the *Law, Society, Policy* series at Bristol University Press. Warm thanks to the whole team at Bristol University Press, especially Becky Taylor, for their very efficient support at all stages of the process. Five anonymous reviewers, as well as Rosie Harding and Becky Taylor, provided very useful feedback in view of the translation, which helped me make a few modifications from the original French book in order to make it more accessible and relevant to an international audience. The time and energy they gave to this task, and their most relevant comments, were very much appreciated.

John Angell, Jessica Edwards, Jennifer Higgins, and Aline Tertre delivered the first versions of the translations of the chapters. Edouard Crocq and Léo Le Roux provided crucial help with formatting.

Finally, I would like to thank the wonderful close support team who supported me and bore with me during the preparation of the original manuscript and its revision for publication: Sophie Kaufman, Mariel Revillard, the Wakim and Kaufman families, Laure Bereni, Reguina Hatzipétrou-Andronikou, Alban Jacquemart, Alexandre Jaunait, Catherine Marry, Sylvain Parasie, Bibia Pavard, Elsa Valtat, and of course, above all, Ziad Wakim, Maya and Elie Wakim-Revillard.

1

Introduction

AR: [The 2005 Act] placed a major emphasis on the rights of disabled people, on citizenship. What does that discourse mean to you?

CL: Well I think there's a lot of blather really. It's a lot of hot air. That's what they say on the face of it, in the media, but behind the talk there aren't necessarily things being put in place. I think there's still an overall mentality – I don't know if it's specific to France or if it's actually specific to disability, but I've had people who've looked elsewhere tell me it's not the same in other places. [In France] there's a real problem recognizing a person with a disability as a person. […] Everyone's happy to talk about disability because it's good to, it's trendy; they're always keen to respect 'the poor old disabled … they're people above all'. But afterwards, in practice, that's not where we're at. (Chloé Lamarche, 23-year-old blind student, April 2015)

Disability has long been perceived as a personal medical issue – having a physical, sensory, or cognitive impairment.[1] But it is also a social reality, often synonymous with poverty, lack of accessibility, powerlessness, and inferior social status (not being 'recognized as a person'). For several decades now, social movements and public policies in their wake have been challenging the inequalities tied to the social treatment of disability, particularly through the use of rights framing.

What does the recognition of rights in public policy change for the social experience of disability? Are rights just 'blather', out of step with what happens 'in practice', or do they have real effects in people's lives? Or, to move past this alternative, are some of their effects not linked precisely to the opportunity they give Chloé Lamarche to denounce them as 'a lot of blather'? This book examines the consequences of disability policy in terms of the realization of the rights of people with visual or mobility impairments in France.

Such an inquiry requires us first to identify the various ways in which rights are mobilized in public policy, from speeches and legislation to policies intended to make rights effective. But we must also clarify how the rights angle can provide a productive framework for understanding the consequences of policy on the transformation of disability-related inequalities. In other words, how do rights have the potential to bring about social change?

The role of public policy in realizing – or not realizing – this potential is captured in this book through the experiences of disabled people. Their stories, collected through biographical interviews, are analysed from a perspective that combines the contributions of the sociology of public policy (a reception-focused approach) and the sociology of law (the study of rights realization at the individual level).

Disability policy, rights, and social change

The experience of disability simultaneously implies the experience of certain physical, sensory, cognitive, or psychological characteristics that lead to long-term impairments, and the experience of the social treatment associated with them.[2] Public policy affects both dimensions: while health policies impact the medical aspects, many other policies influence the social aspects of the experience of disability, which reflect the position afforded to disabled people in society. These interventions concern different sectors (education, employment, social policies, transport, urban planning, and so on), and are based on various definitions of disability, including in terms of the types of disability recognized. Some policies only target certain areas or types of disability (for example, work-related accidents), while others are more comprehensive and raise the question of the position of disabled people in society more explicitly (for example, the French 1975 Framework Act for Disabled People). Disability policies are also diverse in their orientations: they can be egalitarian or based on the idea of inequality (for example, the right to non-discrimination versus wage reduction), inclusive or segregative (for example, education in a mainstream environment or a specialized institution).

In this book, I examine these policies in terms of their role in realizing the rights of disabled people, starting with the idea that the effectiveness of rights, when confirmed, has the potential to bring about social change and improve the position of this group in society. These rights should not be understood in a strictly legal sense. They are first of all 'moral claims' (Sen 2004: 319), which are not necessarily translated into legislation or case law, but are also turned to symbolic and discursive uses (Scheingold 1974). A policy may, to varying degrees, use the reference to rights discursively and frame its purpose in terms of rights. But rights can also be legally recognized and give rise to the creation of policy instruments (Lascoumes and Le Galès

2005) intended to promote their effectiveness, which Pierre-Yves Baudot and I have termed 'rights policy' (Baudot and Revillard 2015). These factors are not necessarily linked. Legal reforms are not always accompanied by the dissemination of a rights discourse. Conversely, a rights discourse does not always translate into law and even less into policy instruments to ensure the effectiveness of the rights that have been recognized (Lascoumes and Le Galès 2005). Rights can thus remain 'empty promises', without legal expression (Hafner-Burton 2005).

Consideration of these different levels of analysis and different types of rights (civil, political, economic, and social) calls for us to re-examine a classic narrative that dates the rise of a 'rights model' in disability policy from the last third of the 20th century (Waddington 1994; Heyer 2015). The rise of a rights discourse and the legal entrenchment of anti-discrimination rights indeed occurred in recent decades, and can be linked to international dynamics. Yet while disability rights have been transformed by these dynamics, they have older origins, which relate to social rights rather than civil rights.

The international origins of the rights framing

The framing of disability as an individual rights issue and the proliferation of references to rights in this area have been fostered since the 1970s by the rise of a disability rights movement, which has asserted itself on the political scene in several countries and in international arenas, particularly the United Nations (UN) (Vanhala 2011; Heyer 2015). As with movements challenging the oppression of other social groups (women, ethno-racial, or sexual minorities), this movement theorized society's oppression of disabled people (Abberley 1987). To this end, it pointed out that disability results at least as much from environmental obstacles (stairs) and social obstacles (discrimination) as from individual impairments (paraplegia). Traditionally considered a personal and medical characteristic, disability was rethought by the 'social model' in its structural and social dimension (Oliver 1990). The theorization of disability as a social injustice rather than an individual tragedy was a powerful driver of demands for rights for disabled people on egalitarian grounds.

The movement led to the establishment of new legal rights. In the United States, the Americans with Disabilities Act (ADA) of 1990 defined a legal framework prohibiting discrimination that includes the provision of 'reasonable accommodations', based on the observation that equal treatment alone is not enough to ensure justice for disabled people. The Act requires employers to provide their employees with the job accommodations they need to work effectively and to take possible accommodations into account when comparing job applications. In other words, the principle of reasonable accommodations recognizes that equality can, and in some cases must, be achieved through differential treatment (Minow 1990). Disability rights are thus understood in the United States chiefly as civil rights (the right to non-discrimination), whereas the UN has defined disability rights more broadly as human rights, including social rights.

The first UN Declaration on the Rights of Disabled Persons was adopted in 1975, followed by a World Program of Action (1982), a UN Decade of Disabled Persons (1983–1992), and the adoption of the Standard Rules on the Equalization of Opportunities for Persons with Disabilities in 1993. Finally, the UN Convention on the Rights of Persons with Disabilities (CRPD) was adopted in 2006 following extensive consultation with non-governmental organizations (NGOs) active in this field and is now the main legal reference at the international level. The Convention defines the rights of people with disabilities broadly, as human rights, including economic and social rights as well as the right to non-discrimination and reasonable accommodations. The assertion of a right to inclusion fostered the principle of universal design, which holds that places and services must be made accessible to as many people as possible from the outset, thereby limiting the need for specific adjustments. Even as it covers a wide range of rights, the CRPD gives a very precise definition of each of them. Furthermore, advanced monitoring systems have been set up to support implementation and thereby improve rights' effectiveness (Flynn 2011; Pinto 2011; Lawson and Priestley 2013).

The US and UN texts inspired similar shifts towards a rights model in many other countries and within the European institutions (Waldschmidt 2009; Halvorsen et al 2017). At the level of the (then) European Community, a similar shift from the medical to the social model of disability was first embodied by the 1996 New Community Disability Strategy, yet at a time when the European Community had limited leverage to impose policy orientations in this matter on member states. The promotion of a rights approach was then reasserted and given further potential by the 1999 Treaty of Amsterdam, which gave the newly created European Union (EU) a competence to combat disability discrimination (Waddington and Broderick 2020). This translated into the adoption of Directive 2000/78/EC of 27 November 2000 establishing a general framework for equal treatment in employment and occupation, which prohibited disability discrimination and imposed that employers provide reasonable accommodations to disabled workers. This was complemented by other EU legislation notably regarding accessibility. The 2000 Charter of Fundamental Rights of the EU includes a broader prohibition of discrimination. This led to the adoption of a 2003–2010 Disability Action Plan, followed by a European Disability Strategy 2010–2020. Disability law thus has become over the years an important component of EU policy, following an approach based on the assertion of disability rights and disability mainstreaming.

The development of rights-based policies at the national level, however, does not only result from the transnational diffusion of norms. When we consider these rights more broadly, their histories also have specifically national origins. France is a case in point.

Older social rights

The Act of 11 February 2005 'for the equal rights and opportunities, participation and citizenship of disabled people', which has since functioned as the main blueprint for French disability policy, marked the endorsement of disability rights discourse in France. References to the UN CRPD, EU legislation, or any other international dynamic, however, have been strikingly absent from the debates leading to the adoption of this law (Baudot 2018). Unlike other European countries where references to supranational rights are more common, especially through the activism of disability rights organizations (Vanhala 2015; Halvorsen et al 2017), these are very rare in France, and were largely absent from policy debates until a the 2017 visit to France of the UN Special Rapporteur on the rights of persons with disabilities, Catalina Devandas-Aguilar.

Far from being simply the repercussion of international rights rhetoric in the title of a law, the uses of rights in French disability policy must be viewed more broadly. It is important to consider the plurality of meanings that rights have been given, how long they have been recognized, and the coexistence of this rights framing with other approaches.

In many countries, what can be retrospectively analysed as 'disability policies' first took the form of sector-based interventions targeting specific groups, according to the type of disability (motor, sensory, intellectual, or cognitive) or to their origin (work-related accidents, war). These measures came under social policy in a broad sense: welfare, education, and health and social care (Ville et al 2014).

In France, before the rise of state social policy at the turn of the 20th century, the first state interventions targeting people who today would be described as disabled were mainly based on the principle of assistance, which was variously combined, depending on the period, with care in separate institutions, work placement, and educational ambitions. An education policy began to take shape in the 18th century, first concerned with deaf and blind children and then, in the 19th century, with children referred to at the time as 'idiots' or 'abnormal', who became the target of special education (Act of 1909). Yet children with severe intellectual impairments or multiple impairments long remained excluded from these educational interventions and were confined to their families or to care in asylums. Mobilization by parents and child psychiatrists led in the 1950s and 1960s to the development of specialized institutions for this group: medico-educational institutes (*instituts médico-pédagogiques* [IMP]), medico-occupational institutes (*instituts médico-professionnels* [IMPro]), and following on from them, sheltered employment centres (*Centres d'aide par le travail* [CAT]) for adults. Born of civil society initiatives, these facilities gradually came to form one of the pillars of the health and social care sector, in which the state intervened as funder and regulator without challenging the role of non-profit organizations as policy implementers (Cret et al 2013). Yet until 1975 at least, these educational and social interventions were not so much a matter of rights as of 'favours' (Buton 2009).

In parallel, disability (as it is known today) was central to the emergence of the welfare state in France, in both its insurance and assistance components, through the enactment of social rights. The first major piece of social legislation, the 1898 Act on work-related accidents, fell within this domain – which it addressed by targeting a group defined based on the origin of disability (a work-related accident). Following an insurance logic, work-related accidents were thought of as a collective risk that should automatically entitle the worker to compensation, regardless of who was at fault (Ewald 1986). At the same time, the Act of 14 July 1905 introduced the principle of a right to welfare for the 'aged, infirm, and incurable' at the national level, and set out its modes of delivery. During the First World War, collective compensation for work-related accidents extended to disabled military veterans while changing in its form: compensation was not just thought of in terms of pension, but came to include rehabilitation (provisions intended to enable beneficiaries to return to work). In 1945, disability insurance coverage was extended to all workers with the integration of the 'disability risk' into the general public health care system (*Sécurité sociale*). The 1971 and 1975 Acts, for their part, consolidated the principle of a right to welfare by introducing a minimum income for adults with disabilities with the disabled adult benefit (*Allocation aux adultes handicapés* [AAH]).

In the area of employment, the context of the First World War thus gave rise to the idea of rehabilitation, reversing the traditional definition of disability (or 'infirmity', in the terms of the time) as being unfit for work: with adequate medical and functional interventions and vocational training, disabled people could take up or return to an occupation (Stiker 2013). Initially conceived of in reference to disabled military veterans, this change of perspective was reappropriated by the victims of work-related accidents and other 'civilian' disabled people, leading to the development of a whole series of measures promoted by several charities and associations.

Rehabilitation centres and job support schemes added to legislative measures to promote the employment of disabled persons in 'ordinary' settings, from the introduction of 'reserved jobs' in the public sector and the 'employment obligation' for disabled veterans under the Acts of 1916 and 1924, to the 'employment priority' defined by the 1957 Act and the 'employment obligation' introduced in 1987. These measures, corresponding to various forms of quota schemes, can be analysed in terms of social rights, or even positive discrimination, with the right to access schemes designed to facilitate employment. Employment under the obligation to employ disabled workers (*obligation d'emploi des travailleurs handicapés* [OETH]) was conditioned on the worker being recognized administratively as a disabled worker through a specific status, the *Reconnaissance de la qualité de travailleur handicapé* (RQTH). In parallel, starting in the 1950s, work centres formed a sheltered employment sector, the consequences of which are harder to describe in terms of rights. It is firmly discredited by the proponents of the anti-discrimination model, who denounce its segregating effects and the sub-citizenship it induces (in France, in the health and social care sector, sheltered work is in derogation of labour law) (Heyer 2005). It nonetheless gives access to work to people for whom mainstream work settings remain very unwelcoming, particularly those with intellectual or psychiatric disabilities (Blanc 1999).

Following and building on these sector-specific interventions, the Framework Act for Disabled People of 30 June 1975 marked the emergence of an integrated policy for this social group, more directly raising the question of their position in society. At the time, this position was described relatively rarely in terms of individual rights. The reference to rights is indeed present in the explanatory memorandum of the bill, the first objective of which was 'to affirm as a whole the rights of the disabled person and at the same time indicate the means of their effective implementation'.[3] In the text of the Act itself, however, the position of disabled people in society is described not so much in terms of individual rights as in terms of a 'national obligation' from a much more holistic perspective: it is the nation's responsibility to give disabled people the position they should have. There is no logical contradiction between these two perspectives: an individual's right is a nation's duty. But at the discursive level, it is the collective dimension that is emphasized rather than individual rights. This Act addressed all areas covered by pre-existing measures (education, employment, social protection) while adding new ones, in particular the accessibility of the built environment and transport, and public information.

While not yet prominent in 1975, the reference to rights became central in the Act of 11 February 2005, which in its very title framed the issue of the position of disabled people in society in terms of 'equal rights and opportunities, participation, and citizenship'. The principles of 'non-discrimination', 'equal rights and opportunities', 'access to *droit commun*',[4] 'equal access', and 'full citizenship' are repeated throughout the explanatory memorandum. The means envisaged for this policy are largely in keeping with those of 1975: schooling, access to employment, social welfare, and accessibility. Yet they are strengthened compared to the previous Act. As regards education, the 2005 Act promotes the principle of inclusion in a mainstream setting more clearly than before, even if it leaves open the possibility of schooling in a specialized institution (see Chapter 2). In the field of employment, it strengthens the quota scheme, as well as introducing the principles of non-discrimination and reasonable accommodations (see Chapter 3). In terms of social policy, it innovates by establishing the principle of a universal right to compensation for the consequences of disability, in the form of a new disability compensation benefit (*Prestation de compensation du handicap* [PCH]). Allocated without means testing, this benefit is intended to compensate for a wide range of disability-related costs (human, technical, and animal assistance, housing or vehicle modifications, additional transport costs, and so on). It differs in its conception from the income security provided by the disabled adult benefit (see Chapter 4). Finally, regarding accessibility, the Act sets an obligation to bring the built environment and transport up to the required standards within ten years, which amounts to establishing, by way of a regulatory obligation at the collective, national level, a right to accessibility for individuals (see Chapter 5).

Thus, in the 2005 Act, as in the UN provisions, different types of rights coexist. Added to the long-recognized social rights that were strengthened by the creation of the disability compensation benefit are the right to non-discrimination in employment (and, more tentatively, in education, with the promotion of mainstream inclusion that does not preclude the possibility of special education) and the right to accessibility. These rights, resulting from the layering of successive measures, may seem partly contradictory in their orientations, between equality and potentially depreciatory protection, between integration and separation. The Act also promotes users' procedural rights through a process of administrative simplification designed to place them 'at the heart of the system'. This involved the creation of department-level agencies,[5] the *Maisons départementales des personnes handicapées* (MDPH), 'one-stop shops' responsible for determining eligibility for social entitlements and providing guidance in accessing the various disability policy instruments (Baudot et al 2013; Perrier 2013). The promotion of 'equal rights and opportunities, participation, and citizenship' therefore involves the recognition of a series of rights for disabled people, some of which are old, some new or renewed.

To sum up, in France, the legal recognition of rights for disabled people (initially known by other names) preceded the rise of rights rhetoric that marked the last third of the 20th century at the international level. The first rights to be recognized were social rights (insurance coverage for work-related accidents), followed by employment rights that constituted forms of affirmative action (reserved jobs, quotas), long before the idea of anti-discrimination policies emerged. Despite these legally enshrined rights, the rights discourse that was constructed internationally (drawing particularly on the American example) based on other rights (equality, accessibility) was slow to assert itself in France. For a long time, the question of the position of disabled people in society was more commonly phrased in holistic terms ('national obligation', 'solidarity') than in terms of subjective rights. The legally recognized rights of disabled people have nonetheless progressed, both in terms of social rights and non-discrimination rights (non-discrimination in employment, accessibility of the built environment and transport, and school inclusion). It is only since 2005 that these legal provisions have been accompanied by the rise, at a more symbolic level, of a rights discourse in public policy.

Rights realization and social change

In what way are rights a potential vehicle for social change for disabled people? From Marshall's classic analyses of social rights (Marshall 1950) to the more recent research of the law and society movement (Haglund and Stryker 2015), many models have theorized the impact of rights on various dimensions of social inequality. In the area of disability, the rights listed thus far are liable to affect the social experience of disability in terms of classic Weberian criteria for analysing inequalities (material resources, social status, and power), but also in terms of the mode of existence (an existence separate from or integrated with the rest of society).[6] For example, social rights in the form of benefits (the disabled adult benefit, disability compensation benefit, and disability pensions) have a direct impact on material resources. The right to education is decisive in that it conditions the socio-professional category to which an individual may have access; but it also has more immediate consequences on the mode of existence, in opposite ways depending on whether it is conceived as a right to special education or to inclusion in mainstream schools. The mode of existence is also centrally affected by the right to accessibility (to which spaces does a person have access?). The right to non-discrimination, meanwhile, has a potential impact on the social status of disabled people (the consideration due to them or that they feel from others), by calling for them to be treated equally (Engel and Munger 2003).

But beyond their content, rights impact the social experience of disability in different ways according to how they are realized.[7] Their reach depends on the confidence individuals have in their sustainability and their consistent implementation throughout the country (temporal and geographical stability that reduces uncertainty). But it also hinges on the degree to which individuals feel they are treated as subjects of rights. This symbolic – and essential – dimension can be relatively independent of the formal criteria of due process. For example, an administrative decision issued on time but involving condescending and infantilizing treatment may well respect due process, and yet the person concerned is unlikely to feel he or she has been considered a subject of rights. This dimension interacts closely with social status. Representations of disability affect whether people are treated as subjects of rights or not and, in return, the recognition that disabled people receive or fail to receive in situations of (non-)realization of their rights affects their perception of their social status.[8] As such, the potential for social change linked to rights must be measured with respect to two distinct criteria: having rights, but also being the subject of rights.

For this potential to be realized, the theoretically stated rights must become effective for the individuals they target. By rights realization, I mean the degree to which and the processes through which rights become real (Revillard 2019c). The notion does not necessarily mean that rights are realized, even if I do not systematically remind the reader of this by writing '(non-)realization'. It aims to capture the full range of possibilities between non- and full effectiveness of rights. Rights realization is commonly considered based on quantified results (how many disabled children attend school, what proportion of schools are accessible, and so on). I approach it instead from the perspective of the processes involved. Through what mechanisms do rights become effective? In the existing literature, two scales of analysis of these processes can be distinguished. The first, at an intermediate level, focuses on institutional and non-profit intermediaries involved in rights realization (Stryker 2007; Haglund and Stryker 2015). The second, which I adopt in this research, is micro-sociological and examines how individuals experience rights. This approach nonetheless requires at least a basic knowledge of the institutional context, which I will discuss briefly before returning to it in the chapters to come.

Due to the plurality of rights and areas concerned (education, employment, social welfare, architecture, and transport, and so on), the realization of disability rights involves a wide range of institutions and organizations. Since 2005, the MDPHs are supposed to act as a 'one-stop shop' through which individuals can access a range of rights, statuses, and mechanisms related to disability[9] (disability card, parking permit, social benefits, referral to specialized institutions, and so on). At the same time, several other public authorities and agencies are involved in rights realization: the family benefits office (*Caisses d'allocations familiales* [CAF]), department councils, job centres (*Pôle emploi*), specialized work placement agencies (*Cap Emploi*), and the Ombudsman (Défenseur des droits 2015). The implementation of employment rights depends on companies and public authorities as employers. Accessibility also concerns both public and private actors, as it concerns all facilities that are open to the public. Within this multitude of public and private actors involved in the production of public policy and the realization of disability rights, the role of associations must be underscored (Barral 2007). Historically, non-profits have played a key role in this sector, both through their mobilization for social rights and rehabilitation, and later for the rights to education and accessibility, but also by being the driving force behind the main institutions and services. They therefore combine activist and administrative stances, in what is sometimes an uneasy relationship between their critique of public authorities and their use as an instrument of disability policies (Revillard, 2017b).

Between non-profits, the private sector and public institutions at different levels of government (from the UN to the municipal accessibility commission), disability policy is a good example of public policy that brings together a plurality of actors to achieve collective goals (Duran 2009) – goals that are themselves complicated to articulate. To complement the many studies in France that explore various aspects of these intertwining mechanisms and orientations (which will be discussed in the following chapters), I shift the attention away from the definition and implementation of disability policy in favour of studying its reception by individuals, to directly address the question of its consequences.

From policies to individuals

Analysing the work of various intermediaries in policy implementation provides only a vague indication of the consequences of public policies. If we believe, in line with the perspective adopted here, that what is at stake in disability policy is the position of disabled people in society, then it is in the experience of these people that the policy's consequences materialize and must be assessed. It is there, ultimately, that rights are realized or not, and that public policy has an effect or not. I consider the relationship individuals have with public policy using the concept of reception.

Studying policy reception

Seen from the individuals' point of view, public policy can be described in terms of its effects, but also of the uses to which it is put. A policy produces effects: for example, minimum social benefits impact beneficiaries' level of income; the promotion of school inclusion and accessibility encourages desegregation (sharing public places with nondisabled people rather than being confined to separate institutions or transport). But individuals also reappropriate public policy. Its orientations are subject to interpretations. People may or may not take up the social benefits they are eligible for. They use the measures in a certain way and sometimes refuse, bypass, or contest them. Because these two dynamics are linked in the individual experience, it is worth studying the effects and uses of public policy together.

While relatively little research has been done in the sociology of public policy on the interaction between effects and uses in the individual relationship to a system,[10] it has been studied in the sociology of culture. Sociologists of culture have theorized the concept of reception to reflect this twofold dynamic. In this field, the concept's *raison d'être* lies in the idea that one cannot deduce the effects from the intentions, conditions of production, or characteristics of the product or producers; reception 'is not the passive absorption of pre-constructed meanings, but the site of meaning production' (Dayan 1992: 144).

Following on from this usage in the sociology of culture, I employ the term 'policy reception' to refer to all the processes through which a given public policy is appropriated and co-constructed by the individuals it targets, and through which it produces its effects on them (Revillard 2018). It is therefore a matter of simultaneously capturing the effects on and the uses of a policy by the individuals it targets, whether or not they are aware of the policy or use the measures it implies (Warin 1999). These effects and uses have both objective and subjective dimensions. The effects of policy are partly material (what level of income do people have? Where do they live? Where do they go to school?), but also correspond to a shaping of individual subjectivity (shaping of categories of thought, perception of one's social status and that of others).

Similarly, the idea of appropriation encompasses both representations and practices. What do those targeted know about the policy in question, and what do they think about it? The meanings associated with the policy are often marked by the way the policy itself characterizes its target population (Schneider and Ingram 1997). The relationship to the measures thus brings into play the identification or refusal to identify as a target. The subjective relationship to public policy is therefore partly compelled by the policy itself. A policy, in its definition and especially in its implementation, influences the meaning ascribed to it. But the individuals it targets also appropriate it differently according, among other things, to social determinants such as social class, gender, generation, and so on. They have room for interpretation and translate it into terms that make sense in relation to their own lives. Inextricably, the reception of a policy involves practices, ranging from compliance with the institutional script to circumvention, adaptation, and non-use (Dubois 2010; Spire 2011; Barrault 2014). As with representations, these practices are partly dictated by the policy: to have a chance of receiving a particular benefit, one must fill out a particular form. But individuals also have variable degrees of leeway, which leads them to turn the policy to unintended uses, to bypass it, or to resist it (Scott 1991).

Moreover, if we adopt a radically sociological definition of these appropriations, they can be analysed as a part of public policy itself. Indeed, the lay uses and representations of public policy, particularly when they deviate from the institutional script, must not, in my view, be understood as merely distortions, failures, or unintended consequences of policy, but as a part of what builds its social reality. This is why I talk about a policy 'co-constructed' by the individuals it targets. Such a change of perspective in the study of public policy builds on the shift initiated by Michael Lipsky, with regard to the work of street-level bureaucrats, when he emphasized their role in the making of public policy and not only in its more or less faithful execution (Lipsky 1980). Similarly, reception can be analysed as 'a "moment" in the production process' (Hall 1973: 3) of public policy if we consider policy in its social reality, as it matters to people, and not from an institutional point of view. In 'bringing everyday life to policy analysis' (Naples 1998), the aim is to give a radically decentred definition of public policies based on what they represent for the groups they target. To take an example developed in Chapter 4, the seemingly common representation of the disability compensation benefit as a welfare benefit despite its universal coverage (that is, it is not means-tested) is part of the benefit's reality, of what it *is* socially. And this representation, insofar as it is widely shared, helps to define the benefit at least as much as the legal texts that underpin it.

A reception-based approach therefore makes it possible to study the effects and uses of public policy jointly, through an interpretative perspective centred on individuals.

The role of public policy in rights realization

To what extent does the reception of public policy enable disability rights to become effective in people's experience? In law and society scholarship, the question of rights realization at the individual level has mainly been addressed through the prism of rights activation, notably through court action. This is consistent with the US context of 'litigious policy', a system of policymaking which relies on litigation for its implementation (Burke 2002). Litigation and collective legal mobilization, however, are only one of the possible ways individuals may strive to make their rights real. Due to the lesser prominence of courts in the French political system, they are likely to be less central than in other contexts. Moreover, an approach in terms of policy reception paves the way for a more comprehensive perspective on how rights may be made real, through individual activation but also through policy implementation (Revillard 2019c).

Indeed, in accordance with the two aspects of reception (effects and uses), rights realization is a matter both of mechanisms specific to public policy and of appropriation by those it targets. Certain direct effects of public policy shape individual experience. And vice versa, individuals act to promote the realization of their rights, including by using policy mechanisms or orientations. For example, in an urban and architectural environment designed for universal accessibility, the right to accessibility is effective for people without them having to take any particular steps. On the other hand, social rights, to become effective, require individuals to submit applications to the relevant agencies (for example, in the case of the disabled adult benefit, the MDPH, which rules on eligibility, and then the CAF, which pays the benefit). These two facets of public policy have been theorized in the sociology of law through a distinction between the constitutive and instrumental dimensions of law (Stryker 2003). While in its constitutive dimension, law shapes individual subjectivities (and bodies and environments, as this example shows), its instrumental dimension refers to the more conscious uses that individuals make of it.

But understanding rights from an interpretative, individual-level perspective also leads us to decouple them from the scope of legally recognized rights, as is called for in legal consciousness studies. This field of research focuses on ordinary people's relationship to the law. In accordance with the two dimensions of law mentioned earlier, the idea is to study both how the law shapes social interactions, including at a distance from legal institutions, and how these interactions help define the social reality of the law (referred to as 'legality'), what it represents, and how it materializes for individuals in everyday life (Ewick and Silbey 1998). Legal consciousness studies thus explore 'lay' conceptions of law and rights. From a rights perspective, this means focusing on what an individual believes they have a right to, regardless of whether or how this claim translates into law (Minow 1987). From this perspective, rights realization corresponds not only to a more or less successful implementation of legally recognized rights, but also to a process in which individuals seek through various means to turn into a reality what they believe they are entitled to.[11] This 'rights consciousness' (Fleury-Steiner and Nielsen 2006) can build on public policy (and often on collective mobilization) but is not necessarily confined to it. A focus on individuals makes it possible to identify sources of innovation in terms of rights, through novel claims to rights that are not (yet) legally recognized (Lovell 2012). More generally, individual narratives reveal how rights are reinterpreted, how they make sense to people.

The concepts of policy reception and rights realization thus allow me to operationalize my initial question about the consequences that mobilizing rights in public policy has on the social experience of disability. Studying the reception of these disability policies as rights-based policies amounts to studying the relationship of individuals to a set of flexible rights, measures, and discourses of varying temporalities (some very old, others more recent). Public policy increasingly addresses the issue of the position of disabled people in society in terms of rights. It legally recognizes a number of their rights and has put measures in place to make those rights effective. This policy helps shape individuals' 'rights consciousness', in the sense of their perception of their 'legitimate social entitlements' (McCann 2006: xii). More structurally, it determines certain parameters of their existence, which may be very material (for example, the presence of access ramps at the entrance to public buildings; audible traffic signals). As the direct outcome of public policy, some rights are therefore likely to be realized without being mediated by people's appropriation of them. Others have to be consciously claimed, mobilized, and sometimes fought for if they are to be realized. Just as the individual relationship to public policy can be understood in terms of the effects or uses of policies, rights realization can be experienced, at the individual level, as self-evident or as the result of an action – with a whole continuum possible between these two extremes. To answer my initial question, I propose to trace out these modes of rights realization in individuals' experience (which rights are concerned and how are they realized?), paying particular attention to the way they interrelate with policy reception: how does the reception of public policy allow rights to be realized? To do so, I rely on biographical interviews.

A study based on biographical interviews

In-depth semi-structured interviews are a classic methodological tool in both disability studies and legal consciousness studies (Ewick and Silbey 1998; Engel and Munger 2003; Shah and Priestley 2011; Malhotra and Rowe 2014; Beadle Brown et al 2018). This research relies more specifically on biographical interviews, semi-structured interviews that elicit a narrative of a person's lived experience, and whose guide broadly follows the person's life course. This method is auspicious for studying policy reception because of its ability to bring to light the interconnection between the effects and the appropriation of policy. Capturing social structures by looking at the course of individual lives is a classic justification for the use of biographical interviews (Bertaux 2016). Similarly, this method makes it possible to trace the effects of policies based on the narrative of people's life experiences. For example, a person's account of their conditions of schooling reflects a given state of educational policies and the way this effect is modulated by other social factors (parental support, location, gender, and social class). But this method also reveals individuals' capacity for action and interpretation: 'biographies make society and are not simply made by it' (Rustin 2006: 147). Biographical interviews therefore make it possible to document the appropriation of public policy by the people it targets, which speaks to social change. For instance, the change in the position of disabled people in French society results not only from the effects of legislation requiring facilities open to the public to be made accessible, but also from all the struggles and negotiations of disabled pupils and students to obtain the accommodations necessary for real inclusion at school and university. Finally, the stories contained in those narratives are 'subversive stories' as well as 'hegemonic tales' (Ewick and Silbey 1995). The interviews show people distancing themselves from public policy, through avoidance or non-use but also critical use or various means of protest.

The life stories at the heart of this study are also a product of it, the result of an interaction between initiatives on my part (the choice of intermediaries for initiating contact, methods of presenting the study, questioning and follow-up techniques) and on the part of the interviewees (coming across an interview request, agreement to participate, statements made). I sought to reach 'ordinary' people targeted by the policies in question, defining 'ordinary' as someone not involved in policy implementation (a 'layperson') and distant from activist collectives. I was careful to include people who do not necessarily engage with the measures in question and to ensure a diversity of social and generational profiles. I limited my study to people with mobility or visual impairments – disabilities that public policy has long recognized – to facilitate analysis of the specific effects of the 2005 reform. This last objective also led me to restrict the scope of the study to people who have had a disability for more than 15 years. These two criteria (type and age of disability) were made explicit in the call for participants (see Appendix 1).

The participants include 17 women and 13 men, aged 23 to 75 years. Fifteen have a visual impairment and 15 have a mobility impairment. Two-thirds of those were diagnosed in childhood. The participants are from diverse social backgrounds and age groups, and their levels of education range from no diploma with schooling interrupted at the end of junior high school, to a doctorate. A third of them live solely on the disabled adult benefit and are far removed from the labour market. The others have jobs of varying degrees of stability and prestige, from sheltered employment to university professor. Most of them (21 participants) were living in the Paris region at the time of the study (but the majority had also lived in other cities), and nine in other medium or large French cities or their outskirts. Almost all currently live in independent housing or with their parents (with two exceptions, one person in a hotel and one in a residential institution), but many have had experiences of living in an institution, either during their schooling (boarding school) or as adults (rehabilitation centre).

The interview situations were marked by the difference in disability status between a nondisabled researcher and interviewees with disabilities. This difference necessarily influenced the conduct of the interviews and what was said, in ways that I cannot claim to capture entirely. To avoid reproducing certain misconceptions that nondisabled people may have of disability, I tended to avoid mentioning the medical and psychological aspects – at the risk, perhaps, of underestimating them – and tied my conduct of the interviews to the social model of disability (focusing on social and environmental barriers). This difference in disability status may have caused some reserve among the people I interviewed on certain subjects, although I cannot identify any topic that was unanimously set aside; the relationship of trust that the interpretative approach encourages was generally established without major difficulty.

To gain this interpretative grasp of how policies make sense for people without focusing the questioning on public policy, I elicited a narrative of the interviewees' entire lived experience, including family context, the onset of disability, schooling, housing, marital status and family life in adulthood, career path, description of current daily life, leisure, and political participation. The intention was to capture how the reference to the various policy mechanisms or orientations emerged as their narratives unfolded. My interview guide (see Appendix 1) also included more specific questions on these measures, which I introduced, if necessary, when they were brought up (for example, administrative procedures, receipt of a given benefit, and so on). I kept a set of questions more explicitly focused on public policy for the end of the interview (for example, perception of the 2005 Act and the role of non-profit organizations).

The empirical material that forms the basis of my analysis is the result of these singular interactions. In reading what follows, it is important to keep in mind the inevitable selection biases linked not only to the acceptance of the interview proposal (volunteers may be more liable to have complaints to voice) but also to the interview situation itself: for example, difficulties with the administration are more memorable than smoother interactions and may be more readily verbalized. The effects of the chosen method may therefore lead to positive experiences in the relationship to public policy being underestimated. Moreover, in taking an interpretative approach, I deliberately chose to adopt the point of view of the interviewees; this means that I did not attempt to check the veracity of their statements, but rather to understand their perspectives, their subjectivities, and the experiences they had in mind when discussing the various public policy measures. It is these experiences, subjectivities, and perceptions that I analyse.

The interviews were transcribed in full and analysed using three methods that correspond to an inductive approach (Glaser and Strauss 1967): the drafting of individual portraits, thematic content analysis (using Atlas. Ti), and in-depth analysis of excerpts (Revillard 2017a). In the excerpts cited throughout the book, the individuals' first and last names have been modified, as have the cities outside Paris. When I cite an interviewee (under a pseudonym), I indicate their age and type of impairment in brackets. These characteristics are compiled in Table A2.1.

By recounting the way policies are perceived, I provide a counterpoint to narratives that focus more on policies' institutional aspects. The two approaches, however, are needed and complementary. Studies focusing on the more institutional aspects of policy implementation help understand what (budgetary restrictions, limited human resources, and so on) shapes the institutional reality the individuals I encountered are faced with. My approach should thus be understood as a contribution to a 'scientific mosaic' (Becker 1977) whose other components (studies of institutional intermediaries, the experience of people with other types of disabilities, quantitative approaches, and so on) are just as necessary to a full understanding of rights realization.

Overview of the book

This book addresses four main areas of disability policy: education, employment, social rights, and mobility. Chapters 2 and 3 follow the participants' life course, dealing respectively with education and work (Priestley 2003). Chapters 4 and 5 cover social policies and mobility. Other aspects of disability policy and rights are addressed in a cross-cutting manner. For example, independent living involves both the allocation of specific social rights (Chapter 4) and an accessible environment (Chapter 5). Political participation, another cross-cutting rights issue, is addressed throughout the book, notably by looking at how people react to rights infringements. Each chapter presents the public policy in the area concerned, then its reception, and analyses how it contributes to the (non-)realization of rights.

Chapter 2 examines the right to education. Based on a study of changes in the way this right is defined at the international level (the United Nations Educational, Scientific and Cultural Organization [UNESCO]'s promotion of inclusive education in line with the social model of disability) and at the national level (promotion of 'school integration' that does not call teaching formats into question), I stress the need to make an analytical distinction between three issues: the type of schooling (mainstream or special schools); the accommodations available; and changes in teaching formats. This distinction, especially the dissociation between the type of school attended and accommodations, enables a better understanding of educational choices (always made under constraint) and how people evaluate their experiences. Individuals negotiate a right to education, which is never fully realized, based mainly on the parameters of access to the mainstream environment and accommodations, variously combined across generations and linked to other characteristics (social class, gender, and parental support). In terms of policy reception, the comparison between different generations reveals an objective effect of the promotion of mainstream schooling on educational trajectories (where one is schooled) and expectations (what one subjectively values). Yet the narratives also show the major obstacles to a full realization of the right to inclusion, and the very active role of students and families to overcome them.

Chapter 3 addresses the complex issue of labour rights, which crystallizes the ambivalence of disability policies: between an assumed inability to work that entitles people to benefits and the promotion of workforce participation; and between sheltered employment, quotas, and anti-discrimination.

Employment might therefore appear to be the area where disability rights are the most fragile. I show, on the contrary, how this coexistence of divergent orientations is their strong point, potentially opening more opportunities for individuals. More specifically, the field of work is a good example of both the enabling and constraining impacts of public policy (which are at the core of the idea of policy reception). From one individual to another, and sometimes for the same person, a given policy instrument (the administrative recognition as a disabled worker, the disabled adult benefit, sheltered employment) can be perceived either as a constraint (an obligation imposed by the employer, an unemployment trap, stigma) or a resource (a means of accessing employment, negotiation of a minor activity that nonetheless confers a social status, or a claim to voluntary unpaid work). Besides all the official employment policy instruments, I highlight emerging mechanisms that fulfil the same function; this is the case, for instance, of employment in the disability sector.

Chapter 4 explores the paradox that marks the reception of social benefits (disabled adult benefit, disability compensation benefit). Although they are factors of empowerment, they are perceived and spoken of negatively. Here, the subjective appropriation of the policies appears to be out of step with their objective effects. I explain this paradox by the link between rights consciousness and the administrative relationship. The relationship to the agency in charge of implementing the rights, the MDPH, sheds light on the perception of these rights and the meaning ascribed to them. While the 2005 Act intended to initiate a virtuous circle between enhancing users' procedural rights in the MDPH and creating a new substantive benefit (the disability compensation benefit), the common perception of fragile social rights can be explained by a difficult relationship with the administration. Many perceive this relationship as stigmatizing, not only because it categorizes the user as a person with a disability, but also because take-up is sometimes perceived as asking for help rather than a citizen taking steps to assert their rights. The high level of social control associated with this relationship accentuates this perception. Finally, the lack of clarity over the time it takes to process applications and how long the benefits will last, combined with uncertainty as to their uniformity across the country, weakens these social rights.

Chapter 5 deals with the right to accessibility. This right is particularly revealing as regards the social status of disabled people, both in its governmental and legislative production, and in the way it is negotiated as people get around on a daily basis. In this area, the authorities have reneged on a legally enshrined right and, what is more, have defended this regression in the name of improving the right's effectiveness. Conducted in this policy context, my interviews reveal its reception by those it targets. The comparison between generations and across one's life course reveals some improvements in the accessibility of the built environment and some public transportation. Yet these improvements remain a far cry from a situation of full accessibility. In this respect, while forestalling the possibility of accessibility litigation, the 2014 reform seems to have had a significant politicizing effect on the people concerned. Through a policy feedback effect, it has produced discontent, fuelling a relative deprivation that, at this stage, is leading more to individual than collective actions. But public space is not only materially hostile to disabled people; it is also symbolically so, as one of the main places in which they experience stigmatization. Taking these various dimensions into account makes it possible to specify the social, and not only material, conditions of a real right to mobility.

Chapter 6, the conclusion, draws on the analyses of each of the areas studied to provide more cross-cutting answers to the initial question on the everyday consequences of mobilizing rights in public policy. Disability rights, while sometimes fragile from the moment they are legally established, suffer above all from major deficiencies in effectiveness. In this context, individuals play an active role in the realization of their rights. They struggle to be considered as subjects of rights as much as to obtain rights. This everyday politics raises the question of its collective and institutional outcomes. Conducted to date largely at a distance from disability organizations or courts, it nevertheless reveals an emerging process of politicization.

2

The Right to Education: A Battle Still to Be Won

Education is a decisive factor in determining disabled people's position in society, not only because of the importance of achieving qualifications, but also because of the role that special schools have historically played in separating disabled people from the rest of society.[1] Over the last few decades, this form of 'special education' has been questioned in favour of the alternative 'inclusive education' model, which implies both 'school integration' (schooling in the same establishment as other children, in a 'mainstream context') and the transformation of school and learning environments to make them accessible according to a universal design that would also allow for the provision of specific accommodations where necessary (see Table 2.1). The ideal scenario evoked both in Disability Studies and in many political speeches about education is thus a progression from being enclosed within specialized educational institutions to liberation via school inclusion. To what extent does a comparison of the school experiences of different generations of disabled people corroborate this scenario?

Accounts from people schooled entirely in special schools are more common among those born between 1940 and 1960 than among those born after the 1970s. Education in mainstream schools has also become a powerful symbolic norm: it's the most favoured option among young people, and when older people describe special education positively, they often do so in defensive terms. However, our interviews also show practices and accounts that differ from this evocation of a smooth transition from special education to school inclusion. Education in special schools was far from systematic among those born between the 1940s and the 1960s. When it did happen, it was not so much because mainstream schools had not allowed disabled children to attend, but more because it was seen as a positive choice, special education being seen as the best way of responding to the person's needs in the absence of the necessary accommodations at the mainstream school.

Furthermore, accounts of schooling from younger people reveal a reality far distant from a situation in which the right to school inclusion functions effectively. The picture that emerges, both of people's experiences (being refused a school place, being excluded or sidelined by a teacher, and so on) and of the way they account for these experiences ('you have to fight for it') is one of a right that is not guaranteed, that has to be fought for, in terms both of access and of accommodations. The experience of having to fight is even more common in the context of higher education.

Examining the difficulties encountered, from primary school through to higher education, and the way in which these difficulties changed, shows the need for a reassessment of current changes. This assessment distinguishes three components within the right to education, which do not necessarily coexist: the right to mainstream schooling; the right to specific accommodations; and the right to immediately accessible pedagogical approaches (which are not necessarily related to one another). Table 2.1 sets out the models of special education, school integration, and inclusive education in relation to these components.

As we study these changes in education from primary to university level, we will ensure that we take account of the diversity of the parameters that structure school and higher education, and that affect the impact and appropriation of changes in public policy. A person's school years are also a key period in terms of integrating their disability into their lives when it emerges during childhood. In these cases, accounts of education are often interspersed with descriptions of medical treatment, evocations of successive stages in the development of the impairment (gradual loss of sight, of grip, of the ability to walk) and the technical solutions adopted (a white cane, a wheelchair, and so on). For disabled children, as for all children, these are also years during which relationships with parents and siblings are key. Relationships with parents, from unswerving support to 'overprotection' and, in some cases, 'denial' of the disability, play a determining role in the

Table 2.1: Special education, integration, inclusion

	Education in a mainstream school	**Facilities provided for the pupil**	**Modification of overall pedagogical approaches/ universal design**
Special education	No	Yes in theory, sometimes poor in practice	No
School integration	Yes	Yes in theory, sometimes inadequate in practice	No
School inclusion	Yes	Yes if necessary	Yes

child's educational trajectory, as do relationships with nondisabled siblings, which, when they are described, are often depicted as aiding integration. All these elements combine, alongside more classic factors (such as gender, social class, and geographic location) to form the experiences of school and higher education that were narrated in the interviews.

In this chapter, after presenting the evolution of public policy relating to the education of disabled children in France, I examine the extent of the change in norms and educational approaches from one generation to the next. I then analyse the negotiation of accommodations in mainstream schools and finish with a focus on higher education.

Which school is best for disabled children?

Analysis of different modes of education for disabled children requires a detour via the historical context: this includes not only the Acts of 1975 and 2005, but also the origins of the idea of education for children with sensorial impairments in the 18th century. The legacy of an educational system based on the principle of 'favour' (Buton 2009) throws light on some of the obstacles encountered by children and teenagers with disabilities in terms of the right to school inclusion, from its expression in law (the terms of the 2005 Act are particularly vague in this regard) to its very efficacy.

From special education to school inclusion

In France, the idea that deaf and blind children are 'educable' dates to the Enlightenment. It translated into access to education, but only in separate specialist institutions such as the Institute for Deaf-Mute People founded by a Catholic priest, the Abbé de l'Epée in 1760, and the Free School for Blind Youth founded by Valentin Haüy in 1785. These institutions were initially conceived as part of a charitable project, education being seen as an integral part of the 'help' needed by deaf and blind people. François Buton shows how this way of thinking was resistant to the move towards the democratization of education which, beginning with the Ferry laws (1881–1882), posited education as a right for all children: 'When injunctions were issued demanding that a right be put into practice, the central administration continued to impose the pursuit of a system of favours, on the basis that this simply needed to be applied more widely' (Buton 2009: 19).

From the early 20th century onwards, in this context of democratizing education, 'inadapted children' became the target of a specific intervention, 'special education', with the creation in 1909 of 'development classes', then the consolidation shortly after the Second World War of a public policy backed by the medico-social sector. Separate institutions, known as medico-educational institutes (*instituts medico-éducatifs* [IME]), were created

(Chauvière 2009). The effect of separation was all the more pronounced because, due to their specialized nature and the fact that they were often far from the children's homes, many of these institutions were for boarders only (Dupont 2016). Quantitative studies reveal lower academic outcomes, overall, than in mainstream schools (Le Laidier and Prouchandy 2016). Special education, then, not only segregated pupils but also had a negative effect on their academic achievement.

As part of the international mobilization for the rights of disabled people that began in the 1980s, inclusive education was proposed as the solution to this dual problem, a system that would enable both desegregation and professional development. The concept is based on disabled children being educated in mainstream schools, in the same classes as their nondisabled peers. Furthermore, rather than thinking of the child as being unsuited to school and needing specific care, it suggests that the school should be adapted to allow for the inclusion of children in all their diversity, following a concept of universal design. By shifting the focus from the unsuitability of the individual to the unsuitability of the educational environment, inclusive education enacts the social model of disability in the educational domain (Peters 2007). In terms of public policy, the concept was soon manifested on an international level. In 1994, following the UNESCO World Conference on Special Needs Education in Salamanca, 92 governments and 25 international organizations committed to promote it (UNESCO 1994). The UN Convention on the Rights of Persons with Disabilities (2006) also promoted the concept in its Article 24.

Education in the 1975 and 2005 Acts

At some remove from this ideal of inclusive education, French policy has been guided more modestly, since the 1975 Act, by an objective of 'school integration', the achievement of which is measured simply by the fact of being educated in a mainstream school, without any guarantees regarding accommodations provided or modifications to pedagogical approaches (see Table 2.1).

The 1975 Act sets out the principle of an 'educational obligation' towards all children and teenagers with disabilities, breaking from previous distinctions between different levels of 'educability' (Plaisance 2009). The education to be received is described as 'either a mainstream education or, failing that, a special education determined according to the special needs of each child by the [Special Education] Commission' (Article 4). Priority is thus given to mainstream education, but special education remains a legitimate option 'failing that', and its organization is also clarified in law with the establishment of Local Special Education Commissions (*Commissions Départementales d'Education Spéciale* [CDES]). The option of special education is even defined in the Act's explanatory memorandum as a right ('right of the disabled child to a special education'[2]).

This Act initiated the promotion of 'school integration', which was understood to mean educating disabled children in mainstream schools. On 29 January 1982, a memorandum confirmed this new direction, without calling into question the role of the medico-social sector. The impact was mixed: during the 1980s there was actually a slight decrease (of -1.1 per cent) in the proportion of disabled pupils educated through a system of individual integration, that is 8.1 per cent in 1989–1990 (Ravaud 1995: 89).

By contrast, the new Framework Act on education passed on 10 July 1989 went further, recognizing school integration as a national priority and formalizing the participation of the medico-social sector as part of this change in direction, most notably with the creation of the Special Education and Care at Home Services (*Services d'éducation spéciale et de soins à domicile* [SESSAD]), which work alongside school integration (Mazereau 2015: 122). The policy of school integration accelerated towards the end of the 1990s (Plaisance 2009). Simultaneously, over the whole 1975–2005 period, accommodations to support disabled children educated in mainstream schools were developed in the context of voluntary work, with, for example, the recruitment from the 1980s onwards of the first school integration assistants, a measure boosted, from 1997, by the framework of subsidized youth employment contracts. These developments reveal the evolving awareness of the accommodations needed to make children's right to education effective, beyond simply providing access to mainstream schools.

The Act of 11 February 2005 gave new impetus to this push for integration. Often described as having established the right to mainstream education, this text is in fact ambiguous in its phrasing on the subject. Although it states that '[within] its field of competence, the State provides the financial and human resources needed for children, teenagers and adults with disabilities to be educated in mainstream institutions', Article 19 then specifies that the child is 'enrolled' at the closest school to where they live, which becomes their 'reference institution', but that they can subsequently be schooled in a different institution (especially a special school) 'on the recommendation of their reference institution and with the agreement of their parents or legal representative'. The law thus maintains special education as a legitimate option. The duty of the state, as summarized in the explanatory memorandum, is concerned less with education in a mainstream establishment than with education in general, whether in a mainstream environment or a specialized one: 'The new legislation formalises the Education Ministry's duty to provide a place for all disabled children in the school closest to their home or to ensure, if necessary, that they are educated in specialised institutions.'

To resolve the tension between promoting mainstream schooling and maintaining special education, the law tries to blur the distinction between the two. It thus focuses on individual education plans rather than on the institutional contexts in which they are situated, leaving open the possibility of a (either diachronic or synchronic) combination of different modes of education. The different modes of education are defined in the framework of a 'Personalized Education Plan' which specifies the type of institution and the accommodations needed (equipment, adjustments of the timetable, learning support assistants, and so on). This euphemistic construction nevertheless struggles to iron out the clear institutional and symbolic difference between school integration and special education (Plaisance 2009).

Furthermore, the promotion of mainstream schooling did not, in 2005, extend to an explicit commitment to the principle of inclusive education. As in 1975, it was a question of educational 'integration' rather than 'inclusion'. Simply stated, a child could be educated in a mainstream school without adequate accommodations and still be counted among the figures for school integration. The desegregating impact of this 'integration' was, furthermore, limited by one of its elements, 'collective integration', through which disabled children are educated in separate classes within mainstream institutions (Localized Units for School Inclusion, *Unités Localisées pour l'Inclusion Scolaire* [ULIS] and Specially Adapted Classes for General and Professional Education, *Sections d'Enseignement Général et Professionnel Adapté* [SEGPA]).

The Act of 8 July 2013 on education reform nevertheless introduced the principle of 'school inclusion for all children, with no distinction', and the rhetoric of inclusive schooling is also continued in the statements from the Ministry for Education. For example, a document produced by the Ministry for Education includes the slogan 'Inclusive schooling. Already a reality',[3] citing a doubling in the number of disabled pupils being educated in mainstream schools between 2006 and 2014 (that is, 258,710 pupils in 2014). The fact that figures relating to the location of schooling are used as indicators of inclusion suggests that the term 'inclusion' has been recast in more traditional terms as 'school integration', confirming the limited extent to which reflections on inclusive education have been assimilated into French public policy. The figures need also to be treated with some caution: the increase in question is partly due to a widening of the formally accepted definition of disability since the 2005 Act (taking better account of learning disabilities and chronic illnesses) and it has not been accompanied by a parallel reduction in the number of children educated in special schools (Dupont 2015).

Despite this, there is a trend emerging, at least in normative terms: the development of political discourse around the education of disabled children suggests a change of direction from special education towards integration – or even inclusion – in schools. To what extent is this change of direction actually happening? Which factors determine these different modes of education and what are their effects?

Putting desegregation into perspective

Our interviews, covering people whose education took place from the 1940s to the 2000s, reveal a great diversity of modes of education: from no schooling at all due to hospitalization or due to the parents keeping the child at home with no home schooling, to school integration with the necessary accommodations, via schooling at home, in special schools or in special classes within mainstream schools.

Comparison of the accounts from people of different generations shows that the norm has gradually shifted in terms of schooling. The experience of having been educated entirely as a boarder in specialized institutions is more frequent among older people, while younger interviewees see integration into a mainstream school as the norm.

This evolution must, however, be put into context for several reasons. Not everyone among older generations attended a specialized institution, and the choice to do so is not necessarily viewed negatively. Conversely, mainstream schooling is far from guaranteed among young people, and is not synonymous with successful inclusion (Shah 2007). Furthermore, the overall evolution is differentiated depending on the type and degree of impairment, and greatly affected by parental resources and support.

From a far-from-universal schooling in specialized institutions …

The accounts given by Geneviève Bertaux and Maryse Cloutier illustrate the fairly linear trajectories that schooling could take in specialized institutions, a trajectory more common among those born between 1940 and 1960 than among younger people.

Geneviève Bertaux was born in the early 1950s on a farm in eastern France, with no running water or electricity. Almost blind from birth, she attended a boarding school for blind children from the age of four. Her parents worked for an aristocratic family from the region, who provided transport to and from the school on Thursdays (the school's day off) and on the weekends. This school closed after Geneviève completed her *cours préparatoire* (CP) at the age of seven, so she continued her schooling right up to the *baccalauréat* as a boarder at the National Institute for Young Blind People (the *Institut National des Jeunes Aveugles* [INJA]) in Paris. Thinking back on her education, she says that she was helped by her 'extraordinary parents',[4] having had a mother who was very concerned that she should lead 'a normal life':

> 'When I was born, my mother's first thought, in a tiny little village, was to go and see the social worker. My mother asked: "What can we do to make sure she has a normal life? She's not going to be a beggar!" She

looked for schools, and I started when I was four, at a school for blind children.' (Geneviève Bertaux, visual impairment, 62, December 2014)

The alternative implied in this choice of schooling does not set mainstream education against special education, but education against the absence of education, which, it is feared, would lead to a life of begging. This allusion is an echo of the ancient association of blindness and begging, which had been established in the Middle Ages by, among other things, the operation of the Hôpital des Quinze-Vingts (Weygand 2003) (a hospital for blind people in Paris). Here, the association with begging is raised as a deterrent. Education in a mainstream school is not mentioned in the alternative scenario: the envisioned schooling is necessarily 'a school for the blind'. The fact that the mainstream option has been set aside is due not to the impossibility of enrolling at a mainstream school, but to a sense of such a school being ineffective because of its lack of accommodations:

> '[At the end of my CP year] this [special] school closed, and a nun from that school said to my parents: "Your daughter has the ability to go on to higher education. Work something out, try to find the best school. She must go to university." [...] My parents couldn't afford to help me. There weren't any services to help with that sort of thing. "We won't have time to read your books to you, we won't have time to support you, so stay in a special school." And I accepted that. I went to the National Institute for Young Blind People, which provided an excellent level of education.' (Geneviève Bertaux, visual impairment, 62, December 2014)

Given the difficulties associated not with gaining access to mainstream schooling but with its inadequate adaptation for visually impaired pupils, special education seems to have been the liberating option, the one that did actually provide access to education, and thus to a 'normal life'. After having passed her *baccalauréat* at the INJA, Geneviève did indeed integrate into a class preparing pupils for literary studies at university (in a mainstream school) and went on to obtain a degree in languages. Given her sex and social origins (rural, working-class parents), special education did not impede Geneviève's social mobility and may even have played a positive role.

Maryse Cloutier was born in 1942 in a village in the south-west of France. Her father was a soldier and her mother ran the home. Her early years were dominated by medical interventions related to her poliomyelitis, diagnosed when she was 18 months old. She describes how, in the first local hospital where her parents took her, her illness was little known ("They talked about infant paralysis. The word polio didn't mean much to them. So, I saw a whole procession of doctors who'd say: 'What's the matter with her? What can we do?', but they didn't really know"). The family then moved to a larger city, where she was hospitalized until the age of five and a half, suffering ill-treatment at the hands of the nuns who ran the hospital ("[T]hey would beat us. The food was bad. They made us eat food again if we hadn't managed to [keep it down]. It was really awful treatment"). She describes how her mother's daily visits gave her some measure of protection ("[L]uckily [my mother came every day] because in that hospital the worse treatment was reserved for children who didn't have visits").

Between the ages of five and seven, Maryse returned to her village, where she was educated at the local state school. She didn't have a wheelchair at that time, so had to be carried, but does not seem to have found this to be too much of a constraint ("everybody carried me. I wasn't heavy"). She was also not the only one in that situation, several of her cousins having also contracted polio. She has happy memories of that time ("[T]he teacher was very nice. She taught me to play the piano with two fingers"). When she was seven, her parents moved to Paris so that she could become a boarder at Garches, a school that specialized in educating children with polio. She continued her schooling there until she was 18. Her memory of Garches is very positive, although overshadowed by her regular hospitalizations in a Parisian hospital where, between the ages of 7 and 11, she underwent a series of major operations that she describes as "more like experiments". These all had the aim of "get people walking" at all costs. "In the old days, the idea was always to get people walking, to get them upright, by doing operations that were often experimental. I was terrified of the operations. It was one after another." Each operation meant a long period in hospital during which Maryse could not go to school, sometimes for as long as ten months. She was once again ill-treated by nuns, as she had been when she was very young. As soon as she could express her own opinion, Maryse said that she didn't want any more operations, and her mother listened: "As time passed, I said I didn't want anyone to touch me anymore, because I was sick of it. And my mother listened. … I'm more independent in a wheelchair than on my feet, there's no doubt about that."

During Maryse's long periods in hospital, away from school, her mother taught her to read. When she returned to Garches on a more permanent basis, she benefited from the support of a teacher who gave her intensive coaching to take the entry exam to go into *sixième*, the first year of high school. She thus managed to catch up on her missed education and continued her studies up to the *baccalauréat*. She is very happy with the education she received at Garches: "[It was] a real school with real teachers … the classes were small, and people liked working, so it worked well … the level was good." She also describes a lively social life alongside her studies during this period:

> 'It was extremely well organized. At the high school, for example, we would go out every Thursday to the theatre or the Pleyel concert

> hall for the youth concerts. It was a dream, really. And then as well as that there were young people who lived locally who'd come over, and we'd go out a lot. I don't think I've ever gone out as much as I did then.' (Maryse Cloutier, mobility impairment, 72, November 2014)

Her depiction of the school is thus a far cry from the image of a repressive, inward-looking institution (Goffman 1961); she describes it as 'paradise' compared to her experiences of hospitalization. She attained her *baccalauréat* at Garches and continued her studies in Paris.

At the end of the interview, I asked Maryse to sum up what had helped her most in her educational development, and the first thing she mentioned was Garches ("what helped me, I can tell you, was ending up at Garches"). She nevertheless felt the need to justify this perception, in the current context of placing high value on school integration: "I haven't even got one bad memory of it, it's funny … it wasn't this integration thing, but it didn't matter, it was still organized in a very interesting way."

For Geneviève Bertaux and Maryse Cloutier, education in special schools didn't happen as a result of denied access by a mainstream school. Access to mainstream school, in the sense of being able to enrol at the school and attend it, was not necessarily a problem. The fact that mainstream schools were relatively open to enrolment by disabled children is confirmed by the experiences of several other people of the same generation who attended such schools. For example, Nadine Trappier did not encounter any obstacles to being educated in a mainstream school in the late 1950s, despite having limited mobility due to having contracted polio. The decision to attend a special school is thus influenced less by the impossibility of enrolling at a mainstream school than by the lack of accommodations at such schools, and by the constraints of social class which meant that families might not have the resources to compensate for this lack.

Education in special schools was not automatic, nor was it necessarily a negative experience: Geneviève Bertaux and Maryse Cloutier have good memories of their experiences at the INJA and at Garches, in terms both of academic success and of relationships with friends and teachers. Maryse Cloutier's account should make us wary of any generalized depictions of experiences of special schooling. For her, boarding at Garches was liberating compared to her other experiences of being confined to another institution, the hospital, which was synonymous with ill-treatment, isolation and a complete lack of schooling. In some cases, attending a special school was also felt to be a liberation from painful experiences of school integration. Educated until the age of seven at a mainstream school during the 1970s, Philippe Tain has a "very bad memory" of this period, when he was the school "punchbag", a victim of other children's cruelty and a lack of support. He describes his parents' decision to send him to board at the Regional School for the Visually Impaired (*Ecole Régionale pour Déficients Visuels* [ERDV]) from the age of seven as "a wise choice". He describes his experience there are a positive one, like "[leaving] one family to join another".

This positive account of attending a special school takes on a defensive tone in the current context of placing high value on school integration. This contemporary norm is especially marked among young people, even though it often fails to become a reality for them.

... *Towards a struggle for inclusion*

Forty or 50 years later, this kind of linear progression whereby (almost) all of a person's education takes places in a special school is rarer. Educational trajectories are now more piecemeal, taking place in different types of institution, and education in special schools is more often a last resort following failed school integration. Integration is still the perceived norm, even though the practice is still rather distant from the theory. The experiences of Chloé Lamarche and Victor Jaucourt illustrate this situation.

Chloé Lamarche is 23, and was born into a middle-class family in the Parisian suburbs. Following a period of illness, she lost almost all of her sight before the age of one. Wanting her to have "the most normal life possible", her parents pushed hard for her to receive an integrated education. She started at a mainstream infant school at three years old, subsequently integrating into a primary school with a special programme for integrating disabled children. There she learned braille while her classmates learned to read "in black and white". She has happy memories of this period. She continued her studies in a mainstream *collège* (school for 11–15-year-olds) which had no special programme, and where she was the first visually impaired child to be integrated. The teachers were informed of her enrolment the day before she started. While some supported her, others were less helpful, such as one Latin teacher who refused to have her in his class. A local service, the Service for the Acquisition of Educational Independence and Integration (*Service d'aide à l'acquisition de l'autonomie et à l'intégration scolaire* [S3AIS]), provided her with braille transcripts of the lessons and exams. Relationships with her classmates were difficult: several of them viewed her with suspicion or even jealousy, seeing the accommodations made for her (extra time in exams, permission to stay in the classroom during the lunch break, and so on) as "privileges". One of her classmates, who later became a friend, described first having seen Chloé as a "vegetable". These difficulties, just as much as the difficulties with her teachers, meant that she finished *collège* "on her last legs".

Having applied to her local *lycée* (sixth form school), Chloé was turned down by the headmaster, who gave the reason that the stairs would be dangerous for her. This happened in March 2005, just when the Act of 11 February had been passed. Although she and her parents were aware of the law, they decided not to invoke it, or to insist on her right to school integration: "We'd heard about that law, but [we thought that] we couldn't fight everything, and we'd let it go this time. Anyway, if we'd forced their hand, the situation would have been bad for the whole year, so. … We let it go this time." Her mother took her exclusion very badly, but Chloé herself was relieved in one sense, suffering as she was from exhaustion after having had to adapt to an unwelcoming school environment.

She went to do her first year of *lycée* at the INJA (where Geneviève Bertaux had completed all her schooling), with the aim of finding some "time to breathe" for a year ("I thought, I'll be able to breathe, I'll take a year and then I'll see how it's going"). She was surprised by the school that she discovered, "a completely separate, completely closed world". She boarded during the week and describes an institution that it was difficult to leave ("[I]t's very very difficult to get out once you're in … it was really a very unusual environment. I could only go out rarely, I was a bit confined"). She also describes the academic level as "incredibly low" compared to what she had known before.

Disappointed by this experience, she went back to mainstream schooling. For a year, she went to a *lycée* that was partnered with the INJA and had a system of school integration for pupils who still boarded at the Institute. The contrast between this elite *lycée* and the low academic level of her previous year made this year a difficult one in academic terms: "Given the year I'd just spent, I wasn't at all ready for that. It was pretty awful." At the end of that year, which was "very educational but very hard", Chloé requested to repeat the year, and went back to live with her parents to finish her secondary schooling in a *lycée* close to their home.

Chloé describes having encountered fewer difficulties at this new *lycée* than she had at her *collège*, in terms of getting the accommodations she needed in order to be able to study at this mainstream institution. She stresses the fact that "more of the teachers used computers [by then]", but also that, because she was pursuing literary studies, the only adaptation needed was the transcription of texts, whereas scientific subjects needed more complex accommodations.

Victor Jaucourt, the son of two engineers, was born in 1985 in the Paris region. At eight months old he was diagnosed with a genetic illness that caused muscular atrophy. He attended nursery school in a town a few kilometres away from his parents' home. It was a mainstream school with an integrated health centre where there was capacity for between ten and 15 disabled children. From the age of seven onwards, this school was only for disabled children. His parents wanted him to be "with nondisabled children too", so they made an ad hoc arrangement with the mayor of their town to have a learning assistant for him in the local primary school: "The mayor acted through positive discrimination, employing someone who'd been working for the mayor's office to be my permanent assistant in class. It was a very good thing for me, but it was a case of special treatment." He was very happy with his experience at this school: "I really liked primary school because I was surrounded by nondisabled children, because I could take the tests and get the same marks as the other children. I wasn't bad, so it was very rewarding."

Victor had to attend *collège* in the nearby town, however, because the buildings at the local school weren't accessible. He was very much affected by this ("It felt to me like a punishment"). The school he went to provided several different arrangements for disabled children, with SEGPA classes "just for disabled pupils" and mainstream classes that included disabled pupils in a system of individual integration (around 15 children spread over all the classes). Victor describes poor relationships both among the children and between children and staff:

> 'The situation quickly became absolutely awful, both with the staff and with the other pupils. With the other pupils it was just because we were teenagers, and it's an age when everyone's nasty to everyone else. And with the staff I had problems because I've always wanted to do lots of things.' (Victor Jaucourt, 30, mobility impairment, January 2015)

His desire to "do lots of things" was, in fact, a straightforward demand for equal treatment (that is, to have access to the same opportunities as nondisabled children). This aspiration was thwarted by discrimination. He was excluded from a school trip organized in the first year of *collège* ("they didn't even invite me to go"). Having put his name down for a theatre class the following year, he wasn't invited to take part. When he protested to the headmaster, he learned that "the teacher of the theatre class didn't want [me] in his class. … The headmaster told me: 'That's the way it is. It's my decision'."

His sixth form years at a *lycée* were better. He was able to go back to the town where his parents lived and, in the late 1990s, integrate into a newly built mainstream *lycée* that was wheelchair-accessible and already had several pupils in wheelchairs studying for their BTS (*brevet de technicien supérieur*, professional or vocational qualifications). He was therefore not the first person to be integrated and benefited from having a youth worker as an assistant. He worked from photocopies and took exams by dictation. His relationships with teachers and classmates were good. On this front, he felt that attending a *lycée* close to home made all the difference: "When you go home in the evening and you live near your classmates, it changes everything: you all spend time with the same people." He obtained good results and chose a scientific *baccalauréat*, known as a 'bac S', against the advice of the school:

> 'As I was good at maths, I chose S because it had more prestige. The *lycée* would have preferred me to take ES [in economics and social science], even though for nondisabled pupils, if they were good at maths there was no problem if they wanted to do S. It was difficult for them [the *lycée*] to arrange for me to do physics because of the practicals. I said to them: 'I've got the grades I need, you can't stop me'. And I did S.' (Victor Jaucourt, mobility impairment, 30, January 2015)

Growing up with visual or mobility impairment 40 years after Geneviève Bertaux and Maryse Cloutier, Chloé Lamarche and Victor Jaucourt had very different educational experiences, reflecting the effects of the increasing promotion, through government policy, of mainstream schooling for disabled children. In their experiences, integration into the mainstream is the norm, and schooling in special schools is the exception. But their accounts, like several others, also show the gap between these experiences and a situation in which inclusive education is perceived as an unquestionable right. Victor Jaucourt's description of the mayor's 'gesture' as 'special treatment' is illustrative of a situation in which the education of disabled children is still perceived as falling within the realm of charity rather than rights. Awareness of the right does not necessarily mean that the right is exercised: when Chloé Lamarche was faced with a headmaster who refused to enrol her based on her disability, she and her parents were aware that she had the right (the 2005 Act having been recently passed) but they chose not to invoke it for fear that her schooling would go badly as a result. Access to mainstream schooling is thus far from automatic; in many cases it requires mobilization or, at the very least, vigilance on the part of the parents. Jérôme Ricordeau (28 years old, the son of a teacher), who has a severe visual impairment, completed his whole education in mainstream schools. He stresses that his mother and father "knew the law and knew who to talk to if anyone refused to enrol the child in the local school".

Furthermore, the level of school integration varies depending on the type and degree of impairment. Chloé's trajectory is close to that of other blind people of her generation who we interviewed, for whom access to mainstream schools was facilitated by support measures initially provided by the voluntary sector before being incorporated into public authorities (the S3AIS, for example). The accounts do also attest to the fact that these services were slow to be put in place, and several of those interviewed were the first to benefit from them. Victor's experience, by contrast, included here to illustrate the possibility of mainstream schooling for a quadriplegic child, is, in fact, exceptional in relation to the experiences of other people with this kind of mobility impairment. For example, Laëtitia Roger (40) was educated in a special school from the primary level. Pierre Béraud (44) and Leila Saddi (31) attended mainstream primary schools and then went to *collège* and *lycée* in a Regional Institution for Adapted Teaching (an *Établissement Régional d'Enseignement Adapté* [EREA]) specialized in mobility impairments. Leila describes a lack of choice once they were integrated into the specialized *collège*: "We didn't have a choice. … Your path is already set out … nobody asked my opinion." Education in the mainstream thus seems more effective for visually impaired children than for those with significant mobility impairments. School integration is more common for those with less serious mobility impairments. Léa Martin (28), who has difficulty walking (she uses crutches or a wheelchair), completed all her schooling in mainstream schools.

Although it is achieved in different ways, mainstream schooling in the local school is still a shared norm and a strong expectation. Attending a special school, or even attending a mainstream school further away, are often seen as signs of failure. Leila Saddi (31) describes her "great regret" at having to attend a special *collège* after having attended a mainstream primary school, saying: "[I]t was a bit of a ghetto." Kader Zyeb (24), who completed a year of *collège* at the INJA, vigorously defends the principle of inclusive education: "In special schools, it's quite sad. There's no more exchange with people, with the outside, with the world. You're somehow disconnected." Léa Martin praises her parents' choice of integrated schooling for her:

> 'My parents and my family always wanted me to be independent, and wanted me to be intellectually stimulated. Going to a special school would have meant … not a regression, exactly, but going against what they wanted for me. They wanted me to have independence, integration into mainstream life, socially. … And so they always fought for that, and that's what made me the person I am today, because otherwise …' (Léa Martin, mobility impairment, 28, January 2015)

Although highly thought of, mainstream schools are far from being easy to access: people have to 'fight' to get into them, but also to obtain the necessary accommodations.

Adapting mainstream schools

Given that schools are not inclusive in the sense that they are not already adapted to accommodate the full diversity of pupils, the quality of mainstream schooling experienced by disabled children now depends, just as it depended in the past, on the specific accommodations that the school can provide: recording lessons and homework, providing note-takers, extra time, and so on. These accommodations are rarely already in place, and usually involve much negotiation and justification.

School integration before and after 'school integration'

Schooling disabled children in mainstream classrooms didn't begin in 1975. Many people born between the 1940s and the 1960s were educated in that way, even though there was no explicit 'school integration' policy, still less any idea of 'inclusive education', with its variety of support, accommodations, and formal or informal teaching adaptations. Conversely, these accommodations are not always made even when 'school integration' is firmly on the political agenda. It is clear that there has always been a *continuum* of arrangements for accommodations, from total absence to more consistent accommodations (as in, for example, the personal education plan).

The complete absence of accommodations at a mainstream school was, as we have seen, the reason why blind children such as Geneviève Bertaux were sent to special schools. However, families with resources could sometimes compensate for this lack of accommodations: Jean-Marc Sernin, who was educated in mainstream schools in the 1960s, managed to complete his education thanks to individual home tuition in braille and typing, paid for by his parents. In other cases, the disability was accommodated in the mainstream by informal arrangements that could be described as passive, in the sense that they amount to tolerance or facilitation and do not involve any active intervention on the part of the school personnel. One example of this is the practice of allowing visually impaired pupils to sit at the front of the classroom for the whole year, or to 'sit up close to the blackboard'. Michel Simon (57) benefited from this type of facilitation. Although such accommodations make education compatible with disability, they can also result in isolation, for example when disabled children are deprived of break times, or do not have access to the canteen or sports lessons. The different experiences of Nadine Trappier and Léa Martin illustrate the change in perception of this state of affairs from one generation to the next, from acceptance to revolt.

In the late 1950s, Nadine Trappier, who had mobility difficulties and used a walking aid and orthopaedic shoes, attended a mainstream school and stayed in the classroom (which was on the third floor) during break and lunch times. Discussing this situation in her interview, she says: "That didn't really bother me. … I haven't got a bad memory of it, actually." Léa Martin, educated in a mainstream school and with a similar disability (serious difficulty walking) in the 1990s, did not take part in sports lessons: "In sport, they said to me 'Well, sit on the bench and look at the sun, or go in the classroom and count up the money in the school cooperative', when they could have found ways of integrating me into the sports." She describes having "suffered a lot" from this kind of experience and criticizes the fact that "nothing was adapted", resulting in a "segregation" that "set the person aside, and didn't integrate them". This different perception of passive accommodation (allowing the person in the classroom but not allowing them to take part in sport) illustrates how expectations of inclusion have increased among younger generations.

In other cases, school staff members took more active measures to accommodate a pupil's disability, without such measures necessarily being part of a formal process. School management teams may have arranged for there to be a classroom on the ground floor for a pupil in a wheelchair, or who had difficulty walking, if there was no lift available. Teachers, for their part, sometimes agreed on certain arrangements with the pupil concerned, to make the teaching more accessible. During the 1950s, Jeannette Houde's primary school teacher provided her with a paper copy of everything she wrote on the board to accommodate her visual impairment. Other school employees also gave informal support. For example, the school assistants used to help Leila Saddi to get to the playground and the canteen.

Other pupils also provided informal support. Michel Simon, who is visually impaired, was helped out by his classmates, who would dictate to him if he could not read what was written on the board: "I would listen, and sometimes the person sitting next to me would dictate if there were words I couldn't write." Jeannette Houde also describes how this informal help made up for a lack of "structure": "I had friends who helped me, who told me things when I couldn't read the blackboards. But it was always individual help, it wasn't … a structure." Dora Moleiro's description of her experience at a mainstream *lycée* in the late 1980s sums up how the combination of support from friends, "little tricks", and "just managing" meant that she could follow the lessons:

> 'Luckily I succeeded. With the help of my friends, of course! And the teachers adapted eventually: they gave me enlarged copies […] What was written [on the board], someone would dictate it to me, or copy it down for me, or I would copy it out again. … I had little tricks. I just managed. But for tests and things like that, the teachers always made enlarged copies for me.' (Dora Moleiro, visual impairment, 47, February 2015)

These accommodations are still the result of informal support, in the absence of any structure guaranteeing them ("there was nothing at all").

The final category of accommodations, which is more common among young people, relates to more formalized support measures mainly obtained through civil society or governmental organizations: the S3AIS, and local educational support associations. Whatever accommodations were obtained, they were usually not given automatically, and had to be negotiated and justified. The issue of accommodations thus comes into relationships with education professionals just as much as with friends.

Negotiating the right to an education with teachers

When accommodations entail modification of pedagogical approaches and evaluation methods, they usually need to be negotiated with teachers, even if they are being made in a formalized context. They are rarely made automatically, and several people attest to having had to be very firm, often with the help of their parents, to obtain them.

Even before any accommodations are made, the very presence of a disabled pupil in the classroom is sometimes contested, even if there has been no problem enrolling them in the school. The following examples involve people with visual impairments. Jean-Marc Sernin (in the 1960s) and Chloé Lamarche (in the 2000s) were confronted with Latin teachers who refused to allow them into their lessons. Jean-Marc changed school and went to a private *lycée* instead; Chloé gave up Latin. Alain Caron (in the 1980s) and Jérôme Ricordeau (in the 2000s) encountered similar vetoes from their physics and chemistry teachers. Alain sat at the back of the class and "did nothing for the rest of the year"; Jérôme complained to the teacher and to his parents, and the matter was referred to the regional school inspectors.

Furthermore, the necessary pedagogical accommodations were often applied unequally depending on the teacher, meaning that pupils lacked what they needed, or had to intervene to ask that accommodations be made. Contrary to how facilities available to disabled children are often represented, negotiating for accommodations was often done in order to ensure that the pupil was not subjected to more lenient evaluation procedures. Chloé Lamarche recounts the heated exchange she had with a French teacher when she asked for her work to be marked in the same way and as quickly as that of her classmates:

> '[T]here was one, a French teacher, who always forgot to mark my homework, because I printed mine out and he put them on one side. He didn't put them in the same pile, and he forgot about them. I know it only got sorted out because I really made things very clear at the end of a lesson and I said to him: "Right, now I'm handing in my work on time, and there's no reason why I shouldn't get it back [marked] on time." He tried to tell me that he was the teacher and that I owed him respect and … I pointed out that he didn't respect me, so. … He took it very badly, but from then on, I didn't have to worry any more.' (Chloé Lamarche, visual impairment, 23, April 2015)

Similarly, Léa Martin had to fight not to be made exempt from the sports element of the *baccalauréat*, an exemption that was made automatically based on her mobility impairment ("nobody asked us; they signed an exemption form with the school doctor"). Being assessed in sport like the other pupils means making accommodations and creating a specific mark scheme, which she finally managed to obtain from her physical education teacher:

> 'I went to see the physical education teacher and I said: "I don't think that's fair, because I'm at a disadvantage compared to the others [...]." She was a bit taken aback – I must have been the first, I think. They discussed it and decided to create an alternative mark scheme for the *baccalauréat*. So, she had to have a meeting with the local education authority to create the accommodations, because I'm slower in my movements, and she had to see what accommodations I needed because it depends on the pathology.' (Léa Martin, mobility impairment, 28, January 2015)

Relationships with teachers were not always defined by such difficulty in obtaining the necessary accommodations, or even in being treated as a pupil in their own right. In many cases, such relationships were characterized by cooperation, and the disabled pupil's education progressed more smoothly. Nevertheless, these accounts are indicative of a right still far from being established.

Complex relationships with nondisabled peers

Most of the people we interviewed describe ambivalent relationships with their nondisabled classmates throughout primary and secondary education. Several report being bullied, which deeply affected their school experience.[5] Kader Zyeb described constant mockery that he finally responded to violently, in the absence of support from teachers:

> 'In primary school, support was non-existent. So, it was a case of who can make fun of whom, and of what. For me, fighting in the playground was constant all the time I was at primary school. There wasn't a week when I didn't get into a fight. Because I was the victim of teasing, and I couldn't stand it. I'd go and see the teacher, but she was tired of me going to see her. ... I ended up saying, if you don't do anything, I'll sort things out myself. Primary school was horrible. [...] After primary, I didn't want to go to school any more.' (Kader Zyeb, visual impairment, 24, March 2015)

Stigmatization of a child's disability was often coupled with jealousy of the accommodations made for them. Jérôme Ricordeau remembers having generally good relationships with his classmates, except for the fact that he often had to explain that although he "had the benefit of extra time, it was not because of favouritism". Finally, several interviewees highlight the difficulty in mingling friendly relationships with relationships built on help. Leila Saddi describes break time at primary school, during which the 'school assistants' would take her to sit in the covered part of the playground. When she was by herself, the adults would ask some of her friends to take turns staying with her, which put her in a delicate position because she was stopping them from going and 'letting off steam' at break time:

> 'I didn't go in the playground with all the other children because … because of all the pushing and everything. At break time children let off steam. … So, I stayed in the covered part of the playground. My friends, the ones I had, stayed. But still, it's true that when it's break time, children prefer to be outside. … So in the end they asked children to take turns staying with me. So it wasn't through choice that they did it, sometimes.' (Leila Saddi, mobility impairment, 31, March 2015)

Analysis of the arrangements regarding the implementation of accommodations confirms the incomplete nature of school inclusion, beyond the simple barrier of enrolment. Accommodations were sometimes insufficient and implementing them involved constant negotiation with teachers. This situation, of a right that was not automatically applied, exacerbated the influence of other individual and social factors, pertaining to both teachers and pupils (with the attitude of parents also playing a key role). Despite successive reforms, the realization of the right to education continues to result largely from struggle, and from arrangements put together in the context of small-scale local negotiations.

Higher education: a new frontier

Education for children and teenagers with disabilities has been part of public policy for a long time, dating back to the 18th century for sensory disabilities, and to the turn of the 20th century for motor and cognitive disabilities. Access to higher education and accommodation for students with disabilities, however, only emerged more recently onto the national political agenda. While the 1975 Act made no reference to students with disabilities, the 2005 Act states, in Article 20, that:

> [H]igher education institutions enrol students with disabilities or who have a disabling illness within the context of the regulatory measures ensuring that they have equal access to other students. The institutions also support their education by making the accommodations necessary

> for their situation in the organization, management, and support of their studies. (Loi n° 2005-102 du 11 février 2005 pour l'égalité des droits et des chances, la participation et la citoyenneté des personnes handicapée, Article 20)

This article also provides for the possibility of support by education assistants, upon notification of the Disabled People's Rights and Autonomy Committee (the *Commission des droits et de l'autonomie des personnes handicapées* [CDAPH]). The *Université/Handicap* charter signed in 2007 by the Ministry for Higher Education and Research and the Conference of University Presidents required institutions to created frameworks dedicated to accommodating students with disabilities (Vérétout 2015).

The recent emergence of this concern for the rights of disabled students in national policy does not mean that disabled people did not previously have access to higher education. Some institutions set up schemes to help students with disabilities well before 2005 (Plaisance 2009). According to figures from the Ministry for Higher Education and Research, the number of students with disabilities attending higher education institutions has gone from 1,500 in 1989–1990 to 18,189 in 2013–2014 (Vérétout 2015). This quantitative indication should, however, be treated with caution. Firstly, it relies on data concerning students with disabilities who declared themselves as such to the institutions involved. However, independent quantitative studies on the subject have shown that students tend to under-declare their disabilities (Ebersold 2014), and may have been more likely to do so in the absence of formal support from the institutions. Secondly, as with primary and secondary education, the rise in numbers results partly from an extension of the perimeter of what is recognized as a disability.

Furthermore, although the few existing surveys give an indication of students' profiles and their professional future, their experiences as students remain largely unknown (Segon and Le Roux 2013; Ebersold and Cordazzo 2015). Our interviews provide useful qualitative elements on this point. What is the situation in terms of progressing to higher education, continuing to study (wanting to continue or wanting to stop after the *baccalauréat*) and choosing a subject? Are choices of qualification limited by obstacles to access? How do students with disabilities experience study and the material conditions of student life?

From the 'fixed path' to broadening horizons

The accounts of pursuing higher education reveal various constraints that come into play either implicitly (self-censorship, seeing the desired course as impossible to achieve) or explicitly (when family, friends or careers advisors pronounce a certain course to be impossible, or dictate the choice of a particular course). The social sources of these constraints are many: the choice of course is not only influenced by the disability, but also by academic results as well as more commonly studied social determiners (social class, gender, and so on). For example, Marie Germain had planned to take a professional qualification in stenography, but didn't actually continue her studies after her *baccalauréat* in 1973 because she received a job offer in the field of specialized training (in a rehabilitation centre). Her choice was not unusual in the context of her social origins: the daughter of working-class parents, and an "average pupil" at the INJA, she "wanted to work, to earn [her] living". The interviews also provide insights into situations in which the disability is a deciding factor in the choice of profession, as well as situations in which, on the contrary, it plays no role at all. Generational differences and social class play an important role in this contrast between restriction and broadening horizons.

For Jeannette Houde, who grew up in the 1950s with a profound visual impairment, the choice of possible professions gradually shrank during the course of her education, under the combined pressures of self-censorship (which led her to give up physics), a lack of accommodations (and an unawareness of such accommodations, which led her to rule out psychology), and explicit external constraints (such as the careers advisor who told her that physiotherapy was her only option). These three elements are all mentioned when she describes how her schooling came to an end after her *baccalauréat* at the end of the 1950s:

> '[I carried on studying] up to the *bac*. After that, it was completely impossible. It was because I wasn't aware of the support I could have had, and I couldn't read the small figures in the algebra anymore, things like that. So, I gave up. … I gave it up, there you go. My idea – well, my idea. … When I was little, it was to be a physics teacher, no less [she laughs at this memory], and then afterwards, when I realized that I couldn't follow the maths, because of the small figures, complicated things, I thought about psychology, but that needed too much reading as well. And no, honestly, I never knew that I could get help, otherwise perhaps I would have done it. After the *bac*, when I was trying to find something to do, a careers advisor said to me [sighs] "The only thing you can do is physiotherapy", but at the same time, he said "You know, physiotherapy is complicated, you have to go into …". Anyway, I remember he didn't encourage me at all.' (Jeannette Houde, visual impairment, 75, March 2015)

Jeannette therefore abandoned the idea of higher education and looked for a teaching job. She came from a working-class background but had been identified as a gifted pupil (meaning that she went from primary school to *collège* a year early). In this case, the disability hampered potential upward social mobility through education. Jeannette states that at the time she didn't see her less privileged background as an obstacle to her studies because she anticipated being able to receive grants. She was not, however, aware of the accommodations available to her for her disability.

Nicolas Barut's trajectory in the 1980s illustrates a situation in which external constraints were stronger, with specific choices being imposed on him by the school for the visually impaired which he attended from the age of 11. He describes a "pre-determined path", according to which the only available professions were "music, answering telephones, or chair-making": "[In that school] my life was more or less mapped out, so they said I could only do music, that I should do music. They didn't ask my opinion, so without any sense of fulfilment." He was told to choose music despite having no enthusiasm for it, and did 15 hours of music a week from the age of seven, but failed in this subject that had been imposed and was not a vocation for him. At the age of 16, he was moved to a class to prepare for work in sheltered employment (known as CAT). He opposed this, wanting to train for call-centre work, but he was too young for the training scheme and was not allowed to enrol on it. He joined the CAT class, describing how he felt "tired" at seeing career options gradually closing off, a feeling that led him to "go with the flow": "I thought 'Just let it happen, take what comes your way and then we'll see'. [I was] tired, really tired, because I couldn't do any of the things they wanted me to do [a reference to music], so I thought: 'I'm just going to go with the flow'." He also evokes the powerlessness of his parents (a mechanic and a housewife) in the face of the school's shaping of his professional future: "For my parents, teachers were gods. Of course, you have to understand, for my parents those teachers were all they'd seen, so if they said I wasn't good enough, I wasn't good enough."

Nicolas resigned himself to the CAT preparation class. In these two cases, the extreme restrictions on the choice of possible professions (only one option suggested, physiotherapy for Jeannette Houde and CAT for Nicolas Barut) derive from a conception of disability which is strongly influenced by gender, social class, level of education, and the type of school attended. To mention other examples of visually impaired people, at the same time, Geneviève Bertaux, in the INJA, didn't encounter the argument that physiotherapy 'was the only thing for her' when she went on to further education after her *baccalauréat*; Louis Resnais, the son of a lawyer, took up a law degree. Other people are steered towards occupations that have long been stereotyped as suitable for blind people (chair making, answering the telephone, physiotherapy, music, sheltered employment), depending on their social class, school, and training.

Sometimes made explicit, the social constraints that reduce the scope of professional opportunities are most often presented in the interviews as having been interiorized, and thus presented as obviousness of what is possible and what is impossible. This, for example, is what is behind Jeannette Houde's amusement when she remembers that as a child, she dreamed of becoming a physics teacher (an aspiration that was probably judged to be triply impossible due to the combined factors of disability, social class, and gender). Similarly, several accounts reveal how initial ambitions were gradually abandoned because they were judged unattainable. Louis Resnais, who studied law in the 1970s, would have liked to go into the field of inspection and surveillance of work conditions, but rejected the idea because he felt that visiting sites would be impossible due to his blindness. At the same time, Daniel Morand, who had been diagnosed with retinitis pigmentosa, didn't fulfil his ambition to be a journalist because he anticipated that the profession would require him to have an independence and freedom of movement that were incompatible with his deteriorating vision. Disability is frequently coupled with economic constraints: Daniel's working-class parents "didn't necessarily have the means to pay [for journalism studies]".

While many interviews describe disability as a constraining factor, to varying degrees, in the choice of a profession, others do not evoke it at all, suggesting an opening up of possibilities. Although Jérôme Ricordeau had gone completely blind, he also dreamed of becoming a journalist when he was at school in the early 2000s. Unlike Daniel Morand, Jérôme never once thought that the profession was inaccessible to him. In this passage of his interview, at a point when he makes fun of himself, he is laughing at the lack of originality of his ambition, which he describes as being exactly like "85 per cent of people" who, like him, would go on to take the exams to earn places at universities specializing in political science ('Sciences Po'):

> 'I was casting around for something to do at that time, I didn't really know, [I thought] "I want to be a journalist" … [laughs]. Like 85 per cent of people who go to Sciences Po… [laughs] and then after five years realize that still being a freelance journalist when you're 42 isn't all that great.' (Jérôme Ricordeau, visual impairment, 28, January 2015)

Whereas Jeannette Houde laughs at herself for imagining she could be a physics teacher, Jérôme Ricordeau laughs at what he sees as his very ordinary ambition for someone who had received an education like his. Later on in the interview we return to the subject of this aspiration and ask him directly if his disability entered into his decisions. He replies: "Not that I know of, I mean, not that I remember" and comments that at the time he had several role models of blind journalists, "who showed that it wasn't completely crazy to imagine myself being a journalist".

Several of the younger interviewees add to this picture of a form of 'normalization' in considering professional pathways, with disability having less influence over such decisions. Chloé Lamarche, for example, finished school and followed a path that was similar to that of many middle-class French students: she began studying psychology, changed to a different university because she disliked the psychoanalytical approach of the first one, and continued her studies after an interruption, when she found a course better suited to her vocation, and then trained in animal osteopathy. She, like Jérôme Ricordeau, attended a mainstream school, suggesting that this experience of contact with the 'norm' and with nondisabled peers opened professional possibilities.

Access to training

Choices about professional training often came up against problems relating to access, either because of direct discrimination or because the chosen training was inaccessible (an inaccessible building, a lack of accommodations, and so on). We came across four cases of direct discrimination relating to access to training, in which students were refused access because of their disability. Two of these cases occurred after 2005. The accounts of these cases illustrate the range of possible reactions when faced with discrimination, from resignation (the word 'weary' comes up often) to individual complaints to the institution, to litigation – going, in the case we encountered, right up to the state council (France's highest administrative court, the *Conseil d'État*). This case occurred in the late 1970s: Louis Resnais, a blind law student, was refused permission to compete for a job as a hospital manager:

> LR: They wouldn't let me. … They said I had to go in front of a committee that didn't exist yet [he later specifies: "In front of the Cotorep public committee, which hadn't yet been created in my department. They never dared say to me 'you can't because you're disabled'"]. They wouldn't let me compete for the job. I appealed and I won [at the administrative court]. […] The Health Ministry appealed. They even put pressure on me to withdraw my complaint because it was embarrassing them. Imagine …
>
> AR: How did they put pressure on you?
>
> LR: They used to phone me. They asked the manager of the university hospital to offer me an internship [instead], and he phoned me. … It was funny. (Louis Resnais, visual impairment, 59, February 2015)

Louis's ability to fight his exclusion from the job application process was boosted both by his social class and by legal knowledge: his father was a lawyer and he was himself finishing his law studies. Although the passage of time and the very fulfilling career that he has had as a law professor allow him to view this episode now with detachment and even amusement ("It was funny"), this act of discrimination nevertheless put an end to his aspiration to become a hospital manager. In the end, the complaint procedure took so long that when the decision came out, he had already accepted a job as an assistant lecturer at the university, thus beginning a university career partly through financial necessity ("I wanted to work, and my father died when I was in my first year at university. I had no choice, I had no money, and I wanted to work").

The second case of discrimination took place in the 1980s. In 1988, Dora Moleiro wanted to enrol for a vocational course (known as a BTS) after her *baccalauréat*, and was accepted by a host company, but they subsequently refused to take her on because of her visual impairment. The impairment was explicitly evoked as the reason for their refusal, something that in hindsight Dora sees as discrimination, but that at the time she did not identify as such. She simply felt extremely disappointed. Following this episode, she "did nothing" for a year:

DM: I was accepted – because I wanted to do a vocational course – so I was accepted by a company who'd seen my application. Except that when they realized that I had a visual impairment, they wouldn't take me. In the application the school hadn't mentioned it either. That was in 1988. So when they didn't take me, I was really disappointed and I stopped everything. For a year I did nothing.

AR: Did they specify then why they weren't keeping you on?

DM: Yes, yes, it was the disability. They told me that. … If it happened today, I'd put it down to discrimination, but at the time it wasn't like that. They said "Don't you realize? Your disability, in front of a client! It would risk … it wouldn't go well." Things like that. And I was very disappointed because based on my written application, they'd accepted me. (Dora Moleiro, visual impairment, 47, February 2015)

The idea that today, Dora could "put it down to discrimination" is the result of the opening up of legal routes to contest the decision, and it also suggests that such a situation has now become less socially acceptable than it was in the 1980s.

The third example of a person being denied the chance to enrol did not lead to litigation either. This is the experience of Léa Martin, who, in the late 2000s, tried to enrol at a private higher education institution of arts and culture. Léa applied without mentioning her mobility impairment. When she was summoned for an interview, it was cut short, with the reason given that "we are not adapted to accept people like you".

> 'I had an interview, I stayed for two seconds because the person said to me "It's not worth my while explaining our course to you, we're not adapted to accept people like you, because we haven't got a lift, because blah blah ..." It was actually quite aggressive. So I left, and I said [to my mother] "I'm not going to waste time on that, I'm going to enrol at the university [rather that at a private institution]. I'm not going to wear myself out trying to prove who I am if it doesn't work".' (Léa Martin, mobility impairment, 28, January 2015)

This final comment ("prove who I am") reveals the importance that this discussion about her enrolment had for Léa in terms of her own identity. The struggle for access is linked to the affirmation of oneself as a bearer of rights.

A few years later, when Chloé Lamarche tried to enrol on an animal osteopathy course, the university initially refused her entry, arguing that there were problems with their insurance. Chloé had already encountered a similar refusal when she was at school and had not fought it. This time, she contested the refusal by contacting the university management to plead her case, and she eventually managed to get a place:

> 'The course administrator said no because of insurance issues. That made me laugh a bit because I said to her: "You know, I'm insured, your university is insured, your excuse doesn't hold water." I asked to see the principal. And so, I said to the principal: "You know that what you're doing is clearly discrimination." I wanted to make him react and it worked straight away. And he replied to me straight away and he arranged a meeting. And he said to me: "No, no, it's not discrimination at all, I just want you to be aware of the difficulties that you'll encounter".' (Chloé Lamarche, visual impairment, 23, April 2015)

It was thus by contesting her exclusion on an individual basis that Chloé Lamarche achieved her integration onto the course she wanted, by putting forward the argument of 'discrimination' which, as Dora Moleiro supposed, had become efficient in the context of the growth of anti-discriminatory policies.

Parallel to those cases of direct discrimination, other people trying to enrol were faced with a less direct expression of reservations that didn't go as far as a refusal. When Jérôme Ricordeau telephoned the reception of the literary preparatory course (a course preparing students for entry to selective higher education institutions, known as *classe préparatoire*) that he wanted to apply for, he was met with the reply that it was "complicated":

> 'I had to convince them a bit ... but not much, actually. ... I mean, convince the people organizing the course. I remember the first time I phoned the secretary for information, and I told her I was blind: "Oh my God! But that's complicated because we're very busy, we can't ..." Well, that was it, and afterwards ... in fact afterwards it worked out fine.' (Jérôme Ricordeau, visual impairment, 28, January 2015)

The hesitation he expresses in this passage ("I had to convince them a bit ... but not much actually. ... I mean, convince the people organizing the course") reveals an in-between situation: he is not refused access outright, but he is made to understand that access is not automatic, so he has the feeling that he needs, to some extent, to "convince" the institution that his application is reasonable.

In all these situations, people actively refuse access to training or express reserve about it being possible. But in many other cases, more material features make access impossible, too dangerous or not sufficient to allow for proper study: this can be because buildings are inaccessible, or because there is a lack of necessary support to enable successful study. Some people were directly affected by such barriers. Pierre Béraud, who is quadriplegic, decided to change to a different university at the end of the first day of teaching at the university where he had initially enrolled ("I got to the end of the day, and I said: 'It's impossible'"). Although the lecture theatre was accessible to wheelchairs, it wasn't well heated enough for him to be able to stay there, and the lift to the seminar rooms was out of order.

Most of the other wheelchair users interviewed anticipated having difficulty accessing buildings and contacted institutions before applying to them. The accessibility of the building thus becomes an important criterion in their choice: "I looked online for information about accessibility, and I phoned about it in advance. ... I made lists, crossed things out, and [only one university] was left" (Leila Saddi). Victor Jaucourt abandoned the idea of the university he had first chosen after the director of the disability services department told him: "We won't refuse to enrol you, but it'll be a nightmare, there are steps everywhere." These preparatory measures meant that people could anticipate obstacles and try to get around them, but the obstacles were, nonetheless, very effective in excluding people.

Student experiences

As one might expect given the statistical evidence of relatively recent growth in the number of disabled students attending higher education, several interviewees found themselves being trailblazers: they were, or at least felt themselves to be, the first or among the first disabled people to integrate into their university or course. Their presence there was not yet taken as given (especially in terms of accommodations) and remained marginal, in both symbolic and material terms.

Leila Saddi, who integrated into a Parisian university in the early 2000s, had the feeling of "opening doors … for other people in [her] situation". She is quadriplegic and uses an electric wheelchair. She describes how when she attended the open days for her university, "just like everyone else", people looked at her "yet again … like an alien". When she was enrolled on her course, she realized that "there wasn't all that much … there wasn't really anyone at all who was in [my] situation", and that the course administrators and teachers weren't aware of the accommodations that she was entitled to:

> 'They didn't know, and I always had to … always had to fight, and shout, and say "I've got the right to that, that and that. … To extra time, to an assistant, to an adjusted timetable." So it wasn't easy. And I was a bit of a thorn in their side. […] Nobody helped me at university. I had to go and see the president of the university, so that he would ask for these things to be done, because it was just impossible.' (Leila Saddi, mobility impairment, 31, March 2015)

As well as negotiating her right to accommodations, Leila Saddi had to fight to make sure that they were actually applied, by taking on herself part of the work that the institution should have done (finding a room, for example) and she sometimes encountered hostility from teachers: "I had to find the rooms myself for my exams. … I even got shouted at once by two teachers, it was surreal." The conflict in question was over her right to extra time, which the teachers were refusing to allow because they said they didn't have enough time ("they haven't got time, they haven't got time"). In the end Leila had to wait a year before obtaining an adjusted timetable, and during that time she sacrificed her medical appointments in order to keep up with her studies ("I didn't do any physiotherapy for a year, and that was awful, because it wasn't possible with my timetable, and that was that, I didn't want to miss my first year at university"). She also describes the feeling of having had to fight for her place as a student with disabilities on a more symbolic level:

> 'I had to find a way of, of getting people used to the sort of student I was. […] When I was accompanied by an assistant, the other students didn't talk to me, they talked to the assistant. […] I could see just how much they saw me as someone … very different.' (Leila Saddi, mobility impairment, 31, March 2015)

The symbolic violence of addressing the assistant rather than Leila herself (something that Leila says is common: "Even now, in administrative situations, places like that, people don't talk directly to me") is symptomatic of a marginalization that was also enacted in the buildings and the accommodations in the classrooms. Leila could only access the higher section of the lecture theatre, "near the exit", which made it harder for her to follow the lectures because "that was where all the people who wanted to talk would sit". The lift to the seminar rooms worked "half the time", and those rooms were difficult for her to navigate because the tables were fixed to the floor. Some of her lessons were in a part of the university where she could not go to the toilet because there was no nurse available (she needs help with this). Aside from the unwelcoming conditions of the university itself, transport from home to university was a problem. Having travelled on public transport for several years with an assistant, Leila now used special transport for disabled people, but she disliked it not only because it was unreliable (often late) but also because of the threat from some of the drivers who were "very aggressive … there were drivers who'd come onto you, it was frightening, because when you're in the vehicle you're strapped in". Furthermore, even where she lived, she was the subject of unpleasant comments from care assistants who mocked her ambition to get a degree: "I had care assistants who said to me: [mocking tone] 'Oh, MADAME is going to university … who does she think she is?"; there was jealousy or … it's impossible to understand." Disability probably was not the only factor in this mockery, which was also addressed to a woman of North African origin whom they were mocking for aspiring to the status of 'Madame'.

The risk of assault in specialized transport, students who looked at her "like an alien" and didn't talk directly to her, teachers who refused to make the accommodations that were her right, and being confined near the exit of the lecture theatre: Leila Saddi's experience is typical of the social production of disability in universities. Despite these difficulties, she persevered with her studies. Her account is certainly one of courage and resilience, rather like those that abound in common narratives about disability, except that in this case the difficulty to be 'overcome' is not the impairment itself but a regime of exclusion and objectification of students with disabilities.

Such isolation and lack of accommodations are not, however, universal, and accounts from older people show that we should be wary of an over-linear reading of the increasing presence of students with disabilities at university. Several of them had positive university experiences. These need to be seen within the context of the university system at the time, which was more elitist, with fewer students and proportionally more financial resources than are available today. Although she describes a "sense of having to clear the way", Maryse Cloutier describes her law studies as having been undertaken without major difficulties in a Parisian university in the late 1960s (she attended lectures and followed seminars by correspondence), at a time when the events of May 1968 had, she says, erased many "differences", including disability ("Nobody noticed my wheelchair, it was of no importance at all. … I didn't even feel disabled any more"). Louis Resnais describes fairly advanced accommodations in the provincial university where he also studied law in the late 1970s: "I was quickly provided with human help, people to dictate to me [in exams], and eventually in the library I had monitors who could do research for me if I had reports to write." He also describes forming a small group with other blind students to organize various actions to challenge the prevalent image of blindness as something that should inspire pity:[6]

> 'There were lots of us. […] We were a group who wanted to revolutionize things and inform people. We created an exhibition of displays and information to inform people about blindness, because we were sick of people just seeing the dogs, or making sympathetic comments. We wanted that to change.' (Louis Resnais, visual impairment, 59, February 2015)

In terms of the accommodations available, the interviews show that, at any point in time, the resources offered by the universities were limited, especially in terms of human assistance. This is a major difference between universities and primary and secondary schools. Chloé Lamarche describes how, when she progressed to higher education, she no longer had "the same rights" in terms of human assistance. Léa Martin criticizes the difference between the provision of learning support assistants (*Auxiliaires de Vie Scolaire* [AVS]) in primary and secondary schools, and the absence of funding for university support assistants (*Auxiliaires de Vie Universitaire* [AVU]) in higher education: "When I finished school I asked the MDPH to ask if there was a solution, they said 'no', and that the AVU wasn't funded, and that there were disability benefit payments that could help pay for it, but at the time I wasn't eligible." Léa had to resort to finding an AVU through a private service, and paying for this herself for five years.

Given the basic lack of adaptations in most universities, support from NGOs has long been an important factor, continuing the role they also play in secondary education. During their university studies, Jean-Marc Sernin and Louis Resnais benefitted from audio recordings of textbooks made by the Group for Blind and Amblyopic Intellectuals (*Groupe des Intellectuels Aveugles et Amblyopes* [GIAA]). Although Jean-Marc Sernin describes receiving a "very warm" and "very considerate" welcome from the Sciences Po administration, the only accommodation provided by the university was extra time in exams – something he refused to take "on principle … so that I could take the exams under the same conditions as the others". In a context of less than cordial relationships with his peers, with whom he was competing in exams for civil service jobs, the only support he received was from the GIAA, whose readers recorded several textbooks for him: "In hindsight, I wonder how I managed to keep up [with my studies]. ... Because I didn't have textbooks. ... Or rather, there were a few textbooks in law, economics, etc, that were recorded by a NGO called the GIAA. ... But still there was very little support."

Support from peers played an essential role. Geneviève Bertaux describes how, in the 1970s, there was an exchange of services between students: she would record the classes and make a copy for other students, who would, in return, make audio recordings of some of the textbooks. Victor Jaucourt, who was a student in the early 2000s, describes a system of "getting by: I'd ask my friends for their notes, and we'd make photocopies". This was supplemented by an hour of human support from a support assistant (paid for by the disability compensation benefit, PCH) every lunchtime "to go to the toilet and eat".

The material conditions of student life

Higher education usually comes at a transitional point in people's lives, when there is a degree of independence that is often incomplete due to financial instability and frequent economic dependence on parents. To what extent does this apply to disabled people? In terms of economic independence, undertaking university studies reveals the ambivalent impact of the disabled adult benefit (AAH), as well as the reappropriation that it can be subject to.

This benefit assumes that the person is unable to work, and it initially seems incompatible with investing in higher education in order to pursue a profession. Commenting on low levels of inclusion of blind students at university, Kader Zyeb describes a perceived instruction to "go home" and remain inactive, an instruction that is legitimized by the allocation of benefits:

> 'University's a disaster. [...] How many visually impaired people get their *bac* with excellent marks, distinctions, and when they get to university, they can't keep up. ... They're told "Go home, you'll get benefits anyway." ... Some people feel that the state prefers to give you money and say, "Stay at home and make sure you don't do anything", than to help you get on in life.' (Kader Zyeb, visual impairment, 24, March 2015)

Alice Perrin heard this same reasoning from her parents when she planned to continue her studies after the accident that paralysed her: "[My parents] said: 'Don't bother carrying on with your studies. You'll never get a job in any case, you can live off your AAH and you'll be all right, it's better than nothing'." Kader Zyeb's personal experience also shows the disincentivizing effect that some benefits can have, in the way that they are currently allocated. Having had to integrate into a specialized institution because of the lack of accommodations on the BTS course where he had enrolled, Kader found that the benefit he received meant that he could only just make ends meet at the end of the month, whereas he would have had a higher income if he had been inactive and not enrolled on the course. In fact, the specialized institution that he was attending (and where he boarded, because there was no reliable and affordable transport from his home) was considered as a medical establishment, so Kader's AAH and PCH benefits went down, even though he was having to pay costs that were not easily covered by the small payments he received in the context of his training. For example, he had to buy his own food, because his chronic digestive illness made the canteen food impossible for him to eat. In his case, the choice to stay in education was only financially justifiable when it was seen as part of a longer-term calculation of the usefulness of the investment.

Despite the disincentivizing effect of the initial philosophy of the AAH, several people reappropriated it (sometimes in combination with another benefit) as a form of study grant. Indeed, it provided some financial security during university courses that were often made difficult by the lack of accommodations:

> 'I was lucky to pursue my studies without having to think about all that, in the sense that I had reasonable benefits and I lived decently. It's true that I was very lucky, it's true that there are lots of students who don't have the luck to have what I had. Obviously there was the disability on top of everything, but at the same time I was very lucky, and then I've always had help from my family. The benefits were a useful source of income.' (Alain Caron, visual impairment, 48, January 2016)

Among the younger interviewees, Jérôme Ricordeau and Chloé Lamarche make similar comments about the financial security provided by the benefits, which were especially useful during years of hesitation or transition between courses that punctuated their university careers (as they do for many students). In Chloé's case, she gave up one course to take up another, and in Jérôme's case he spent a year preparing for the ENA (*Ecole nationale d'administration*, a prestigious French school training higher civil servants) 'without conviction'.

If the benefit provides such objective improvement in their living conditions and student experiences, how do people view the fact that they receive a benefit even though their situation (studying with a view to working) means that they do not fulfil its initial logic? When they outline their justifications for receiving the AAH while studying, they don't compare themselves to disabled people who are excluded from work on a long-term basis, but to nondisabled students:

> 'When I saw that my brother and sister could work during the summer, they were earning money. I wasn't working. Inevitably it's. … It helps us and it still helps us. When you don't work. … It means you can have a bare minimum socially, I mean, at least a bare minimum.' (Dora Moleiro, visual impairment, 47, February 2015)

In this extract Dora Moleiro presents her inactivity during university holidays as an inevitable state of affairs, according to the logic of the initial function of the AAH, a basic social benefit providing 'aid'. The same reference to student holiday jobs appears in interviews with Chloé Lamarche and Jérôme Ricordeau, but they outline the difficulties encountered by students with disabilities when seeking work, both in terms of holiday jobs and of long-term jobs after their studies. The implicit reference to discrimination in their accounts gives a different tone to this justification for receiving the AAH. It no longer seems like an 'aid' but as a form of compensation for systemic discrimination. Chloé Lamarche also describes how her difficulties in finding holiday work made her change her mind about receiving a benefit about which she initially felt "uneasy", because of the different ways in which she and nondisabled students were treated:

> 'Initially I did it for convenience, but I felt uneasy about it, because I … I didn't really understand why I needed a benefit. Why as an individual, why I could be paid just like that, even though I hadn't done anything in particular. […] I admit that I've stopped asking myself that question ever since I've been through my training, which cost a fortune. Because I suddenly realized that it was much harder for me to find summer work. Or to have a side-job in the evenings or at weekends when I was a student.' (Chloé Lamarche, visual impairment, 23, April 2015)

When he describes the difficulty of finding a job, Jérôme Ricordeau comments that: "[Without the AAH] I don't know what people would do." A benefit initially based on the idea of people being unable to work can thus be reappropriated as a social right that supports entry into professional life, or as compensation for systemic discrimination (when allusions are made to discrimination on the job market). The reappropriation of existing resources thus constitutes one of the ways in which students with disabilities cobble together a right to higher education that is still not being implemented at an institutional level.

Conclusion: Individual battles for the right to education

Comparing the trajectories and school experiences of different generations of people reflects, to a certain extent, transformations in public policy. The promotion of 'school integration' since 1975 has meant that there are now fewer people who complete the entirety of their schooling in special schools than there were in preceding generations. But this integration is especially noticeable in terms of changing norms, in the growth of the idea that integrated schooling is more desirable and more valued, a norm that reinforces the idea of special schooling representing some kind of failure for younger generations. While the right to education demanded by older generations was essentially a right to an effective education (whether in a special school or in the mainstream), it is now strongly defined, among young people, as a right to mainstream schooling.[7]

This intergenerational comparison also reveals the weight of factors that affect the impact of public policy on individual cases – something that also limits the possible precision of differentiating between generations. Location, social class, and support from parents and schools all have a strong influence on educational trajectories. The local availability of resources (how close people are to a sufficiently accommodated school, support from municipal teams or civil society organizations) influences whether schooling takes place in an integrated way in a mainstream school or in a special school, and whether students live at home or board. In situations in which a mainstream school is receptive but has no formal accommodations (as was the case in many places until the early 2000s), social class combined with parental support influences the mode of education. Finally, the attitude of teachers is decisive, especially when formal accommodations are non-existent, but also in schools in which integration is more advanced.

The interviews give an insight into the very active role that individuals play in negotiating their right to education from primary to higher education, in terms of access (when it becomes necessary to argue against a discriminatory refusal of enrolment) and in terms of accommodations (to implement them effectively). Despite the growth of a strong norm in favour of mainstream education, the right to education still implies the need to 'fight'.

3

Rights at Work

In France as elsewhere, disabled people suffer from structural marginalization in the labour market.[1] Their situation can be described in terms of marginality in relation to employment (with an unemployment rate of 19 per cent and an activity rate of 35 per cent, compared to 10 per cent and 64 per cent respectively in the general population) and within employment (less qualified jobs, more frequent part-time work, lower pay) (Barhoumi and Chabanon 2015). What rights can they claim in this area, and what are the effects of existing policies?

The question of the realization of rights in employment is more complex than in the other areas analysed in this book. Unlike educational or social policies, where the public authorities have a central responsibility for the implementation of policies and the (non-)realization of users' rights, in the field of employment their action, in a capitalist market economy, takes the form of mediation in relations between employers and employees. Although the state has been able to put in place, in the field of disability, binding measures vis-à-vis companies with the quota scheme (OETH), its capacity to influence access to employment and professional progression remains limited. The impact of public policy is strongly modulated by the economic context, the level of qualifications, the sector and the effect of other social inequalities (class, gender, ethno-racial inequalities).

Moreover, contradictory orientations coexist in public policy: between inability to work giving entitlement to benefits (AAH, disability pension) and rehabilitation and occupational integration policies, between sheltered and mainstream work, but also between categorical labelling within the quota scheme, and the promotion of non-discrimination.

To answer the question of the effects and uses of this public policy, we will first look at the individual relationship to employment. In a context where public policies make it possible to assert both a right to work and a right to not work (Bertrand et al 2014), how do people position themselves? The strong desire for employment comes up against the reality of a labour market that often allows only marginal forms of participation. This chapter will pay particular attention to the link between the effects of the gender system and disability in the relationship to employment. In this context of marginalization of disabled people with regard to employment, policy provisions (for example, sheltered work, quotas) play a role that is both instrumental and restrictive, facilitating employment while reproducing marginalization. As for other populations far from employment, self-employment can be part of the same ambivalent dynamic, allowing access to a professional activity while keeping people on the margins of more stable forms of employment. Finally, other ambivalent modalities of labour market participation are more specific to the disability sector: alongside more formalized policies, the confinement to employers pertaining to this sector plays such a role. After a review of the history of disability policies in the field of employment, this chapter analyses how disabled people negotiate a marginal place in the labour market, in dynamics that combine structural inequalities and the reception of public policies. It then focuses on the effects and appropriations of the flagship measure in this domain, the quota scheme.

The central but ambivalent role of work in disability policies

Questioning the place of work in disability policies reveals a series of contradictions. While unfitness for work has defined disability since the Middle Ages (distinguishing the 'deserving' poor), it was based on the apparent oxymoron of the 'disabled worker' that the term disability first appeared in a French legislative text in 1957. A few years later, the Law of 30 June 1975 established both a right to work and a right not to work for disabled people, by instituting a national obligation to integrate them into the workforce, while consolidating the right to assistance with the creation of the AAH (Ville 2008, 2010). This duality was maintained by the 2005 law, which also introduced a principle of non-discrimination. A historical detour is therefore essential to understand the contemporary interweaving of different intervention logics.

From unfitness for work to the quota scheme

The notion of disability is 'historically based on inability to work' (Ville 2008: 82). This characterization has been present since the Middle Ages, when the criterion of inability to work (combined with domicile) was used to distinguish among the poor those who deserved assistance, according to what Robert Castel called a 'handicapology' grouping together the most diverse profiles based on their commonly recognized inability to work: 'destitute old people, children without parents, cripples of all kinds, blind people, paralytics, scrofula sufferers, idiots' (Castel 1995: 29). Initially a church and charitable initiative, this assistance was later structured on a municipal basis and was recognized as a right by a law of 1905.[2] It is this same principle of the right to assistance that guided the creation of the disabled adult benefit in 1971.

Compared to this assistance-based logic, the 1898 law on workplace accidents innovated by introducing an insurance-based logic. The compensation due to victims of workplace accidents became automatic (although limited to a fraction of the salary), based on a conception of the accident as a collective risk and no longer as an event for which fault must be attributed individually (Ewald 1986). Thus, part of disability, defined from its origin (a workplace accident), moves from the register of assistance to that of insurance. Here, work is both the cause of the disability, the criterion by which it is defined (unfitness for work), and what enables its insurance coverage (employee status). This insurance logic linked to employment was extended in 1945 by the introduction of a 'invalidity risk' in the Social Security system, giving entitlement to a pension regardless of the origin of the disability.

The laws relating to compensation for disabled soldiers adopted during and after the First World War marked a break with this initial interpretation of disability as an inability to work. In parallel with the pension system defined on an insurance basis by the Law of 31 March 1919, several laws promoted the professional reintegration of 'war invalids', through coercive provisions (system of reserved jobs or quotas) aimed at both public and private employers. The Law of 17 April 1916 gave disabled soldiers of the ongoing war a 'right of preference' for 'reserved jobs' which, in the public administration, had previously been reserved for soldiers who had completed at least four years of service. The Law of 30 January 1923 extended the scope of this first law and specified its application. The Law of 26 April 1924 'ensuring the compulsory employment of the war-disabled' imposed an obligation to employ them in the private sector: companies with more than ten employees had to employ them up to 10 per cent of their workforce, subject to having to pay a fee to the National War-disabled Office (*Office national des mutilés*) (Omnès 2015).

The First World War and its aftermath were thus the cause of a historical destabilization of the equivalence previously established between disability and incapacity for work. This turnaround is explained first by economic reasons. The budgetary possibilities of increasing the level of pensions were limited given the very large number of people concerned (more than 600,000 disabled people). Professional integration, which was demanded by veterans' organizations, seemed to be a way of providing pensioners with a supplementary income. The parliamentarians thus considered pensions and employment as the two complementary pillars of the reparation due to war victims (Bette 2006).

The strength of this reparation imperative, linked to a feeling of national debt towards disabled soldiers, explains the choice of rather coercive measures towards employers: reserved jobs in the public sector, quotas in the private sector. While policies aimed at promoting the employment of socially subordinated categories (women, ethnic minorities) have since mainly had an incentive dimension and have targeted candidates rather than employers (until the more recent rise of gender quotas targeting higher-level positions), this is an early example of a particularly voluntarist policy, both in its choice to target the latter and in the use of binding means. The combination of the pre-existing system of reserved jobs for professional soldiers and the war's hecatomb, which called for reparation, makes possible a type of public policy that is not very common in the history of anti-discrimination policies in France. This comparison should not, however, be anachronistic: these employment policies for the war-disabled were conceived as reparation policies, with employment acting as an alternative form of 'social assistance' (Romien 2005: 233), and not as anti-discrimination policies with an egalitarian aim. As proof, the 1924 law provides for the possibility of underpaying pensioners by 20 to 50 per cent compared to other employees.

The professional integration of disabled soldiers was therefore initially a response to an economic imperative for those concerned and a moral commitment to reparation on the part of the community, and was then fuelled by the discourse of 'rehabilitation', advocating work as a response to the impairment, with a view to social integration (Stiker 2013). From the 1920s onwards, this discourse was promoted by associations of so-called 'civilian' disabled people who, as they were neither covered by work-related accidents nor by military policies, were not covered by the legal provisions described.

However, it was not until 1957 that a law was passed to promote the professional integration of all 'disabled workers', regardless of the origin of their disability. The Law of 23 November 1957 defines a disabled worker as 'any person whose possibilities of acquiring or keeping a job are effectively reduced as a result of an inadequacy or reduction in their physical or mental capacities' (Article 1). The relationship to work remains central to this definition of disability. However, it is not formulated in terms of incompatibility or inaptitude, but in terms of 'reduced possibilities' to acquire or maintain employment. The legal definition of the disabled worker in 1957 thus formalized the reversal initiated by the 1916 law from inaptitude to encouragement to work, by generalizing it regardless of the origin of the disability. The recognition of this status of disabled worker was devolved to department-level commissions (the *Commissions départementales d'orientation des infirmes* [CDOI]). With a view to 'ensuring the right to work of all disabled people who are able to exercise a profession', the law reserves a 'priority of employment' for disabled workers, in the public and private sectors, up to 10 per cent. This provision is limited to a procedural obligation and has little effect.

At the same time, this law officialized the development of sheltered employment, including the CAT and the sheltered workshops (*ateliers protégés*). The CATs are medico-social establishments that do not come under the Labour Code and are intended to accommodate disabled people whose estimated working capacity is less than a third of their 'normal' capacity. The sheltered workshops, which must employ 80 per cent disabled workers, operate like ordinary companies, although they receive specific subsidies from the state. They target a disabled public with a working capacity higher than one-third of the 'normal' capacity.

This promotion of the professional integration of disabled people, which has been taking shape since the First World War, does not put an end to a right to assistance based on the presumption of unfitness for work – a right whose continuity, as we shall see, is vital in view of the real difficulties of professional integration and promotion. A disabled adult benefit was created in 1971 and confirmed in the 1975 law. While reaffirming the 'right to work' set out in the 1957 law, the 1975 law thus consolidated a right to assistance based on the recognition of an inability to work. Administratively, the CDOI was replaced by the Technical Commissions for Vocational Guidance and Reclassification (Cotorep). Sheltered work was always included in the law, and the simultaneous adoption of a law on the medico-social sector[3] signalled its importance in the eyes of parliamentarians and the government. In the following years, this sector continued to develop rapidly, while employment in the mainstream environment made little progress (Velche 2009: 250).

This discrepancy is one of the reasons for the 1987 law. Since sheltered work was more expensive for the public authorities than promoting employment in mainstream work settings, the law was an attempt to refocus policies on the latter (Velche 2009). Thus in 1987 a new law was passed 'in support of employment for disabled people', and this time it imposed an obligation of result on employers, rather than simply a procedural obligation. The 'employment priority' established by the 1957 Act was replaced by a 'disabled workers' employment obligation' (OETH). People who had obtained official recognition of their disabled worker status (RQTH) were eligible to be counted as part of the quota, as were victims of work-related accidents or illnesses, those receiving civil or military invalidity pensions, and the widows and children of soldiers who had died in combat. The employment quota, which fell from 10 per cent to 6 per cent, was intended to apply to private companies as well as to the public sector (from 20 employees or agents). However, non-compliance is only subject to financial penalties for private companies. The financial penalties are collected by a national agency called the *Association de gestion du fonds pour l'insertion professionnelle des personnes handicapées* (Agefiph). However, this promotion of employment in the mainstream is not unilateral: the law also provides that employers can contribute to the 6 per cent quota by subcontracting to the sheltered employment sector.

Anti-discrimination and the promotion of diversity

The 1980s and 1990s were marked by the rise of the 'rights model' in disability policies at the international level, of which the anti-discrimination law in employment, embodied in the United States by the ADA of 1990, is the archetype (Heyer 2005). This model reverses the way work is conceived for disabled people: it is no longer thought of as a protection, an innovative form of social assistance, a lever for economic security, social integration, or even normalization through rehabilitation, but becomes a right: the right to work, of course, but also the right to professional equality with nondisabled people. Professional activity is no longer granted or invested as a reparation, it is an area of existence where, like all others, one is entitled to expect equal treatment. This approach leads to a reassessment of discriminations in hiring, working conditions, and experience.

Legislation prohibiting discrimination against disabled people has been adopted in many countries, sometimes as a result of the dissemination of the US model (Heyer 2015), but also in response to local mobilizations and under the influence of supranational law (Vanhala 2015), in a context of more general dissemination of the anti-discrimination framework (targeting racial, gender, religious, and other discriminations). In the European Union, Directive 78/2000 prohibits discrimination on the grounds of disability as well as on the grounds of religion, belief, age, and sexual orientation.[4] Like the ADA, the concept of non-discrimination promoted by this directive includes the obligation for employers to provide reasonable accommodations. The 2006 UN CRPD also enshrines this anti-discrimination framework, in matters of employment as in other areas.

In France, the first legal translation of the principle of non-discrimination on the grounds of disability dates from 1990.[5] The criminal law on non-discrimination then included the grounds of disability and state of health, which were prohibited in recruitment and dismissal situations, except in the case of 'medically proven unfitness' (Article 3). This is therefore a strict principle of non-discrimination, which does not include reasonable accommodations. On the other hand, reasonable accommodations were incorporated into the Law of 11 February 2005, which marked the real acclimatation of an anti-discriminatory approach in French disability policies (Joly 2015), in a broader context of a rise in anti-discrimination policy (the High Authority for the Fight against Discrimination and for Equality [HALDE] was created that same year [Chappe 2011]). In the explanatory memorandum to the law, this anti-discrimination rationale is explicitly linked to the need to bring French law into compliance with Directive 78/2000, which requires the introduction of the possibility of 'reasonable accommodations'. The expression is mentioned in the explanatory memorandum, but not in the text of the law, which refers to 'appropriate measures':

> In order to ensure compliance with the principle of equal treatment for workers with disabilities [...] employers shall take appropriate measures, as needed in a specific situation, to enable workers [...] to have access to, or to remain in, employment commensurate with their qualifications, to perform it or to progress in it, or to receive training appropriate to their needs, provided that the costs of implementing such measures are not disproportionate, taking into account any assistance which may compensate the employer for all or part of the costs incurred.
>
> These aids may concern, in particular, the adaptation of machines or tools, the adaptation of workstations, including the individual support and equipment necessary for disabled workers to occupy these positions, and access to workplaces. (Law of 11 February 2005, Article 24)

The law specifies that these 'appropriate measures' do not constitute discrimination, however, an employer's refusal to provide them 'may constitute discrimination' (Article 24). Without being named as such, reasonable accommodation, under the term 'appropriate measures', is therefore well recognized and clearly guaranteed by the law. However, recent studies show the limited diffusion of this concept, in its link with anti-discrimination, within French companies (Lejeune 2017).

While anti-discrimination policies are classically theorized as antinomic to quota policies in political science work on disability (Waddington 1994), in France the adoption of anti-discrimination provisions in 2005 was accompanied by the maintenance and even strengthening of the quota scheme. Not only are the penalties payable to Agefiph for failure to meet the quota increased, but these penalties now also apply to the public sector, feeding a new Fund for the Integration of Disabled People in the Public Service (*Fonds pour l'insertion des personnes handicapées dans la fonction publique* [FIPHFP]). The law also maintains the sheltered employment sector, as well as the possibility of subcontracting to this sector as a means of meeting the OETH. Sheltered workshops are transformed into 'adapted firms' (*entreprises adaptées*), and CATs into establishments and services for assistance through work (*Établissements et services d'aide par le travail* [ESAT]). ESAT, medico-social establishments hiring only disabled people, form the sheltered employment sector in France, while 'adapted firms', which are formally part of mainstream employment but must employ at least 80 per cent of disabled people (at the time of this study), are designated as the 'adapted sector'.

The rise of diversity policies, initially driven by the private sector, is another important contextual element in the transformation of disability policies at work since the mid-2000s. An American invention imported into France from 2004 onwards, the promotion of diversity has brought about a 'managerial transformation of anti-discrimination', removing its legal and militant dimension and emphasizing the contribution of diversity in terms of 'human resources (HR) performance', while offering companies a new way of promoting their image (Bereni 2009: 97–99). Initially focused on ethno-racial discrimination, the promotion of diversity rapidly extended its scope to other criteria, and in particular to disability, which often occupies a prominent place in company policies (Doytcheva 2009).

This pre-eminence is explained by the fact that disabled workers constitute a pre-existing category of intervention within companies thanks to the quota system, which also indirectly provides these interventions with financial resources. For disabled people, as for women, diversity policies have thus been based on pre-existing social policy interventions (Bereni 2018). In the case of disability, since the 1987 law, companies have been able to substitute their contribution to Agefiph with a branch, company or establishment agreement providing for a programme in favour of disabled workers. The incentive to waive the Agefiph contribution has thus fuelled the development of companies' disability policies. In addition to hiring, training, job adjustments, and support for disabled workers, companies' disability missions work on communication initiatives to promote diversity by promoting the 'business case' of disability (Roulstone 2012: 214). Indeed, contemporary managerial rhetoric on disability includes the founding arguments for promoting diversity: valuing social responsibility and promoting the 'HR' contribution of disabled workers, often portrayed as superheroes.

From unfitness for work to 'HR performance', from quotas to non-discrimination, public policy in the field of employment has led to the coexistence of various orientations. The result of the sedimentation of different public policies over the decades, this plurality is also adjusted to the diversity of capacities and aspirations of disabled people, in a context marked by strong discrimination (Revillard 2019c). The proliferation of measures adds to the complexity of this public policy: while this historical account has mentioned the main ones (AAH and pensions, RQTH and quotas, non-discrimination law and accommodation, diversity policies), one must also list policy instruments aimed at professional integration (*Pôle emploi*, *Cap Emploi*, subsidized contracts) and job retention (reclassification, professional rehabilitation centres). The diversity of interventions and orientations that make up this policy makes it particularly difficult to evaluate. In the following two parts, the analysis will focus on two key issues. The first concerns the relationship to employment and the way in which it is constructed and evolves in the light of experiences of (non-)work, and at the intersection of structural social inequalities and the effects of policy measures (AAH, support towards employment, non-discrimination). The second concerns the flagship mechanism of French policies, the quota scheme, considered here from its administrative translation for users, the RQTH.

Employment: between aspirations and discrimination

Public policy is marked by a fundamental indeterminacy concerning the compatibility between disability and employment, with the right to work and the right to not work coexisting. In a context where activity and inactivity are equally defensible options, what conceptions and aspirations are expressed by the persons concerned? Do they seek first and foremost to exercise a professional activity, or do they defend an 'inactive' status? What role do policy mechanisms, and in particular the AAH, play in these aspirations? After showing that the almost unanimous aspiration to be employed comes up against structural obstacles, we will see how disabled people negotiate participation on the margins of employment.

An almost unanimous but discouraged aspiration

None of the research participants considered impairment to be necessarily in itself synonymous with inability to work. Practically all of them aspired to work, at some point in their lives or on a more permanent basis. In practice, this is reflected in the intensity of the steps taken: increased submission of CVs, participation in forums, frequent professional reorientation (training courses, resumption of studies). While other incomes are available (albeit limited: most of the people concerned are eligible for the AAH as well as the PCH or *Allocation compensatrice pour tierce personne* [third-party compensation benefit (ACTP)]), these practices reflect the persistent strength of the integrating function of professional activity, which is coupled, for some, with a distancing from the stigma of assistance (Abberley 2002; Méda 2010).

This value placed on paid work is sometimes verbalized. This is particularly true for those who are most marginalized in the labour market: Luc Vallat, who became mobility impaired as an adult, started applying for jobs while he was still in rehabilitation: "For me, I had to work. I had to have a place in society." This 'place' must be understood first in its symbolic dimension: given the income expected at the time, the parameter of material resources is secondary at this stage. It is more a question of regaining, through work, a form of social status that the disability has undermined. When we asked him about his decision to go to work in an ESAT (sheltered employment) following a failed business start-up a few years later, Luc commented: "I couldn't stay without work." For Philippe Tain, this aspiration to work takes on the meaning of a challenge in the face of a society that he perceives as "pushing aside" disabled people: "[I]n any case, my whole journey was, each time, with the aim of finding a job, of integrating myself into this society that … tends, even now, to push us aside."

Situations of non-seeking employment do not therefore correspond to a hypothesis of a priori incompatibility between disability and work but bring other factors into play. For several women, the phases of inactivity can be explained by the effects of the gendered division of labour, which assigns them primarily to taking charge of domestic and parental work, and to a role of supporting their spouses' careers (Wajcman 1996; Delphy 1998; Kergoat 2000). Jeannette Houde (75), who is very visually impaired, worked for several years as a teacher and then as a trainer before interrupting her activity to follow her spouse on a career move abroad. Maryse Cloutier (72) never looked for a job after her studies. But these two cases simultaneously illustrate the complexity of the interactions between gender and disability. Indeed, one might think that for disabled women, the injunction to inactivity would be twofold, under the joint effect of gender and disability. However, these two trajectories, as well as those of several other women we met, show, on the contrary, a strong initial ambition to have a professional activity, in particular in response to the disability, with the classic objective of social integration but also of economic autonomy in a context where the disability can lead to less reliance on the material security linked to heterosexual conjugality. The mechanism of distancing oneself from assistance, combined with the anticipation of a more difficult marital market and the threat of returning to or remaining in the parental home, can lead to over-investment in studies and professional activity among women who, without disability, could also have gone straight to the status of housewife – particularly for the oldest generations (born in the 1940s and 1950s). Disability then works against the injunctions of the gender system.

Before the interruption of activity due to her spouse's mobility, Jeannette Houde was active 'although' a disabled woman. In her case, we can therefore hypothesize that it is the effects of the gendered division of labour (priority given to the spouse's career), and not the disability, that lead to inactivity. In a reciprocal and equally classic way, several of the men interviewed benefited from the support of female relatives (mother, partner) in their professional ambitions: encouragement, moral support, taking charge of domestic and parental work, administrative tasks related to the disability, but also in some cases support for the professional activity (for example, typing work).

Maryse Cloutier's trajectory illustrates in a similar way the complexity of the interactions between disability and the gender system. Disability initially functioned as an important driving force in her relationship with her studies. When she went to university to study law, it was, in her words, to avoid returning to her mother's house where she would have remained inactive, "with a tartan blanket on her lap". However, after finishing her studies while married and having a child (the second was born a few years later), she did not look for a job and concentrated on raising her two children. She describes the turning point at the end of her studies as follows:

> '[During the last years of my studies] my husband looked after the child and I went to school, but I must admit that I was less motivated. It was always my idea that my life should be like everyone else's, so I had proved to myself that I could study. I had just proved to myself that I could have a baby. I was more focused on my daughter than I was on anything else at that point.' (Maryse Cloutier, mobility impairment, 72, November 2014)

The drop in motivation for studies and the distance from the prospect of professional integration can therefore be explained by the fact that employment is no longer seen as necessary for the normalization process ("that my life be like everyone else's"), since studies and motherhood have fulfilled this function satisfactorily. Thus, inactivity sets in, whereas the disability initially pushed Maryse towards a professional activity. The risk of social marginalization linked to the disability having been 'overcome' in some way by access to education, marriage, and motherhood, it is as if the gender system was taking over again, in a situation that is initially relatively undetermined. Maryse, who was studying, could just as easily have invested in a professional activity to ensure that her "life was like everyone else's". This aspiration is even more clearly present among women of more recent generations, for whom the aspiration to engage in professional activity is unanimous, despite the major obstacles encountered.

It is precisely these obstacles, rather than an a priori incompatibility between disability and employment, that can lead to discouragement and in some cases to the abandonment of the job search.[6] These difficulties in finding a job are more frequent among people from working-class backgrounds or with a low level of education, so that it is difficult to separate the influence of disability from that of social class on these chaotic career paths, which are also the lot of many able-bodied people, particularly in a context of economic crisis and mass unemployment.[7] However, we can at least identify the role of disability in the many situations where there is direct discrimination on this ground – discrimination that is also attested to by quantitative studies (Ravaud et al 1992; Bellemare et al 2017; Ameri et al 2018). Dora Moleiro, who holds a bachelor's degree and has long applied for administrative jobs (secretarial), has faced such discrimination on a recurring basis:

> 'They said that maybe they wouldn't be able to adapt a work tool for me, that if I was in contact with customers it might cause

> problems. … Things like that, which were not always rewarding. […] Each time it was: "Yes, but a disabled person, we haven't been asked for a [disabled] person. … We are not entitled to take on a disabled person, we don't have an adapted position".' (Dora Moleiro, visual impairment, 47, February 2015)

The first part of this quotation evokes an argument, that of the difficulties linked to 'contact with clients', which frequently underlies other situations of discrimination, notably ethno-racial discrimination. The second part reveals a mechanism more specific to disability. In the idea of a necessary adaptation, or even 'entitlement', we find traces of the historical construction of the issue of the professional integration of disabled people. In a complete reversal of the legal injunction to non-discrimination, the idea that one must be 'entitled' to be able to hire a disabled person illustrates the position of strangeness in which disability can be constructed: it is not part of normality, of the company's ordinary routine, to the point where its integration would require a particular authorization ("we are not entitled").

In addition to discrimination in recruitment, discrimination in the workplace contributes to a weakened relationship with employment. This is what Nicolas Barut's experience reveals. As we saw in the previous chapter, Nicolas had finished his schooling, against his will, in a sheltered employment preparation training. After having worked in a sheltered employment structure (CAT) between the ages of 20 and 29, he trained for three years as a receptionist, at the end of which he took up two successive salaried jobs in mainstream employment. He first worked as an agent for a public services information structure, then as a remote customer advisor. In the latter job, he initially had a good relationship with the people who had recruited him, but then relations deteriorated following a change of managers:

> 'They were fired [the people who had hired me], so new ones came along who didn't understand anything about my difficulty, so at a certain point I gave up. I did what I could and then when it was really no longer possible, I left, because it was really no longer possible.' (Nicolas Barut, visual impairment, 40, January 2016)

He describes these difficulties as harassment, several occurrences of which are clearly linked to disability. Having left his job with a contractual termination, he hesitated to take legal action for harassment, but then gave up, mainly for two reasons. Firstly, he anticipated that the pension he would earn if the judge ruled in his favour would reduce the amount of his disability benefit by the same amount – a concern that reflects his anticipation of a limited probability of professional reintegration. Secondly, he doubted his chances of success in legal terms. In addition to the difficulty of establishing proof of harassment, he was worried about being the only one to take the step, and feared coming up against stereotypes: "Would it [litigation] have worked if I was on my own? 'What is he doing with his disability? He can just go to a CAT!' That's what we [disabled people] are often told." After unsuccessful searches, at the age of 40 Nicolas resigned himself to the absence of a job. Although he is still a statutory job seeker, he no longer has any hopes of finding work ("I know very well that work is over"). In the absence of a job, he developed a voluntary activity to help disabled people with their administrative procedures, using the skills he had acquired in his first job to provide information on public services. He defines himself as a "disability resource person", an activity that has ended up giving him more satisfaction than he could ever hope for in a paid job. When discussing his relationship with work, he mainly emphasizes its importance in terms of identity ("at least to show that before being blind you are a person") and feeling useful to society ("you have to be useful"), two functions that his current voluntary work satisfactorily fulfils:

> 'I wish not to work because I can't find any work, or if I do it's going to be very complicated. Right now, I'm busy every day, I've had a hard time getting what I have now. So how to be, if not the best connected, at least to show that before being blind one is a person? [...] And now that I cannot work, what use am I? There, one has to make oneself useful somewhere.' (Nicolas Barut, visual impairment, 40, January 2016)

The succession of the two modalities ("I wish not to work" and "I cannot work") summarizes the persistent ambivalence of the relationship between disability and work in social representations, and how it may translate for disabled people. The reality of Nicolas's work experiences (in a CAT and then in two jobs in the mainstream) objectively contradicts the idea of an inability to work, which seems to be invoked in the "I cannot work" much more as a label to be referred to than as an intimate conviction – unless one is to retranslate the "cannot" into a potential stifled by social barriers rather than the more common understanding of disability. "I wish not to work", on the other hand, appears to be a more personal formulation, if only because of the deliberate nature of the assertive construction ("I wish not" rather than "I do not wish"). This wish is clearly related to the obstacles to employment. The poor chances of professional integration and the anticipation of the lack of interest in potential employment compared to voluntary activity finally led to the re-translation of the constraint into an opportunity, in the defence of an aspiration to "not work" (in a paid way). The difficulties encountered in finding or keeping a job can thus lead some people to resign themselves, at least temporarily, to not having a paid job, substituting work with benefits (a substitute for work in its income function) and voluntary or individual commitments (a substitute for work in its social function).

If the disability benefit (AAH) offers financial security in the event of joblessness, to what extent does it push people into inactivity? For one research participant, the cessation of professional activity was directly linked to an 'inactivity trap' effect induced by the social benefit (prior to its reform). Laëtitia Roger reported that she was forced to stop all paid work as a journalist (freelancer), as her income had too negative an effect on the amount of her AAH: "The CAF, every time I did freelance work, for example if I worked one month in the year, they cut my AAH by half for a year, because my salary was a little bit higher. So I had to stop working."

As illustrated by trajectories such as those of Laëtitia Roger and Nicolas Barut, the boundary between activity and inactivity is far from rigid but can be renegotiated according to the obstacles encountered in the professional sphere (discrimination) as well as on the side of social policies (reduction in the amount of the AAH disproportionate to the income from activity). Moreover, in the case of Nicolas Barut, the voluntary activity is highly professionalized and claimed as a strong identity. There seems to be a fine line between this situation and the frequent situation of a very limited professional activity, whether part-time or occasional. Several people were combining occasional income from work with an AAH supplement. There is a *continuum* of situations between total inactivity and earning an income corresponding to the amount of the AAH from their activity. Although they are on the fringes of the labour market in terms of income, these situations nonetheless allow disabled people to benefit from the social and identity functions of professional activity.

Overcoming barriers to employment: self-employment, sheltered or specialized work

In a difficult context, people show great persistence in their efforts to access employment. One of the contemporary forms of this resilience, in line with the current transformations of the labour market, is the development of self-employment or self-entrepreneurship (Abdelnour and Lambert 2014). This is seen as a way of circumventing discrimination in hiring, but also the lack of accessibility of certain workplaces and the lack of adaptation of existing jobs. In this respect, it represents an attempt to make a place for oneself in the labour market while recognizing its structural maladjustment to disability. Let's look back at Laëtitia Roger's life before she stopped working. Tetraplegic, Laëtitia had been forced to abandon her studies at the end of secondary school against her will and despite her dream of becoming a journalist. After several years in a rehabilitation centre, when she finally moved into her own apartment, she followed up on this long-held aspiration by training in journalism – only in the written press, as radio and television were "strongly discouraged" because they were "too fast" for her. After an internship as an editorial secretary, she then worked for seven years as a journalist, doing a succession of freelance jobs – not without having to face the reservations of a *Pôle emploi* advisor who told her that she was "not in the right category to work". Describing this period of freelancing, she said that she "didn't want a [permanent] contract, to be able to rest". The decision to work on her own is the result of an incompatibility between the individual's capacity to work and the requirements of a professional sphere that cannot be sufficiently adapted to accommodate the individual's specificities. In another example, Carole Perret, a secondary school teacher, developed an independent coaching activity partly as a result of the difficulties she encountered with school management in having her fibromyalgia recognized as a disabling illness requiring accommodation.

In other cases, the adoption of a self-employed status follows the failure to obtain a salaried job. Luc Vallat and Dora Moleiro followed such trajectories. After an initial failure to set up a business and several fixed-term contracts with no follow-up, Luc Vallat took a training course in computer-aided design through *Pôle emploi* (the French public service for job placement), after which he intended to work in this sector on a self-employed basis. After suffering the discrimination mentioned earlier and failing civil service exams targeted at disabled people, Dora Moleiro became a self-employed entrepreneur and made decorative objects. Her business was profitable for two years, but from 2010 she no longer had enough customers, which she linked to the economic crisis. She then decided to become a "well-being practitioner". After a training course provided by an association for visually impaired people, she obtained a fixed-term contract in a beauty salon that went bankrupt within six months. Dora then became self-employed, selling massage services through several providers.

Other mechanisms for overcoming barriers to employment are more specific to disability. This is the case of sheltered employment. Conceived as a tool for integration into and through work for certain categories of disabled people (particularly those with intellectual disabilities), sheltered work has also been a lever for their segregation and statutory inferiority on the labour market. As such, it can be perceived as assigning second-class citizenship. This is, for example, what Philippe Tain expressed in his refusal of sheltered employment, invoking his desire to work "like everyone else" after his CAP (*certificate d'aptitude professionnelle*, or certificate of professional competence) in cooking: "I just had a disabled worker recognition (RQTH), that's all. But … I didn't go to what are now called ESATs, before that they were CATs. No, no, no, I really wanted to work in a kitchen, in a kitchen, like everyone else." A hierarchy is visible in this quotation between employment provisions. While the RQTH is acceptable, sheltered work is distanced as a form of relegation. In fact, the experience of sheltered work is in the minority among research participants, which results from the choice to focus on mobility and visual impairments, whereas intellectual and psychiatric conditions are in the majority in ESATs (Blanc 1999; Boudinet 2019).

Two people, however, had had experience of working in sheltered employment (CAT or ESAT). Nicolas Barut worked in a CAT for nine years before "fleeing" an institution of which he has very negative memories: "I used to put sweets in a bag every day, the same place and the same robotic gesture. ... I was looking for ways to escape the CAT ... because you also realize that being robotized, somewhere I was going crazy." Luc Vallat worked in a CAT for two years after his attempts to start a business failed. Unlike Nicolas Barut, he describes an overall beneficial experience. Suffering from serious mental health problems at the time, he felt that it was beneficial to have been able to work in an ESAT rather than remain inactive: "[I]t kept me busy. ... It allowed me to have a certain social fabric. Because I had become a bit isolated." The experiences of Luc and Nicolas warn against any one-sided reading of sheltered work, whether emancipatory or critical. This type of employment can have very different meanings for individuals depending on the way it is included in their biographies, and depending on the institutions (Boudinet 2019).

In addition to self-employment, a method of managing precariousness that exists for all groups, and sheltered employment, which is aimed at the disabled public, another means of circumventing obstacles to professional integration more specifically concerns disabled people, although it is not part of a formalized employment policy: this is specialization in the disability sector, which consists of working for an institution in the sector (for example, a specialized education establishment) or specializing in this area in one's activity (for example, a lawyer specializing in disability law, a journalist working for a specialized magazine in the sector) (Revillard 2022). Thirteen of the 30 people interviewed had been involved in this type of specialization at one point or another in their career. For some people, this specialization is a positive choice, in view of the working conditions and the interest of the job: Geneviève Bertaux, a teacher, defends the interest of working in a specialized institution where she works with smaller numbers of pupils; Kader Zyeb, a computer science student who has designed an accessibility tool based on the use of barcodes, sees his professional activity as a lever to promote better accessibility for blind and visually impaired people.

But for many others, specialization in the disability sector is a stopgap measure, in the absence of other professional opportunities. It is then what makes the professional activity possible, while often being experienced as a relegation. After training in communication, Joséphine Tournut, who became mobility impaired after a ruptured aneurysm, could only find jobs in the disability sector. She currently manages the communication of a company in the sector. After an internship with a general publisher, Laëtitia Roger did freelance work for a magazine specializing in disability for a few years. As a performing artist, Léa Martin regrets that she is always referred to art therapy offers, even though she claims her practice as an artistic practice:

> 'I cannot claim to be considered a, say, mainstream artist. No, it is not possible, because we are not there yet. So, it is not possible for me, it is too early. They are not even capable to hire different artists, disabled and nondisabled, in the same artistic creation. [...] The day I will be hired for a project I do with nondisabled people and without talking about my disability, that's when pigs will fly.' (Léa Martin, mobility impairment, 28, January 2015)

Comments such as "we are not there yet" and "it's too early" indicate an awareness of the inscription of personal experience in an unfinished dynamic of social change. Léa Martin is aware of being a pioneer in her field in France, and of the resulting impossibility of claiming an 'ordinary' status.

Dora Moleiro works freelance for companies that sell massage services to businesses. When she tried to register with a 'mainstream' service provider, she was told "If you are disabled, we will need your RQTH, and you will go only if needed, during the disability week." She therefore resigned herself to working mainly for companies that specialize in the employment of disabled people and built her public image around this feature. One of these companies is an adapted firm: the services it sells to other companies can be deducted from its employment quota. The fact that Dora works through these intermediaries means that she is always identified as a person with a disability in the companies where she works, rather than based on her job:

DM: When you arrive at the reception desk and you say that you are the masseuse coming for the massage service, [they tell you]: "Oh, it's for the disability awareness? Oh so you are disabled?" I think we came for something else than disability, but you know ...

Interviewer: Yes, it must be weird situation, as you come to offer a service ...

DM: Yes, to work, to offer a service. [Imitating the person at the reception desk:] "Oh, so you are the disabled person? You're coming for the massage? What are you disabled from?" [She sighs] and you know, on the telephone, at the reception desk, when they call the person whom we are supposed to meet, they say: "It's the disabled person!" They don't say "It's the masseuse," it's: "The disabled person has arrived." That's …

AR: Indeed, they could use some awareness raising …

DM: Indeed, yes. (Dora Moleiro, visual impairment, 47, February 2015)

This framing of the service by companies in terms of corporate social responsibility (doing a good deed for disability) leads to a strong seasonality of Dora's activity. The European Week for the Employment of Disabled people (EWEPD) is, not without irony, her busiest week of the year, to the detriment of the others. The EWEPD, which is held every year in November, causes companies to show a surge of 'social responsibility' regarding disability, which is reflected in the occasional use of this type of service, alongside other 'disability awareness' actions that are just as seasonal. This calendar coincidence meant that Dora was able to witness an intervention of this type involving a simulation, which she experienced in a particularly violent way:

DM: The other time I was [in a company], there were two of us [well-being practitioners]. There was an association for disabled people. They had small workshops. We were right next door, doing our massages. I could hear the association speaking to raise awareness. For example, at one point it was about the visual impairment, blindness. They had blindfolded the employees and made them touch objects. But it was a joke, you see, and I didn't appreciate it at all, because in fact people [*mimicking the amused astonishment of the person who guesses an object*]: "Oh well, that's it!" As if it was a game. But that's not putting people in the situation. Because for us, it's not a game every day. And you see, they were laughing at nothing, at little things that we don't find funny at all. And besides, I pointed this out to the company where I was, I told them: "Next time they could do that somewhere else, not next to us", because we wonder if disability is not the world of … of …

AR: It's the distraction …

DM: Distraction, absolutely. (Dora Moleiro, visual impairment, 47, February 2015)

This exoticization of disabled people in an able-bodied workplace is all the more difficult for Dora because it is coupled with the lack of consideration for her and her colleague's presence ("they could be doing this somewhere else, not next to us"). This episode symbolizes the marginalization of disabled people in employment, a context in which working in the disability sector allows participation while reproducing a form of marginalization.

In a policy context which, for the people we met, opens options of activity and inactivity, the aspiration to have a job is generally very present. The more distant subjective relationship to employment of some women born in the 1940s and 1950s seems to be linked to the effects of the gender system rather than to disability. For the people interviewed, the AAH does not have an immediate deterrent effect on employment; its existence does not lead to an a priori inactive role. On the other hand, it is an essential safety net in situations of inactivity caused by repeated failures to find and keep a job, implying direct discrimination. Faced with these repeated exclusions, several mechanisms make it possible to negotiate a place on the margins of the labour market: as for all people with a precarious relationship to employment, self-employment can provide work while maintaining precariousness. Sheltered and adapted work, a specific tool of disability policies, is subject to varying degrees of appropriation; lastly, specialization in the disability sector is an often-constrained form of professional integration, for lack of (better) options in the rest of the labour market.

The quota scheme, between constraint and resource

What about the quota scheme, conceived as the main facilitator of access to and retention in employment? People's reception of this policy can be analysed through how they relate to the disabled worker recognition, the RQTH, the administrative status one needs to apply to so as to be counted as part of the disability quota when employed. In addition to other studies (Bertrand et al 2014), this study highlights the diversity of meanings and effects of this system.

An obligation ... for whom?

Legally, the RQTH is a status that can be freely applied for, which is not imposed on individuals; if there is an obligation, it concerns companies, the quota scheme being termed 'employment obligation'. However, in the interviews, this recognition is often evoked at least in part from the angle of constraint ("you have to", "it's compulsory", "I am obliged"). For example, Dora Moleiro says: "[W]hen I started working, I had to ask for it." When I asked Nicolas Barut if he had the RQTH when he took up his first job in a mainstream workplace after having worked in a CAT, he commented: "Obligatory! For work in the mainstream, it is compulsory."

The effect of constraint is exercised in two ways. Firstly, in the form of an administrative automatism, for all the people to whom the Cotorep or the MDPH proposed the RQTH as an extension of the administrative procedures previously or otherwise carried out in relation to the disability. Philippe Tain describes how the RQTH and the AAH were the logical extension of the special education allowance (*Allocation d'éducation spéciale* [AES]) for him, once he had reached the age of 18:

AR: Did you apply for the RQTH as soon as you finished your CAP?
PT: Yes, yes. So before, we[8] already had the AES, the special education allowance, so there was already a file at the ex-Cotorep. And then, yes, I did the recognition to find work, still in quotes, "more easily" ... supposedly, and ... that's what. So RQTH and then ... the AAH. So that's what we do from the age of 18. As soon as you leave the AES. (Philippe Tain, visual impairment, 47, January 2015)

While describing an administrative trajectory written in advance (AES–RQTH–AAH), this evocation reveals a distancing of the RQTH, whose significance in terms of professional integration is contested ("in quotes, 'more easily' ... supposedly").

Similarly, Jérôme Ricordeau describes the application for the RQTH as an extension of the AAH, which he received during his studies. Dora Moleiro presents it as an additional box to be ticked in her application to the MDPH:

DM: It's done at the same time [...] when you fill in your file for the AAH or for the disability card or for the parking card, everything is ... we tick boxes in the file. There are headings. And there is the section for the disability card, the section for the disabled adult benefit, the section for the parking card, and you also have the ...
AR: RQTH ?
DM: Yes, but they put it under 'vocational guidance', something like that, and depending on what you do, you ask for it. But sometimes you can have it and not work! You can have it for five years and not work. But at least if, for example, within five years you find a job, at least you have it. (Dora Moleiro, visual impairment, 47, February 2015)

The comment that "you can have it and not work" points, through a literal reading (and without irony on the part of Dora, from a legalist concern), to the non-performative character of this administrative status: the RQTH does not *really* make its beneficiary a 'disabled worker', because it is not enough to turn them into a worker. A facilitator of access to employment in the minds of its designers, it is neither a right to employment, nor the recognition of an already existing job, but a mere potentiality.

While the creation of a 'one-stop shop' with the MDPHs may have encouraged a form of automaticity in the granting of the RQTH, this was not the case before 2005. Applications for the RQTH were then more often in response to another form of constraint, coming from employers – a means by which applications for the RQTH are also often made, more recently, for people who have not yet taken any administrative steps related to disability. Marie Germain applied for the RQTH shortly after it was created (she had been employed for several years at the time) "because [my] boss needed it, he needed it to prove that he employed disabled people". In a similar way, Nadine Trappier took the step to "be recognized by Cotorep" at the request of her manager. Although he presented the process as a right for her, Nadine initially felt pressured:

> 'I remember when I applied for Cotorep, to be recognized as Cotorep, because my director had told me about it and that it was … that I was entitled to it, that there was no point in me not applying. So I did it under a bit of pressure, I didn't really see [the point].' (Nadine Trappier, mobility impairment, 61, January 2015)

This quote clearly illustrates the tension between resource and constraint, right and obligation ("he told me … that I was entitled to it", "I did it under a bit of pressure"), which is found in other comments about the RQTH. For example, Pierre Béraud stated: "I am obliged to have the aids [adaptation of the workstation], otherwise I would not be able to have the aids." These formulations therefore reveal a system that is both restrictive and enabling: one is 'obliged' to go through this process, in order to access resources.[9]

Effects on professional integration

What are the effects of this status? The RQTH often appears in the accounts as a facilitator, or even a condition of access, not only to jobs, but also to training and job adjustments. Several examples suggest an increased effect since 2005. Dora Moleiro notes that this status is in some ways 'more in demand', while stressing that it does not solve the structural difficulties of access to employment:

DM: I find that it [the RQTH] is more [searching for words] it is more in demand now, I find. Today, for example, if you apply for a job as a disabled person, you will be asked straight away. It's: "Do you have your disabled worker status?"

AR: Whereas before, the first few times you applied, it wasn't a reflex?

DM: No, it wasn't automatic.

AR: So, for you, did the RQTH play a role in one way or another in your job search?

DM: Yes, but even if we had it, sometimes it wasn't easy. Not always. ... You know, to get into a company, it's still. ... To get into a company, it's still difficult. It's very, very difficult. ... So it turns out that we have lots of friends with disabilities or visual impairments, or blind people, many of whom don't work. It's not for lack of trying, it's mostly that. (Dora Moleiro, visual impairment, 47, February 2015)

Dora's mistrust of the capacity of the RQTH to counter disability-related discrimination is reflected in her choice not to mention it on her CV when applying for a job ("it is never mentioned on the CV"), unlike other people who have got into the habit of mentioning it:

> '[I had sent] more than 1,000 CVs between 2007 and 2008. I would either go to job fairs, I would send out ... always targeted if sent, with a personalized cover letter, and so and so. ... And I would put "disabled worker" because I had gone through a training course through Cap Emploi, and they advised us, given that the 2005 law had passed, to say that we were disabled, that it was a new law, and so and so. But in fact, it's a falsehood.' (Julie Ferandi, mobility impairment, 39, March 2015)

This testimony shows how public policies shape the uses of the instruments they put in place. It was on the advice of a specialized employment intermediary, *Cap Emploi*, that Julie mentioned her RQTH at the application stage, revealing a disability which, in her case, is invisible. This question of mentioning the RQTH on the CV reveals a tension between quota policy and anti-discrimination policy at the implementation stage of these policies. While the strategy of not mentioning one's disability on one's CV can be defended, in terms of principles and effectiveness, from the perspective of preventing discrimination, the conception of the RQTH as a facilitator of employment leads to a declaration that can lead to discrimination. The users then tinker with their self-presentation strategies on the CV according to the advice they have received to this effect (as in this case, from *Cap Emploi*), but also according to the visibility of their disability and their past experience. Julie Ferandi's critical distance from *Cap Emploi*'s recommendations ("and so and so") should also be noted: she follows them without believing in their effectiveness. She expresses weariness about advice on professional integration, which one feels has been heard repeatedly from various employment policy intermediaries ("targeted" CVs, "personalized cover letters"), without producing the desired effects.

Philippe Tain and Jérôme Ricordeau, however, offer two examples of recruitment clearly favoured by the RQTH. Philippe Tain found his current job after a 'job breakfast' organized by his town hall to encourage the hiring of disabled people: "I was taken on in the context of a search for disabled workers." Jérôme Ricordeau was recruited by a local authority at a time when external recruitment was relatively rare in a budgetary context that favoured internal mobility:

> 'I was replacing someone who had changed jobs, but in fact, as all local authorities are going through periods of restructuring and downsizing, there is a strong priority given to internal recruitment. And so, the fact that I was disabled, as there was also a strong disability policy, enabled my bosses, who liked my profile [...] to recruit someone straight away [...] whereas otherwise they might have waited six or eight months.' (Jérôme Ricordeau, 28, visual impairment, January 2015)

It seems that in this case, the hiring would have been more difficult if his status as a disabled worker had not allowed the local authority to reduce its contribution to the FIPHFP by employing him. The disability was thus able to "work in [his] favour", mediated by public policy.

In addition to the access to employment that it is likely to promote, the RQTH is mentioned as the entry point for accessing training, services (access to *Cap Emploi*), workstation adjustments, or even benefits that are more specifically related to the company's disability policy. This is the case of Nadine Trappier who, when she mentions the RQTH, points above all to the advantages to which this recognition entitled her: a workstation near the printer, a discount on the automatic gearbox for her vehicle.

The RQTH thus appears to be both enabling and constraining in the accounts: constraining because it is often perceived as an obligation (sometimes verbalized by the employer) and because of the stigmatization potentially induced by the categorization, but also enabling because of the resources to which it gives access, and which are not limited to the possible facilitation of access to employment.

Conclusion: The power of fragile rights

Of all the rights studied in this book, labour rights may seem the most 'fragile' a priori, if only from a legal point of view. Firstly, because the idea of the right to work has generally fragile legal foundations. Although it is enshrined in the Constitution, it is denounced by legal experts as a largely incantatory right, because it cannot be enforced (Diatkine 2016). Secondly, because public policies in this area involve the coexistence of models that are often theorized as contradictory: quotas and sheltered employment versus anti-discrimination, promotion of employment through rehabilitation versus assistance schemes based on the assumption of unfitness for work. Rights relating to work thus appear to be flawed rights, which are therefore vulnerable to theoretical and political criticism, which they have indeed not failed to arouse (Heyer 2005).

However, from both points of view, these rights are in fact stronger than they appear at first sight. Firstly, while the idea of the right to work remains for most people a public policy objective without a solid legal translation, for disabled people it has given rise to the implementation of binding legal provisions for public and private employers. When fines must be paid for not meeting the employment quota, when non-compliance with the obligation to provide reasonable accommodation can be sanctioned by a court, the intervention goes beyond mere incantation. Disability is therefore an area where the very vague idea of the right to work has in fact given rise to precise and binding legal translations for employers in France.

Secondly, the coexistence of contradictory normative orientations (promotion of employment, recognition of incapacity to work) is, in our opinion, a strength rather than a weakness of these rights. Far from weakening them, their unsteady nature makes these rights more solid, because they are fairer, and because they open possibilities for individuals. The recognition of a right to non-work embodied in the right to assistance via the AAH is both adjusted to the reality of the vulnerability of disabled people on the labour market, and thus does justice, in principle if not in amount, to this group and the inequalities they suffer. The same applies to specific measures aimed at promoting professional integration: quotas, support measures. The affirmation of a right to non-discrimination recognizes the legitimate aspiration to participate equally in the labour market. But to reduce the right to work to this egalitarian fiction would be to fail to recognize a very real vulnerability, just as to reduce it to protective measures would draw a line under the equally strong aspiration to equality.

The coexistence of different orientations finally opens possibilities for individuals. Firstly, on a material level, by facilitating the professional integration of some while allowing others to live outside of work, albeit in an insufficient manner. But also on a symbolic level, through the appropriation of these measures. Thus, for example, the recognition of a right to not work could be reappropriated as being based not on a diagnosis of inability to work (which the individuals we met overwhelmingly rejected), but on the idea of compensation for discrimination, whether it was directly experienced or perceived as structural.

But while opening possibilities, policy provisions can also act as constraints on the individual's relationship to work. Public policies thus appear to be both enabling and constraining, particularly in this area, which also illustrates in an emblematic way the limits of their scope in the face of structural inequalities.

4

Autonomy under Supervision

Disability-related rights in France have been first and foremost social rights.[1] From collective compensation for work-related injuries (1898) to the incorporation of the disability risk in the general *Sécurité sociale* (public health care) system (1945), and from assistance for the infirm (1905) to the disabled adult benefit (1971), the rights of disabled persons have been integral features of the rise of the modern welfare state. Indeed, even prior to its recognition as a policy category in 1975 and later in the Law of 11 February 2005, disability was covered under French social policy. The prominent role of the departments (*départements*, the 94 French administrative territorial units) and the *Direction générale de la cohésion sociale* (General Department of Social Cohesion) in administering disability policy reflects this strong anchoring in social policy. This social policy translates into a series of statuses such as the disabled worker status (RQTH), and the disability card, as well as disability benefits,[2] which include the AEEH (*Allocation d'éducation de l'enfant handicapé*, or disabled child education allowance), AAH, ACTP, and PCH, that are distributed based on an administrative qualification of individuals as 'disabled' by specific public agencies.

This chapter explores the effects and appropriations of these disability-related social rights, with a focus on two specific benefits: the disabled adult benefit (AAH), which is a means-tested welfare payment designed to guarantee a minimum income for disabled persons, and the disability compensation benefit (PCH). Created after the third-party compensation benefit (ACTP), the PCH covers a range of expenses encountered by disabled persons (particularly for personal and technical assistance) regardless of their income or resources.

Understanding the reception of these programmes entails analysing both their empirical effects on beneficiaries' living conditions and on the configuration within which their autonomy is defined, as well as how these programmes are appropriated (that is, how the benefits are used and the significance that users assign to them). The data reveal a broad gap between the objective impact of a given benefit, which, however inadequate, may be assumed to be positive (in providing a minimal degree of income security and covering disability-related expenses) – and the predominantly negative tone of users' comments about the benefit and how it is administered. Negative perceptions of public services and benefits are not necessarily synonymous with non-take-up, however (Warin 2016). Although such perceptions occasionally contribute to non-take-up, they may also be associated with critical or distanced take-up (for example, claiming the benefit after a period of hesitation, valuing certain uses of a benefit as opposed to others, or imposing conditions on sustained take-up of the benefit). Negative perceptions can also contribute worried take-up, when one is anxious that benefits are unstable or will prove unreliable over time. How, then, can we interpret this symbolic distancing from a set of guaranteed social rights, despite their positive material effects, if compared with a lack of any public assistance?

These phenomena of non-take-up, distanced take-up and worried take-up result from the connection between social rights consciousness and the administrative relationship (Dubois 2010). This administrative relationship is defined as the relations between benefit recipients and the agencies responsible for administering their rights. Beneficiaries' narratives regarding this relationship reveal systematic patterns in how they represent the administration and the roles that the administration assigns to them. These representations include the extent to which they feel welcomed, marginalized, or respected by the administration, the nature of official expectations of users, and whether the relationship is based on trust or demands constant justification. They may also include expectations concerning the administrative process, including the timeframe within which the administration responds to an application, whether it is rapid or occurs within a predictable – or indeterminate – period of time. Other variables encompassed by the relationship include the degree of user confidence – or lack thereof – in the reliability and fairness of administrative decisions. In tandem with these representations, the relationship between users and the administration is enacted through specific practices, ranging from initial contact, preparing, and submitting documents and files, requesting information about the status of an application, and receiving a decision. In some cases, the relationship can also translate into non-take-up. For its part, the way in which an institution or agency responds to user requests encodes a particular level of respect for user rights, not only in terms of their final decisions, but also of their treatment of prospective beneficiaries (including welcome, timing, information, and so on). Users' procedural rights, beyond their social rights, are at play in the allocation of benefits.

The Law of 11 February 2005 had great potential as the beginning of a virtuous cycle between a new public benefit – the PCH – and the strengthening of beneficiaries' procedural rights. Indeed, in a rhetorical convergence between new public management and the promotion of disability rights (Bezès 2009; Chevallier 2011), the law sought to resituate the user 'at the heart of the system' by creating a one-stop shop, the MDPH, where disability organizations were represented (Baudot et al 2013; Perrier 2013).

The participants in the present study repeatedly demonstrated the central importance of this link between rights consciousness and administrative relationship, although in a way that sharply contrasts with this virtuous circle promised by the Law of 2005. Although experiences differ, an image of fragile rights dominates in participant narratives. This can be connected to participants' relationships with the MDPH (or the earlier Cotorep) in three main ways. First, benefits continue to be perceived as associated with a stigma because they involve being labelled as a disabled person, and they are perceived as putting beneficiaries in a situation of 'asking for help'. Relatedly, although they succeed in a variety of ways in promoting autonomy, benefits also perpetuate a traditional feature of welfare policy: heavy-handed oversight and supervision of beneficiaries. Finally, the uncertainty surrounding benefits stems from the often extended and unpredictable period of time required to process applications, as well as a lack of confidence in the stability and reliability of payments and services, particularly in the case of the PCH.

Between non-take-up and critical take-up

Theoretical discussions about social policy often suggest that welfare benefit programmes have the potential of promoting greater beneficiary autonomy. This is consistent with the enhanced autonomy found among the participants in this study. The study's findings also indicated, however, that benefits often tend to be mistrusted, which may or may not be a contributing factor in non-take-up. The question is how to explain this phenomenon of distancing from available benefits that have the potential of substantially improving the quality of life of their beneficiaries.

Benefits that make a difference

Comparative studies on the welfare state offer important insights concerning disability benefits, including the anticipated effects of such programmes on the lives of disabled individuals. A central factor in general discussions of welfare state impact is autonomy (Esping-Andersen 1990; Orloff 1993; Lister 1997). Although often narrowly viewed as purely economic, autonomy merits broader consideration as the potential contribution of a given benefit to the promotion of a more independent life for disabled individuals (DeJong 1979). This includes housing, as well as performing certain everyday tasks without assistance from family members and friends. Autonomy is not absolute, but instead involves the interplay of a range of bonds of dependency between individuals and the market, the state, and their families as well as the third-party sector and social relationships.

In his initial conceptualization, Gøsta Esping-Andersen, through the idea of de-commodification, emphasized independence from the necessity of selling one's labour on the labour market. From the perspective of the gendered division of labour, feminist authors such as Ruth Lister and Ann Orloff then pointed to the need to evaluate welfare benefits based on their potential for 'de-familialisation' (Lister 1997) or 'autonomization' with respect to conjugal relationships (Orloff 1993) (defined as the degree of reliance or non-reliance on family and/or conjugal ties). In the field of disability studies, these approaches have been criticized for implicitly reducing disabled people to a 'burden' that nondisabled women have to care for (Morris 1993; Fine and Glendinning 2005). By promoting the idea that 'the private is political', however, these feminist approaches have helped to open the 'black box' that the family typically represented in early comparative studies of the welfare state, while also calling attention to the importance of encouraging autonomy from family ties. This form of autonomy is a fundamental tool for analysing the potential effects of disability assistance programmes. Two key criteria thus appear: de-commodification and de-familialization – in attempts to evaluate the role of benefit programmes such as the AAH and PCH in supporting the development of user autonomy.

The contribution of these benefits to greater autonomy may not seem obvious. Indeed, the AAH is often criticized as a benefits programme whose payments are too modest to nurture genuine financial autonomy. However, by comparison with no disability benefit whatsoever, the AAH nevertheless clearly offers a modicum of immediate financial security that limits reliance on the job market, family ties, and private charity.[3] It is also demonstrably superior to other minimum income support programs such as the RSA [*Revenu de solidarité active* or Active Solidarity Income Payment], although both programmes fall below the poverty line. In 2016, at the time of this study, the monthly AAH benefit for a single adult with no children was €808, compared to €535 for the RSA, and €1,139 for the monthly minimum wage.[4]

The objective of the PCH is to provide funding for technical, human, and animal assistance, as well as transportation and residential accommodations. The PCH promotes the autonomy of disabled people in several ways: It supports the ability to independently perform tasks by allowing for technical aids, for example, for visually impaired or blind people, including scanners, braille consoles, and voice-recognition software. Such tools enable a degree of communicative autonomy, while a white cane and guide dog support autonomous mobility. The PCH also allows recipients to minimize dependency on family members and friends by paying for personal assistants.

For example, when he was living alone as a student, Jérôme Ricordeau's mother initially helped him once a week with the housekeeping, but after he began receiving the PCH, he was able to hire a housekeeper. Michel Simon, who shares his residence with his brother, also points out that the ACTP allows him to separate his family relationship from assistance by enabling him to pay for professional housekeeping:

> 'My brother is not my personal assistant. [...] I've always been careful not to impose constraints on the people close to me. OK, if I need an occasional hand, sure, I'll ask him. But I use the ACTP to pay people to help me with household, personal, administrative, and small computer-related tasks, as well as some shopping. So, yeah. I believe that things need to be clear in life.' (Michel Simon, visual impairment, 57, February 2015)

By making independent housing possible, the PCH plays an even more decisive role in reducing dependency on family ties (Beyrie 2015). This is the case for Victor Jaucourt, who requires around-the-clock assistance that he could not afford prior to the creation of the PCH. The PCH can also contribute to the formalization of economic exchanges surrounding domestic tasks that are otherwise customarily naturalized within a gendered division of labour. Jean-Marc Sernin, for example, uses his PCH to pay his girlfriend, who assists him daily, thereby in turn allowing her to supplement her retirement pension. In this case, the benefit encourages the accompanying person's autonomy by providing an income and a benefit that is independent of the couple, in addition to the disabled primary recipient.

'A disability card means you're blind'

Although demonstrably encouraging autonomy, however, these programmes are often the target of negative remarks, a distancing that is explainable because the designation of an individual as 'disabled' that these programmes imply can be perceived as stigmatizing (Wang 2013). Most of the participants in this study did not mention administrative categorization as an important biographical turn, however. Indeed, because most participants have lived since childhood with their disabilities, their adult relationships with the administration (through the Cotorep or the MDPH) logically follows the relationships established by their parents with agencies such as the CDES or the MDPH. Shifting from one benefit (the special education allowance, AES or AEEH) to another (AAH) thus does not have any major consequences in terms of one's identity as a disabled person.

On the other hand, the relationship with the disability administration can play a significant role in identity construction in cases in which the impairment develops during adulthood, particularly following an evolving illness.[5] Although seriously visually impaired since childhood, Michel Simon, whose impairment was not identified at the time, completed his schooling in a mainstream academic environment. He became certified as a teacher and taught in a mainstream school for several years until his relations with students became problematic and he was advised to accept a position at an ERDV (a regional school for visually impaired students). Only there did he discover the world of disability, initially through professional socialization, teaching visually impaired students. While this professional change did not cause a genuine change in his sense of identity, Michel's initial reaction to his colleagues' suggestion that he declare his disability to the Cotorep was negative:

> 'When I arrived at the school for the blind, I met visually impaired colleagues, some of them who could not see as well as I could. And they were the ones who said "You need to apply for your disability card. You might qualify for compensation." That seemed bizarre to me, because a disability card meant being blind or walking with a white cane, but I could see. ... And that's when I began to realize how little vision I had, which was about one-twentieth.' (Michel Simon, visual impairment, 57, February 2015)

Despite some reservations, he decided to take the next step:

> 'I was motivated. There was a benefit involved. So, I went to city hall to talk to social services, picked up an application, and went to see my ophthalmologist. [...] But I was the one who had to file the application. [The ophthalmologist had not mentioned that he could perhaps qualify for benefits.] Because it would never have occurred to me that I could be eligible. ... I'm not really for. ... It's not an abusive behaviour about things. You're either eligible or you're not. There are criteria – you meet them, or you don't. If I fulfil them, there's no reason I should be prevented from receiving the benefits for which I'm eligible. So, he filled out my medical certificate, and in fact I was recognized at 80 per cent [disability].' (Michel Simon, visual impairment, 57, February 2015)

In Michel's case, administrative recognition appears to have influenced the development of an adult identity as a disabled person, within a professional environment that supported this identification (the ERDV). He also found himself in a setting that encouraged critical steps in the visually impaired itinerary (Blatgé 2012), such as learning braille and how to walk with a white cane.

His application at the Cotorep coincided with a certain instability in the development of his identity as a disabled person, although he was motivated by the prospect of being compensated for his disability. His defensive attitude when he described the application process included imagined accusations that could be addressed to him: "It is not an abusive behaviour." It also shows that agreeing to take up a benefit was the result of a reflective process that required a specific justification which, in this instance, was of a legal nature: "We either have the right or we don't. There are criteria. We either fulfil them, or we don't." This need for self-justification suggests that the perception that this right is legitimate is not necessarily a given.

Refusing to 'ask for help'

Michel Simon initially resisted being labelled as disabled. For others, the stigma held at a distance is the idea that taking up a benefit will be equated with 'asking for help' or even as a form of begging. When we asked if she received the ACTP before 2005, Jeannette Houde explained that until recently she had not tried to learn about her eligibility:

> '[In response to a question about this benefit] the ACTP, I have never heard about it. [...] I mean, it's not my style to ask. Now that I'm involved in disability organizations, I'm more informed, so I'm doing like everybody else, but before, it's true that. ... It's always this nasty habit of autonomy, getting by on my own and being totally self-taught. It's been both useful and not useful to me. [...] My idea isn't necessarily to go begging in the street or whining. ... No, I didn't know about it. I didn't know, and I wasn't trying to find out. So, I didn't ask.' (Jeannette Houde, visual impairment, 75, March 2015)

The autonomy described here is diametrically opposed to that described at the beginning of this chapter: An autonomy against public intervention, not nurtured by it. 'Not trying to find out', in the context of a perception of take-up as 'begging', constitutes a hybrid type of non-take-up in the light of existing typologies. Although a priori a case of non-take-up due to non-familiarity with available benefits ("I didn't know about it"), a more explicit statement, such as "I wasn't trying to find out about it, so I didn't ask," suggests that Jeannette is enacting an active, voluntary type of non-take-up. This appears all the more valid, given that she often justifies her position by self-distancing from any action that resembles an appeal for help (Warin 2016). This could be interpretable as a form of non-take-up via 'active non-familiarity', a clear illustration of her ambivalence about disability programmes. Ultimately, because she frequented civil society organizations in the field of visual impairment after retiring, Jeannette reconsidered and concluded that she might as well "do like everyone else" to benefit from these programmes. The fact that she took this step due to associative networks took precedence over her earlier tendency to stay detached from disabled programmes out of fear of losing her autonomy and her refusal to "beg" or "whine".

This narrative concerned the ACTP during the era of the Cotorep. Did the creation of the MDPH change this belief that to apply for disability assistance was the equivalent of asking for charity? Only one participant offered a very positive assessment of the MDPH in this respect. After he became disabled at the age of 40 following an illness, Lucien Rémo enjoyed a successful career as a coach and was openly critical of the paternalism of various contemporary discourses regarding disabled people. His praise of the MDPH is consistent with this perspective, unlike the experiences of his mother and sister, both of whom had been disabled for a longer period and had had the impression of being reduced to 'begging' the Cotorep:

> '[My mother and my sister] experienced living hell with the Cotorep. I had the impression that they spent their time begging and asking for charity. But here you get the impression that you just fill out an application. … We're not treated as beggars. We're considered users. Just like normal human beings. And society has an obligation towards us to enable us to gain access to things like everyone else. I find that pretty good. I like that mentality. I don't have the feeling of being a beggar. Which I'm not.' (Lucien Rémo, mobility impairment, 56, January 2015)

Lucien Rémo's quote amply illustrates the extent to which being treated as a client and as a 'normal human being' is a prominent expectation towards the administration among study participants. Expecting to be treated like individuals with rights and not 'like beggars' is as important for disabled individuals as being approved for benefits. They refer rights and payments as only one dimension of society's 'duty towards us', in echo of the law itself with respect to a national obligation and the duty of solidarity.

Nevertheless, Lucien did not apply for the PCH even though he had take-up to the services of the MDPH for his RQTH and his *station debout pénible* ('painful standing card', giving priority seating on public transportation due to difficulty standing). He reported that his disability required him to limit the length of time that he spent on transport, which led him to use a motorcycle rather than the RER (light suburban railway) to travel to the airport. When asked whether he would apply for the PCH to compensate for the additional expense, he found the question strange and mused about the MDPH staff's reaction to an application for benefits from the disabled director of an independent company:

AR: In fact, have you ever thought of applying for the PCH to cover costs like those?

LR: No, it never occurred to me. It would be funny. You think I should have the right to something, as a company boss? [Smiles] Yeah, that's amusing. I'm going to apply – I'll keep you posted. (Lucien Rémo, mobility impairment, 56, January 2015)

His reaction shows that due to his professional success, he does not identify as a member of the target population of the programme. This distance can be compared with a comment from another beneficiary regarding a comparable use of the PCH. As a recipient of a PCH flat-rate blindness stipend, Geneviève Bertaux explains she notably uses it to pay for taxis to travel to the airport. She comments on this use being at odds with common representations of disability:

> 'I, for one, say: my PCH, if I take a taxi or two ... for example – it costs €120 round-trip when I go to [the airport]. When I travel ... OK, you're going to answer, "If you're blind you don't need to travel." I don't know what to say to that. That might be the answer I'd get at the MDPH. Should a disabled person attend conferences? What does it mean to be disabled? Is it clear to people that a disabled person might be an engineer or a professor or teach at a prestigious institution? What goes through the mind of the legislator? Does everyone always think of us as being sick?' (Geneviève Bertaux, visual impairment, 62, December 2014)

Despite the benefit's being universal (non-means-tested), Geneviève voices doubts about the fact that it could be intended to be used to finance transportation and other expenses related to an intellectual profession such as 'attending conferences' or 'being a professor'. This perceived gap does not imply non-take-up, but instead a distanced type of take-up, with a sensation of not fully belonging to the target population.

In other cases, however, the gap can trigger non-take-up. Louis Resnais, a blind university professor, reported that he decided not to "ask for assistance" by applying for the PCH in order to "leave it for people who don't have much":

> 'I could probably get some PCH, but with my salary, I find that rather inappropriate. I still think that asking for assistance. ... I have an elevated civil-servant salary. I make 5,000 euros a month, so I'm not going to request compensation for my disability. I don't need it, if you will. You see? It's a matter of principles. You have to leave it for those who don't have much.' (Louis Resnais, visual impairment, 59, February 2015)

This reference to 'principles' exemplifies Philippe Warin's finding that non-take-up is a form of 'active citizenship' with political meaning in populations fully aware of the benefits for which they are eligible (Warin 2016: 12). This form of 'active non-take-up' shows the extent to which disability benefits are symbolically associated with assistance in ways that are potentially indistinguishable from popular views of charity. As a result, the PCH remains to some extent stigmatized as welfare, which leads to a perception among potentially eligible individuals that applying for it signifies 'asking for help'. Some individuals without pressing financial 'needs' clearly feel the necessity of distancing themselves from the benefit, despite its universalist goal of compensating for a structural inequality between able-bodied and disabled people. Because it is universal, the PCH is distinct from a guaranteed income, but this difference is not easily perceived. Yet this distancing phenomenon also results from the close institutional supervision that is associated with the benefit.

'Sure, we have rights, but we also get to be policed'

Central among participant's frequent criticisms of the MDPHs is the idea of 'being policed'. Participants used this expression to describe administrative oversight, reinforced by additional, less well-defined strategies of social control. Administrative supervision is a heritage from older social welfare policies intended to prevent or limit welfare fraud (Dubois 2009). In the case of disability, the monitoring and supervision that participants most often criticized involved methods to establish disability levels and compensation needs associated with them, as well as the requirements to justify expenses under the PCH benefit. Users also described less direct forms of social control that took the form of value judgements about lifestyle choices. Geneviève Bertaux's narrative demonstrates this fear of intrusion into her personal and family life. Because her income was above the threshold level, she had never been eligible for the ACTP. After the PCH – for which she is eligible – was created, she was initially hesitant to apply out of fear that it would be deducted from her inheritance, but also out of fear of a home visit by the MDPH to assess her need for compensation. Indeed, she had traumatic memories of a home visit by a social worker from the *Protection maternelle et infantile* (PMI) after her daughter was born. At the time, she was afraid that she could lose custody of her daughter because of her disability and dreaded the prospect of official home visits. Her narrative reveals constant, diffuse anxiety of being required to provide justifications to a welfare agency, as well as more specific concerns related to the PCH:

> 'It all scared me. And I admit that if it wasn't for one of my friends having to convince me and certify it wouldn't affect my inheritance, I wouldn't even have asked for it [the PCH]. [...] And then I didn't

> want a hearing. They told me … and I didn't feel like it. They also told me that people might come to my home. This, I really did not want it to happen! I mean – I'm disabled, but my family … and I'm afraid of them playing cops. We have rights, OK, but we also get to be policed. […] I can understand that the state needs proof. But how should they request it? I didn't want them coming to my home for one precise reason. When I had my first daughter, I had a tough time because right after I came home, the PMI was all over me saying "We have to come see you, you understand, you are disabled, do you mistreat your daughter?" … They came to the house and […] the only thing they could find to complain about what that I put too many blankets on my daughter. So yeah, sure, whatever. And you know what? It's stupid but when they came, I was afraid that they might take my daughter away. … It really scared me. It was totally unjustified – I knew it. I had no reason to be afraid, but inside that's how I felt. And it was the same for the MDPH. I don't need personal assistance at home – so why would they need to come?' (Geneviève Bertaux, visual impairment, 62, December 2014)

Geneviève Bertaux's description of her fear of losing custody of her daughter as 'unjustified' is a result of her socioeconomic status, combined with the fact that she is in a couple with a nondisabled husband. It is conceivable that a single mother from a more modest background would not consider such fears unjustified.[6] This is also an indication of her perception of the supervisory mentality underlying the PMI, which she correctly identified as targeting women from lower socioeconomic circles. Her disability placed her in an unusual situation for someone of her more comfortable socioeconomic status, that is, being forced to be accountable to a welfare agency. Later in the interview, she vigorously defends a flat-rate, universal PCH that does not require 'proofs': "[In the field of vision-impairment] I don't think that it's normal to ask people to provide evidence of what they do with these payments. Once you have your disability card and you're in compliance, I don't think it's acceptable for them to demand proof."

In short, there appear to be two main explanations for this perception of social rights as stigmatizing. First, these rights are linked to a categorical view of disability based on being certified as a 'disabled person'. Second, benefits are closely tied with being 'assisted'. Participants report distancing themselves from two specific dimensions of assistance: the administrative procedures involved in 'asking for help' and the social control that follows these procedures and requires perpetually justifying oneself to the administration. In this respect, the primary source of conflict between users and institutional evaluators centres on the assessment of individual need for compensation.

Assessing needs: users versus public institutions

The fears of stigmatization and social control that are expressed in the distancing of social rights reveal the administrative relationship behind the relationship to benefits. The way in which social rights are perceived derives in a central way from the relationship with the administration and the people who grant them, a relationship often described by participants as marked by social control mixed with condescension. Before describing more specifically how beneficiaries experience benefits such as the ACTP and the PCH, it is thus worth reviewing their relationship with the MDPH, the public agency responsible for implementing disabled benefits since the passage of Law of 2005. Indeed, it is important to recall that the stated purpose of the 2005 law was to dramatically reform the administration–user relationship by placing users 'at its heart'. This does not correspond to the way the majority of participants experience the MPDH, which they describe as an institution where they do not feel welcome, an administration demanding proofs and controlling rather than an administration providing services. This impression is especially true in the context of PCH allocation. The needs assessment process generates conflict between users' experiential knowledge of their own daily needs and the ostensibly 'multi-disciplinary' professional expertise of the MDPH, which often determines the final assessment. The restrictive conditions for receiving the PCH explains why many users opt to continue their enrolment in the ACTP, an earlier benefit programme with less stringent conditions and less monitoring. The ACTP, as well as the PCH flat-rate payment directed at blind people, raise the question of how users appropriate these benefits. In other words, given fewer constraints and oversight, what meanings do users assign to the ways in which they spend these benefits?

An inhospitable 'house'

The establishment of MDPHs was one component of a broader programme of decentralization that began in 1982 and, more recently, of regrouping of French public services. In 2005, the MPDH system was proposed as a way of providing a one-stop shop that would centralize disability-related administrative procedures, which had previously been overseen by multiple institutions such as the CDES, Cotorep, prefectures, and others. MDPHs arbitrate people's eligibility to benefits which are then distributed by other agencies, including the CAF for the AAH and the Departmental Council for the PCH (Baudot and Revillard 2014). Despite differences in how MDPHs function from one department to the other, there are three main phases in processing benefit applications. First, users submit applications for 'initial processing' – verification that files are complete and data entry – before they are transferred to the 'multi-disciplinary team' to determine eligibility and issue an allocation proposal (Perrier 2013; Borelle 2015). The explicit emphasis on multi-disciplinarity indicates a desire to go beyond a strictly medical apprehension of disability, although in practice, medical opinions remain of crucial importance. The evaluation process, particularly regarding the need for compensation, sometimes involves home visits, as well as summons to appear in person at the MDPH. Finally, the ultimate decision regarding rights eligibility and allocation is made by the CDAPH (Bureau and Rist 2011; Revillard 2017b). In several MDPHs, however, the CDAPH actually reviews few applications in detail due to their high volume, leading to procedures such as validation 'by list', that is, bulk approval by the commission of batches of applications assembled by the multi-disciplinary team. As a rule, CDAPHs follow the teams' recommendations, which are in effect the final authority concerning needs assessments, although the CDAPH retains final authority. The CDAPH is also a place where the law intended to enhance the participation of users, through the possibility for them to come and defend their case before the committee, and through the presence of association representatives within it.

Unlike this political rhetoric insisting on a major institutional change, the transition from the Cotorep to the MDPH is most often not experienced as a rupture. Research participants were associated with ten different MDPHs. With the exception of the narratives of Lucien Rémo (mentioned earlier) and Laëtitia Roger, who recalled "idealizing" the MDPH when it was created,[7] other participants answered questions regarding this transition (which they never spontaneously mentioned) in a neutral or negative manner. Jérôme Ricordeau and Philippe Tain both responded "nothing" when asked to comment on the shift from the Cotorep to the MDPH. Jean-Marc Sernin observed that the transition was managed "in a completely transparent way. … It didn't change a thing". Other participants reported negative experiences, however, including Claudine Durand, who "liked the Cotorep much better. … [For example, the MDPH] ask me all the time how long it's been since I've been disabled. At the Cotorep, they knew." Dora Moleiro reported difficulty even finding an interlocutor at the MDPH: "Before, we always had the same person when we had a problem with the paperwork. Now it's more complicated. You call and you get an operator."

Beyond these general impressions of the transition from one institution to another, participants expressed a range of impressions of MDPHs. Out of 30 participants, all of whom had been in contact with a MDPH, five reported a globally positive experience with no significant problems with the administrative process and an impression of being properly treated. On the whole, other opinions regarding the MDPH were negative, although with some variation. Descriptions of institutional experiences with the Cotorep were similar to those of MDPHs, the dominant impression being of objectification: "60 per cent, 80 per cent. ... We're not just pieces of meat!" (Lydie Sonnet); "We're not just a stack of paperwork" (Leila Saddi); "You don't feel like telling them your story because you know very well that they don't give a damn" (Daniel Morand). For some participants, the impression of not being appreciated or respected by MDPH staff also corresponds to specific accessibility issues. Daniel Morand, for example, observed that the waiting room of his MDPH was ill-adapted to visually impaired people because there was no audio announcement when one's number flashed across the screen:

> 'At the reception desk, they give you a ticket and ask you to sit down and wait your turn. But how do you know when it's your turn? You have to be able to read a number on the digital banner on the wall. ... [As a visually impaired person] you could wait a long time in your chair for your number to come up.' (Daniel Morand, visual impairment, 58, November 2014)

Beyond this general perception of an institution that is inattentive to its users, programmes specifically intended to grant users a central role in the MDPH by the 2005 law merit closer examination. The law provides for representatives from disability organizations to be present during CDAPH meetings, where users also are supposed to have an opportunity to defend their applications in person.

No participant spontaneously referred to the presence of associative representatives in the CDAPH. When explicitly questioned about this, the issue seemed irrelevant: participants either did not know about this representation of disability organizations among CDAPH members, or had no comment to make about it. Clearly, being represented by associations did not provide users with the sense of being 'at the heart' of the management of their benefits – which does not mean that this participation had no influence (Revillard 2017b). Comments on the possibility of defending one's application in front of the Committee are even more revealing regarding the limit of the MDPH's capacity to foster a sense of citizenship among its target population. Legally, the MDPH is supposed to inform claimants, 15 days ahead of time, of the date their application will be discussed by the CDAPH, as well as of their right to come and argue their case on this occasion.[8] Studies of MDPHs reveal highly variable – and sometimes illegal – practices regarding this policy, however (Baudot et al 2013; Borelle 2015). Particularly given the length of time often required for CDAPHs to issue their decisions, even 'by list' approvals, some MDPHs do not inform users of their right to support their applications, leading to what Céline Borelle refers to as a 'form of non-take-up that is integral to the functioning of an institution' (Borelle 2015). Participant interviews confirmed that a lack of information contributes to non-take-up. Indeed, only Victor Jaucourt and Julie Ferandi asked to be heard by the CDAPH. Non-take-up does not necessarily reflect a lack of knowledge. Élise Bastien described the obstacle of travelling to her MDPH, which was in another city, and the numerous public transportation challenges facing visually impaired people:

> 'We're allowed to attend the commissions. [...] But for visually impaired people, going to [City X, where the MDPH is located], taking the bus, the train, the subway. ... It's the other end of the world. It is a place that we are unfamiliar with, and no one in [Department Y] except the inhabitants of [City X] is going there to ... defend their cases in person.' (Élise Bastien, visual impairment, 47, January 2015)

Non-take-up often results from the ways in which users interpret the right to attend a CDAPH hearing as tantamount to a summons or demand for justifications. When asked about speaking to the commission, Dora Moleiro referred to a colleague who had been 'summoned' by a commission as part of an AAH application review:

AR: [A]fter the MDPH was created, were you informed by the MDPH that you could attend a hearing?

DM: No. Now, I know that when some people ask for home assistance. ... I have a colleague who, not long ago after she'd been laid off, they asked her to be recategorized because her vision had deteriorated, and she could not do her job anymore. She was obliged to file a request at the MDPH, and then she got a summons. Because she had worked for 25 years and all of a sudden, she asked for the disabled adult benefit. So, she received a summons and went before the committee.

AR: But you – that didn't happen to you?

DM: No. I think that when they are cases ... from a long time ago [that is, when one has been administratively certified as disabled for a long time] I think ... maybe someday we'll need to appear before them? (Dora Moleiro, visual impairment, 47, February 2015)

It is probable that this 'summons' was issued by the MDPH multi-disciplinary team and not by the CDAPH, which generally try to keep users at arm's length. This confusion surrounding the question of summons – as opposed to rightfully attending commission meetings – is nevertheless revealing. The confusing series of administrative episodes going from an eventual summons by the multi-disciplinary team to the right to attend a CDAPH hearing, means that it is unsurprising that users potentially perceive the hearing as a new summons and hence a demand for justification as opposed an opportunity to defend their right to receive benefits. Even Julie Ferandi, who attended a CDAPH meeting to argue for her right to the AAH, mentions having gone to "have her card renewed in front of a jury", an allusion to the criminal justice system that underscores the perception of being repeatedly held accountable by the administration. Daniel Morand's remarks well describe this no-man's-land between a right and a command ("If they think it's necessary, you might be heard") that the "possibility of a hearing" can represent for users:

AR: Were you informed about the possibility of committee hearing?

DM: I am aware that hearings are possible, but I think. ... I was told that if they thought it was necessary, you could be heard, but it wasn't me who. ... I couldn't participate in the commission if they didn't think it was necessary. It seemed to me. On the other hand, if you appeal a decision, you can make your argument before the appeals commission. Sure, I know you can do that. (Daniel Morand, visual impairment, 58, November 2014)

The burden of continually owing justifications to these institutions is also revealed, although in a different way, by Leila Saddi's narrative. Although she had clearly understood that she had a right to a hearing and that it was not an order, Leila refused to exercise her rights on the grounds that it would entail having to justify herself. She rejected the idea that anyone could conceive that an applicant for the PCH would commit fraud on the application to finance homecare assistance: "Having to justify yourself ... I mean, it's surreal, once again. OK, why not in an extreme case if it's about equipment? But for homecare, I mean, there is no way. It's no fun having someone at home, needing someone 24 hours a day." This apprehension about the prospect of a hearing illustrates that the administrative relationship with the MDPH is primarily seen through the prism of social control. This explains users' near-uniform expressions of discomfort regarding the institution. The fact that few users attend CDAPH meetings means that clashes over needs evaluations tend to take place outside of the commission, either beforehand, as part of the MDPH's evaluation of the application, or afterwards, when users appeal the decision.

'I don't need anybody to think for me'

The administration's power to determine compensation levels assigns PCH beneficiaries a rank analogous to that of social welfare recipients in terms of bureaucratic intrusion into their daily lives. In his foundational article, 'The Law is All Over', Austin Sarat describes the omnipresence of the law in the daily lives of 'the welfare poor':

> Law is, for people on welfare, repeatedly encountered in the most ordinary transaction and events of their lives. Legal rules and practices are implicated in determining whether and how welfare recipients will be able to meet some of their most pressing needs [...] because being on welfare means having a significant part of one's life organized by a regime of legal rules invoked by officials to claim jurisdiction over choices and decisions which those not on welfare would regard as personal and private. (Sarat 1990: 344)

Although unlike welfare, the PCH is a universal, non-means-tested benefit, it wields similar control over certain aspects of recipients' personal lifestyles, including adapted equipment and technical aids as well as homecare. The principle of individualization that governs the needs assessment is ambiguous in this regard. On paper, this principle takes an individual's unique needs into account, but in practice, experiential expertise is not really recognized, and institutional expertise prevails. Instead of encouraging greater attention to users, the individualization principle results in increased monitoring: this is exemplified by the transition from a fixed-rate benefit – the ACTP – to the PCH, an individualized benefit whose amount is based on an assessment of compensation needs over which the institution has the final word.

Participants often objected to the way the administration assessed their needs, on several grounds. Geneviève Bertaux, for example, was opposed to any pretense on the part of the administration to "think for [her]": "Maybe it's because I have true awareness of my needs, but I tell myself 'I'm old enough to formulate them. I don't need anybody to think for me'."

The first problems with PCH needs assessments begin with the application. Several participants contended that the assessment is based on a reductionist view of disability that fails to reflect actual needs. The administrative definition focuses on functional limitations that result in an inability to perform specific daily tasks that are unchallenging for them (for example, bathing by oneself with a visual impairment), leading to difficulties in knowing "which box to assign [ourselves] to":

> 'When you're sitting there with the documents, you don't know which box to assign yourself to: "Do you get dressed by yourself? Do you bathe by yourself?" [...] It's not really addressed to us. ... It's true that the questionnaires are pretty broad, but they're not about us. So as a result, you never know where to situate yourself in all that. Because

it's true that we can dress unassisted. But going grocery shopping is complicated. Travelling around is a bit more complicated, too.' (Dora Moleiro, visual impairment, 47, February 2015)

Geneviève Bertaux described similar difficulties that led her to "declare more limitations than you really want to declare" to avoid having them "drain your benefits" because the forms did not match her needs.

In addition to inadequately identifying which needs merit compensation, expertise acquired through personal experience sometimes conflicts with institutional expertise in terms of specific personal factors. Claudine Durand, a paraplegic 56-year-old, disagreed with the MDPH occupational therapist who conducted a home evaluation of modifications needed in her bathroom. Claudine maintained that she needed a shower, but the occupational therapist insisted on a pivoting chair for her bathtub, which she initially refused to use:

> 'I'd asked for a shower because it's hard to step into a bathtub. There was an occupational therapist who came, sent over by the MDPH. At the time he thought – I'll show you in a minute – he thought it was better to place a chair in my bathtub, a pivoting chair. I didn't agree at all. ... I accepted it, but I wasn't pleased – I wanted a shower! In the beginning, I was fixated on it – "I'll just use the sink!" – but now, well, little-by-little I've grown to like it. Whatever.' (Claudine Durand, mobility impairment, 56, November 2014)

When Claudine shows me the bathtub installation at the end of our interview, it becomes obvious that she was reluctant to accept the chair because it was so blatantly medicalized, which clashed with her own attempt to make her disability less visible by the way in which she arranged the rest of the apartment. Handrails on the walls and the placement of the furniture, for example, enabled her to move from room to room without a wheelchair, which she reserved for use outside. The aesthetic dimension of her living space was obviously important to her, but it was considered secondary by the occupational therapist responsible for making the decision.

Leila Saddi, who is quadriplegic, experienced a more significant mismatch between her assessment of her needs and the official MDPH assessment. Following a deterioration in her health, she requested an increase in her hours of at-home personal assistance. The request was initially denied on the grounds that she had not been tracheotomized. Leila insisted on her ability to estimate her own needs, but she also based her appeal on an interpretation of relevant official regulations. The MDPH evaluator who visited her home had retorted that she was doing "very well" and that there were cases "far worse than hers". Because Leila continued to insist that she should receive the amount of homecare assistance that she believed to be necessary, the MDPH asked the association for whom she herself volunteers to provide additional volunteers to cover some of her assistance:

AR: And otherwise, at the level of the benefits that you receive, have you already had conflicts with the MDPH? Have you already been involved in a disagreement with them?

LS: Yes. This summer. … Maybe that's why I got sick. I renewed my application and requested that, in view of my situation – my disability – my condition had really deteriorated. … I asked for 24-hour homecare. But I was told I didn't need it and that I wasn't dying, that I didn't have a tracheotomy. But when you look at the regulations, it's clearly written that to prevent bedsores. … For assistance, you need someone to be present. We have the right. So I had to fight for more hours. And I was visited by different people who were supposed to help me complete the application, but they all just downgraded me.

AR: People from the MDPH?

LS: Yes. I had one. … What do you call them? An evaluator, who was completely out of it and told me I was doing very well and that there were far worse cases than me. … They conducted an inquiry into my activities. They also called the association where I volunteered and asked them if they couldn't help me in order to reduce my demand for hours so that they didn't have to pay for them. […] Normally, that's not legal … it's my private life. (Leila Saddi, mobility impairment, 31, March 2015)

Leila was ultimately granted an increase in at-home personal assistance, but the administration reproached her over her combativeness: "When you defend your case, they tell you you're mean. Because you're using the correct terminology and you defend yourself, you're accused of being aggressive and mean."

Leila's experience illustrates the two facets of control, both in terms of the needs assessment and of intrusiveness into one's private life (in this instance, the association for which Leila was a volunteer). Compounding this two-pronged control was the fact that the official assessments explicitly undermined Leila's claiming process. When she insisted that her rights be respected and protested how she was treated, she was labelled "aggressive" and "mean". Not only did Leila deplore the monitoring and suspicion, but she also resented the fact that the process invalidated her personal experience and that she was not recognized as having rights and a private life and of being capable of communicating her needs and making claims.

Diverse appropriations of a fixed-rate benefit

Even though the 2005 law was innovative in establishing a universal right to compensation, a pre-existing programme – the third-party compensatory benefit (ACTP) – had been established by the Law of 1975. The parameters of this benefit, whose beneficiaries prior to 2005 are allowed to choose to continue (they were offered the choice between the ACTP and the newer PCH programme), are more restrictive than the PCH in two ways: it is means-tested, and funds for homecare are typically restricted to fewer than three hours per day (Beyrie 2015). On the other hand, while the PCH imposes close surveillance of expenses (direct payment upon receipt of bills), the ACTP is paid directly to the beneficiary, with expenditures at their discretion. Blind people, however, are targeted by a separate system in which fixed compensation is provided via the ACTP (the 'blindness payment' of €880 per month at the time of the study) or through the PCH blindness benefit (at a lower rate of €620 per month).

The fact that the ACTP imposes less monitoring of expenses explains why enrolees whose needs were met by ACTP payments remained with the programme after 2005. Because of the specific nature of the blindness payment, this is particularly true of visually impaired participants. Philippe Tain described the PCH as a "trap for idiots" that most eligible blind individuals avoided because of widespread awareness of the lower flat rate of the PCH. The only study participants enrolled in the ACTP prior to 2005 who changed to the PCH had physical disabilities that required homecare levels that surpassed ACTP coverage. One visually impaired participant, Jean-Marc Sernin, also had to withdraw from the ACTP after moving to a new department because the method used to assess eligibility by his new MDPH caused him to exceed the ACTP income ceiling. All other participants had become aware of the advantages of strategically maintaining the ACTP through friends, personal inquiries, associations ("people advised me to stay where I was", as Lydie Sonnet reported), or even through the MDPH itself, which "told us to just keep the old one", according to Dora Moleiro.

How do people receiving these fixed-rate benefits (ACTP or a flat-rate PCH blindness benefit) account for their uses of the latter, in a context where other benefits are under close administrative scrutiny? The interview context is not neutral in this respect: it is possible that study participants modified their discourse, facing a nondisabled interviewer, as opposed to fellow beneficiaries. They may have oriented their discourse towards legal criteria for compensation. It is nevertheless worth noting the diverse ways in which participants accounted for how they spent their benefits during interviews. Original conceptions of justice emerge in these narratives, through reinterpretations of legal criteria.

The cases of individuals whose only other source of income is the AAH warrants separate discussion. These individuals describe the ACTP/PCH as an indispensable supplement of the modest income provided by the AAH. These two benefits are thus often described as connected in such a way as to provide a basic income. Lydie Sonnet, for example, observed "I had the AAH. ... And [since 2001] I get the third-party payment." A comparison between these two payments suggesting they originate in the same programme is implicit in Dora Moleiro's remark that the ACTP "is something that you get even if you work", unlike the AAH, which varies according to recipients' earned income. Alice Perrin describes the ACTP as a "phenomenal help", confirming that "Just living on the AAH at €800/ month, I couldn't have managed."

The fixed-rate payment hence functions as an income supplement, particularly for AAH beneficiaries. This does not mean the payments are not intended for specific expenses in the minds of beneficiaries. The variety of attitudes towards fixed-rate payments illustrates the variety of relationships between beneficiaries and the regulatory framework, ranging from conforming as closely as possible to regulations to insisting on independence, including occasional idiosyncratic interpretations of the notion of compensation.

Michel Simon expressed the most legalistic argument among study participants.[9] He refused to consider the ACTP as an "income supplement", preferring to consider it "normal to use these payments for what they are intended for":

> 'At first, I used it to pay for housekeeping, mainly housekeeping. Housekeeping but then the ACTP was more than enough, and I started not hesitating to take taxis. ... I just told myself that what I receive from the ACTP I need to use because it's intended for that. It's not an income supplement, it's not intended for us to save money. It's really supposed to be spent for the disability. So I don't hesitate. I don't hesitate to buy specialized equipment when I need it and to take taxis when I need to. Yeah. Calling professionals for repairs. Those are the kinds of things that, if I had good vision, I'd certainly do myself. [...] I think it's normal to use these payments for what they're intended for.' (Michel Simon, visual impairment, 57, February 2015)

Describing how she spends her flat-rate PCH, Marie Germain stresses that it compensates for the extra costs of shopping at her local grocery store as opposed to a large supermarket, which is not accessible for her:

AR: And you were saying that the problem with these technologies [technical assistance for blind people] is that it's often fairly expensive. Is this something you have been compensated for?

MG: There are some compensations. There's what is called the PCH, a compensation payment for disabled people, that you apply for and that's paid every month to compensate for all the ... additional financial costs, in fact, that can be caused by our disability. For example, when I go shopping, well, I go to my small neighbourhood grocery store. I don't go to the supermarket because I'm not going to take the car to go grocery shopping [Laughs]. (Marie Germain, visual impairment, 60, November 2014)

The idea of compensation for extra costs associated with purchases at a local store instead of a large supermarket marks an interesting departure from the initial conception of the PCH focusing on individual 'needs', to what could be described as a compensation for structural discrimination (not having access to the same opportunities for consumption).

In another example of how individuals give specific meanings to benefits according to their own situations, Alice Perrin complained about the lack of consideration of maternity-related needs. As a paraplegic person, she receives the ACTP and did not apply for the PCH because the needs she needed compensation for, particularly those related to her maternal role, were not recognized by this programme:

> 'They don't take into account the help you need to take care of your baby. Can you give a baby a bath when you're in a wheelchair? You'd lose your balance. Just putting the baby in the car-seat, you lose your balance because the child's weight makes you fall forward. It's super-dangerous!' (Alice Perrin, mobility impairment, 40, February 2015)

This insistence on compensation for expenses related to parental duties reveals two significant biases in the traditional workings of disability compensation in France. The first concerns the relationship to care and caregivers. By conceiving of intended beneficiaries above all as recipients of care, the programme neglects the caregiver roles that they themselves also perform. Relatedly, the programme reveals an obvious gender bias: by omitting needs linked to parenthood, it fails to compensate needs which currently are much more present in women's than in men's lives due to the gendered division of labour. Although parallel compensation programmes exist related to wage-earning professional activity, no similar compensation, at the time of the study, addressed the unpaid but considerable family caregiving labour that is overwhelmingly performed inside the home by women.[10] For lack of formal recognition, the ACTP, a payment that was initially intended to transform individuals into care recipients, is appropriated by users as a tool that reconstructs them as caregivers.

Finally, in a demand for autonomy that is even more distanced from official regulations, Maryse Cloutier openly proclaims that she uses the payments to pay for leisure activities. She presents her right to leisure as how life differs from survival. Underscoring the fact that "you can't live on the AAH", she describes how the surplus provided by the ACTP allows her to "go out" or "take a trip", which would no longer be possible if she applied to the PCH programme, which would only pay directly for at-home personal assistance:

MC: If you're on the PCH, they're going to require you to justify your expenses down to the last cent, and I can't do that.

AR: OK, so [when the choice was presented following the 2005 reforms] you preferred to remain with the ACTP programme …

MC: And use the money the way I want. […] I mean, I want to be able to go out and if I want to travel, to be able to do it. If I spent all of my money on home assistants, it will be so sad. (Maryse Cloutier, mobility impairment, 72, November 2014)

Autonomy, understood as including access to leisure activities, is defined here in a conflictive relation to disability-related social rights, objectively relying on them while departing to some extent from their initial purpose and avoiding or contesting the social control often associated with them. As a counterexample, Maryse Cloutier cites a friend who was forced to change from the ACTP to the PCH by a decline in his health. She describes her friend as confined to his home after the change, without any margin for expenses other than the needed homecare: "He's at home! He doesn't do anything anymore! All his spending goes to this [homecare]."

All these comments provide useful insights into people's relationship not only to the law, but also to the justice due to disabled people. To be sure, rights as evoked in the interviews are to some extent linked to legally encoded rights. Legal recognition of the right to compensation due to a disability contributes to the subjective perception of this right. As subjectively defined, however, these rights encompass a broader perimeter than legally recognized rights, including for example the right to parental support, to leisure activities, and to compensation for additional costs associated with shopping in smaller shops. The room for manoeuvre left, where applicable, by the system (ACTP or flat-rate PCH) is then invested, allowing the use of legally enshrined rights to serve the more personal conception of rights. This discrepancy is sometimes perceived, and its investment claimed. Maryse Cloutier and Alice Perrin are aware of using the payment in a way that deviates from regulations (maternity, leisure activities). In other cases, benefit uses are thought to fall within the perimeter of legal criteria, of which they reveal personal interpretations. This is the case, for example, of Marie Germain when she talks about the compensation for having to shop at the local grocery store rather than in a supermarket.

While the assessment of disability as well as of compensation needs seem to be typical examples of contemporary processes of governmentality, bringing state discipline as close as possible to the everyday behaviour of individuals, the accounts of experience show that this hold on bodies and subjectivities is never complete (Lebeer and Moriau 2010). In fact, participant interviews revealed a high level of critical reflection among disabled people in the face of the policy interventions in which their daily lives are involved to varying degrees. Whether they are objecting to being treated like objects ("60 per cent, 80 per cent. ... We're not just pieces of cheese!"), refusing to accept the results of a needs assessment, even when they fail to have the last word ("I preferred to just wash myself in the sink!"), or defending their autonomy against administrative control ("using the money as I see fit"), disabled individuals demand their independence and express these demands concretely through a range of practices that represent acts of micro-resistance against the administration (Scott 1991). Further, users' sometimes innovative ways of appropriating their rights, as exemplified by their understandings of a flat-rate benefit, could provide a rich resource for regulatory reforms, including recognition of the right to leisure activities, compensation for maternity-related expenses, and compensation for structural discrimination.

A situation of uncertainty

One of the fundamental characteristics of formal-rational law, according to a Weberian analysis focused on its social effects, is the predictability that it enables (Coutu 1995). The law induces a particular type of relationship to time, limiting uncertainty. Legal rationalization consequently constituted a necessary precondition for the development of modern capitalism by guaranteeing private property and regulating exchanges. This is similarly true of social benefits, whose guarantee is intended to foster a particular relationship with temporality marked by the reduction of uncertainty, regardless of the contingencies of life. This idea is the founding principle of the development of social policy. Envisioned from a perspective centred on citizens' rights consciousness, this link between rights and time suggests an evaluation of the efficacy of rights through the prism of citizens' confidence in their effectiveness. A right completely fulfils its purpose only when citizens have total faith in its effectiveness. Short of this trust, the right fails to reduce uncertainty. In the case of disability-related social rights, eligible citizens are often uncertain about their future as beneficiaries. This uncertainty about rights derives from the uncertainty that marks the administrative relationship. This uncertainty concerns obtaining a response, the continuity of payments, and geographical consistency. It often flows from the past experience of delays, interruptions, and unannounced changes in benefits.

Chronically unpredictable processing times

A key component of the administrative evaluation of the quality of services provided by MDPHs is the length of time required to process applications. This question is also a primary source of user dissatisfaction. Ever since the MDPHs were created, chronic delays have been a frequent complaint, despite the fact that reducing the long delays of the earlier Cotorep system was an explicit objective of the 2005 reform (Baudot et al 2013: 245). Although the law stipulates a maximum application processing time of four months,[11] at the time of this study, the average exceeded this period in half of the MDPHs, reaching as many as 12 months in some departments (CNSA 2014) according to administrative data provided by the MDPHs themselves (which need to be interpreted with caution given unstable data and the political dimension of this key measure of institutional effectiveness) (Baudot 2015).

Most participants in this study reported extended delays in the processing of their applications. Daniel Morand's request for occasional technical assistance (a computer) was simply lost:

> 'They lost the file I had put together, along with all of the supporting documents. They couldn't find any trace of it. They require medical exams, which are only valid for three months. So, a lost file, if it takes six months [to realize the file is lost], it means you have to start your medical exam completely over. So, I said no way. I was outraged. I told them that it was out of the question for me to return. … Because in addition, medical exams are done at the hospital, and it takes six months to get an appointment. It's just unthinkable. I told them it was out of the question [for me to redo the exam] and that I would give them a photocopy, since I had luckily taken the time to copy the whole file. Otherwise, there's just no solution. And it happens to plenty of people with the MDPH. So maybe there aren't enough employees, or the people aren't well-trained. Maybe the budget's too small, too. But it's unforgivable.' (Daniel Morand, visual impairment, 58, November 2014)

Long delays are such a common occurrence that users expect them and act accordingly rather than following recommended timeframes. For example, they learn to anticipate that a PCH application will take up to a year to be processed. Users also learn to anticipate extended delays for benefit renewal requests by filing renewal applications as long as a year in advance of the deadline. According to Dora Moleiro, "You have to start the process a year early. … Before [with the Cotorep], you reached three or four months. … Now, you get an answer a year later."

The most significant problems associated with long delays involve requests that cannot be anticipated, such as increase in homecare needs during periods of poor health or when adaptive equipment requires urgent replacement. Claudine Durand wryly observed, after her MDPH refused to reimburse her for the replacement of her hearing aid, that the device did not warn her before it broke:

> 'When I changed hearing aids, for example, I wrote the MDPH so they would reimburse me part of the cost. But I find that absurd, because the first one broke, and I had to buy another one. So, I wrote the MDPH and explained, and they answered me, "Once you already have one, we can't do anything. You should have told us before you bought it." But the device didn't, like, warn me "Six months from now, I'm going to break, and you'll have to replace me."' (Claudine Durand, mobility impairment, 56, November 2014)

Waiting for an application to be processed is a significant problem for those who use the PCH to pay for technical assistance, often culminating in their being forced to use their personal funds. After several refusals by the PCH following extremely long processing times, Léa Martin recalled exhaustion that led her to pay for the equipment herself:

> 'I needed to redo my application, but after all that, you're just tired of it. You give up because it takes two years for your application, and it still has to be accepted. So, yeah. … A wheelchair is something you need right away! And you need an accessible bathroom right away, too!' (Léa Martin, mobility impairment, 28, January 2015)

Not every disabled person is financially able to pay for such urgent needs, particularly given the considerable cost of homecare. After a delay in her PCH renewal, Leila Saddi owed money to the organization that provided her caregivers, which even threatened to suspend her homecare services. During a period of unemployment, Philippe Tain experienced an interruption in his AAH benefits: "Wham. It's zero. Nothing. Not a dime. Try explaining that to your leasing agent. What are you supposed to do after that? Go to a soup kitchen? Apply for the RSA?" Dora Moleiro, whose ACTP was suspended after she received a late renewal notice, described the difficulty of the long wait for the commission to reach a decision:

AR: In that case, did you try to appeal the decision or take other steps to unblock things?

DM: Ah, unblock them, I don't know. On the other hand, it's true that afterwards, they pay you the full amount. It's retroactive. The worry is that sometimes you don't receive a dime for three or four months. That happened with the third-party benefit because the commission hadn't met. For several months we didn't get anything. Then afterwards, of course, we received the full amount. But I mean. … In the meantime, though, you can't do anything since they tell us "Your application is going before the committee." There is nothing you can do, no way to accelerate things. (Dora Moleiro, visual impairment, 47, February 2015)

Unpredictable processing times can have far-reaching consequences for users, leading to non-take-up but also to interruptions in payments that have financial but also potentially life-threatening consequences. These negative effects are internalized and anticipated by users, either based on experience or through hearsay from their networks. As a result, benefits become a source of unpredictability rather than functioning as vectors of stability. Strategies for avoiding such problems include submitting applications far in advance of deadlines, thereby reintroducing a degree of predictability although not necessarily shortening the timeframe. Indeed, not only are unpredictable events not covered, but the continuity of payments is frequently reported as an additional source of anxiety.

Uncertainty about the long-term stability of payments

Unpredictable processing times are exacerbated by other uncertainties about services and benefits. These doubts extend to concerns about the stability of the level of payments (in connection to the recognized level of functional limitation as well as assessed compensation needs) and even of the benefit itself. For some, this concern derives from the experience of interrupted payments, or interruptions experienced by acquaintances. In the 1990s, Philippe Tain, whose visual impairment was stable or even deteriorating, saw his official disability level reduced from 100 per cent to 60 per cent, entailing an important decrease in the level of his AAH. After two appeals to the Cotorep, his case was eventually settled in court "after a two-and-a-half-year battle". After moving to a different department in France, one of his friends had recently seen his disability level reduced by a single percentage point, from 80 per cent to 79 per cent, that caused him to lose his full-AAH eligibility, a direct consequence of budget-reduction policies in his opinion:

> 'These men, since there is fewer and fewer [budget], want to invest less and less, so they raise the ceilings. Meaning one day you're at 80 per cent. You haven't gone to Lourdes or been operated on. Your case

> is classified as incurable. Nothing can be done. And from one day to the next, wham! You're at 79 per cent. Yep. That's it. The end of your AAH payments!' (Philippe Tain, visual impairment, 47, January 2015)

Alice Perrin expressed similar concerns about renewing her ACTP after noting that the criteria used to establish disability levels had been made "stricter": "Now I don't even know if they're going to maintain it ... because the rules are stricter." Independently of their likely impact on the evaluation of disabilities, cost-cutting policies cause concerns among beneficiaries about the continuity of their payments. After receiving PCH payments for ten years, Marie Germain expressed anxiety, as her renewal date approached, due to the difficult economic context and the fact that "lots of things are called into question". This common representation of unstable rights is revealed by the apprehension that accompanies the 'paperwork' (Mesnel 2017) when applying for renewals:

> 'I tremble every time I have to renew it.' (Maryse Cloutier, mobility impairment, 72, November 2014)

> 'I know people who get depressed and stressed out or can't sleep when their applications are due.' (Élise Bastien, visual impairment, 47, January 2015)

When asked what needs "to be improved about the administration", Lydie Sonnet suggested automatic renewals, an idea derived from the experience of an impromptu home visit by an MDPH evaluator after she forgot to apply for her ACTP renewal:

> 'It was when I made the change to receive third-party compensation, until 2015, ten years ago. ... I put away the paperwork and didn't think about it again. I forgot. One of the people who work in those offices phoned me and said, "I'm coming by to see you tomorrow or else we're cancelling everything." She came. I told her "Listen, ma'am. I made a mistake. Please don't take away anything because I'll be forced to file a complaint." It scared her, because it's unacceptable. And it would be great if it was automatic. They just say, "Madame Sonnet in 2015. Wham."' (Lydie Sonnet, mobility impairment, 73, November 2014)

Lydie reported that she no longer trusted herself to fill out the forms and now asked for help from associative volunteers out of fear that one day they would send her an announcement that said, "you have made an error – we're stopping everything":

LS: I was doing it myself, but since it was getting complicated, I asked for help.

AR: And it's the people at the MDPH who help you, or …?

LS: Yeah, or else the volunteers [at a foundation]. And I filled them out, too, but now it's more and more complex, so I prefer not to be sent a paper saying, "You've made an error – we're stopping everything." You see what I mean? There needs to be … sometimes it makes you think there should be disabled people working in this field. (Lydie Sonnet, mobility impairment, 73, November 2014)

The uncertainty surrounding benefit renewals, combined with the sheer administrative weight of the process, helps explain that participants criticize the five-to-ten-year eligibility renewal requirement, which is a particularly useless burden on individuals whose disabilities have not changed:

> '[Referring to a mobility impairment] A body part doesn't just grow back all of a sudden! […] Whenever I go to the ophthalmologist, he asks me "Ah, so this is for your renewal application?" […] He complains about it every time. He says it's just crazy!' (Philippe Tain, visual impairment, 47, January 2015)

> 'It [reapplying every five years] is abnormal. We shouldn't have to justify ourselves for being disabled. We're not going to be cured – we're disabled. So, it's really, really hard [sighs].' (Léa Martin, mobility impairment, 28, January 2015)

In addition to the frequent complaints about the administrative process, participants often express resentment about repeatedly being required to prove that their disability still exists even though, in their cases, it is stable over time. The renewal requirement – which is consistent with a definition of disability as situational – clashes with the experience of individuals whose disabilities are a permanent feature of their lives.[12]

Geographical uncertainty and awareness of territorial disparities

Geographical variations further complicate the stability of benefits, both in terms of transferring a MDPH file from one department to another, and in terms of widely reported and documented territorial disparities in the operations of MDPHs and the attribution of benefits (Baudot et al 2013).

Several participants reported problems transferring their files to a new MDPH, which took Jérôme Ricordeau over a year after he changed departments for professional reasons: "[F]rom MDPH to MDPH, it took a year to get it taken care of. … Because there was no form or process for moving.

After that they made a mistake, and my file was processed wrong." He pointedly observed that he had no such difficulties transferring other administrative files such as the CAF (family benefits) and *Sécurité sociale* (national health insurance). This suggests the existence of specific problems in the MDPH system that Jérôme Ricordeau derides as stemming from ignorance: "[T]hey don't know that disabled people ever move." Daniel Morand reported similar struggles with his MDPH file that he transferred when he moved.

Jean-Marc Sernin also experienced territorial disparities when he transferred his file following a move, only to find that his ACTP benefit was reduced by two-thirds due to a different method of calculating income:

> 'There seemed to be a big difference in how the regulations were interpreted in terms of resources from one department to the next. [In my home city] I had an ACTP of 80 per cent that was divided by three when [I changed departments]. So, given this substantial reduction. ... I never understood why, because I figured the payments were at least standardized. ... So that's why I switched to the PCH programme.' (Jean-Marc Sernin, visual impairment, 61, February 2015)

Without personally experiencing such issues, a number of other participants spontaneously complained about territorial variations: "What's deplorable is that the same rules don't apply to everybody between different regions."[13] Nicolas Barut referred to differences in the evaluation of disability levels between departments as an issue he commonly provides advice about as a disability-resource advisor:

> 'We know things are OK [in X city]. Because you know it's the departments that pay ... so it depends on how much is in the local piggy bank. If you go to [department Y], you're not going to get the PCH or ACTP because they don't have any money.' (Nicolas Barut, visual impairment, 40, January 2016)

He continued by pointing out problems transferring files between departments:

> 'You really have to be careful about transferring your files too often because, for one thing, it can take two months. ... It's easy to picture how departments don't communicate with each other, especially since they can't even manage what's in their own department. So, expecting them to know what's happening somewhere else is just impossible.' (Nicolas Barut, visual impairment, 40, January 2016)

Knowledge of these territorial disparities, as well as the difficulty of transferring files, contributed to Nicolas Barut's decision not to transfer his file when a several-year training programme caused a temporary move to a different department: "You just have to avoid transferring it. You should keep it where it is unless you're moving permanently." For this reason, he maintained his original address as his "assistance residence".[14]

Systemic problems such as extended or unpredictable processing times, concerns about the continuity of payments, territorial disparities, and problems with inter-departmental transfers demonstrate that disabled benefit programmes are failing to realize their potential as vectors of predictability for their beneficiaries. In combination with the social control the programmes involve, these uncertainties render disabled benefits more tenuous, despite their potential role in increasing autonomy.

Conclusion: Rights consciousness and the administrative relationship

The enshrinement of substantive social rights in law is not enough to make them exist for individuals. This study of the reception of social rights reinforces earlier pessimistic research findings concerning the ability of MDPHs to make these rights real (Baudot et al 2013; Baudot and Revillard 2014; Borelle 2015). It also underscores the strong connection between the 'having' and the 'being' of rights, that is, users' rights consciousness significantly depends on the degree to which they feel respected by the administration as rightful subjects of rights.

The effectiveness of benefits is diminished by the ways in which they are implemented and by users' perceptions. The experience – and expectation – of heavy supervision, conflicts over needs assessments and disability levels, interruptions in payments, and unmanageable delays create a lack of trust and predictability, as well as a perception of disrespect. Social rights then fail in their capacity to reduce uncertainty and to act on people's perception of their social status by making them subjects of rights. Whether the eventual outcome is non-take-up, or distrustful or reluctant take-up, rights consciousness is therefore tenuous and unstable.

This fragility of social rights is particularly surprising in a country that is known for its long-standing and strong social policies. Indeed, this does not mean that these benefits to not have true, positive impact on their beneficiaries' living conditions and autonomy. Clearly, however, the scope of these beneficial effects is attenuated by both material failings, such as when payments are reduced, cancelled, or not paid in a timely manner, and symbolic flaws such as social control, inefficiency, and unpredictability. Without being reduced to this, these fears relating to social rights can be linked to the experience of a retreat from acquired rights which is taking place, at the time of our study, in another area: that of accessibility.

5

Freedom of Movement: A 'Sweet Dream'?

> 'Going to friends' houses whenever I want, without any limits. That's my "sweet dream".' (Laëtitia Roger, mobility impairment, 40, November 2014)

> 'There is nothing more gratifying and satisfying than being free to move, free to travel, to be independent.' (Léa Martin, mobility impairment, 28, January 2015)

When nondisabled people consider freedom of movement or travel,[1] they tend to associate it with border-crossings or being deprived of freedom by incarceration, because mobility seems so natural for them that they are only able to conceive of it through its absence.[2] This conceptual presence-via-negation is incarnated in sites of deprivation of freedom such as prisons, detention centres, and re-education camps. For many disabled people, this fundamental right is violated daily, leading to a conception of unfettered mobility as a 'sweet dream'. In this dream, independent mobility takes a variety of forms but generally includes moving without assistance that is often made necessary by inaccessible physical environments. Another common feature of this dream is spontaneous mobility ('whenever I want') unlike the advance planning often required by adapted transportation services – and mobility at the same transportation cost as that afforded by nondisabled people (unlike when one needs to take a taxi for lack of availability of accessible public transportation). This dream may also include being able to move about like others and benefiting from non-segregated public transportation.

For disabled people, this still unrealized fundamental freedom imposes important limitations on access to employment, leisure activities, and numerous other forms of social participation. This disparity in access to features of life that many nondisabled people take for granted is deeply revealing of the social status of disabled people. Beginning in the 1980s, their demands to increase their freedom of movement occupied a central role in the actions of advocacy associations that quickly came to be represented by a single word: accessibility (Mor 2018). For disabled people to be able to enjoy unobstructed, spontaneous mobility, the physical environment must be rendered fully accessible. This key axiom of the disability movement has gradually gained some influence over public policy. Because of its very material dimension, this claim provides one of the clearest illustrations of the shift from the medical to the social model of disability (Oliver and Barnes 2012): providing mobility for a paraplegic person does not require developing medical treatments that enable them to walk (medical model), but instead replacing a staircase with an elevator or stairs with ramps (social model).

Accessibility was initially somewhat tepidly introduced in France by the Law of 1975. It was more clearly defined in the Law of 11 February 2005, which imposed a ten-year period for accessibility modifications to the built environment and public transportation systems, a period after which sanctions and penalties would have been imposed in case of non-compliance. This legal guarantee was intended to ensure the timely execution of a nation-wide accessibility programme, raising hopes that were ultimately unrealized following a September 2014 ruling that postponed the 2015 deadline. This chapter focuses on the effects of this accessibility policy, which was initially voluntaristic but whose ambitions proved to be thwarted by the postponement. As discussed in the first section of this chapter, this broken promise as well as the material effects of the partial implementation of this accessibility policy exerted a mobilizing influence on disabled people. While the focus of struggles and politicization, the question of accessibility, however, does not entirely encompass the notion of mobility. Although the physical environment can be modified to improve material accessibility, significant social barriers to mobility remain. This invites us to investigate public spaces as sites of stigmatization, marginalization, and discrimination, as well as the attendant fears associated with mobility that accompany them.

Accessibility: an unrealized political imperative

How have successive disability policies in France recognized accessibility rights, and what has been their impact?

Two steps forward, one step back

The first legal reference to the concept of accessibility in France dates to the Law of 1975. Article 49, which relates to the built environment, stipulated that '[a]rchitectural designs and organisation of residential facilities and sites open to the public, in particular schools, universities, and training locations, must ensure that these sites and installations are accessible to disabled persons'. Article 52, which relates to public transportation, opened two parallel pathways 'to facilitate the mobility of disabled people': ensuring the accessibility of public transportation, and the development of specialized transportation services. As is the case for education through the development of both mainstream and special education, the law promotes perspectives on accessibility that are theoretically contradictory according to classical models of disability policy: specialized modes of transportation that sustain segregation, and making standard modes of public transportation accessible.

During the three decades that separate this law from the Law of 2005, a two-fold dynamic could be observed (Larrouy 2011). The policies developed by transportation agencies tended to prioritize specialized transportation services, while modifications to standard means of public transportation were initially designed to focus on disabilities that were considered 'light', and more broadly on improving comfort for the entire population. At the same time, the 1980s and 1990s witnessed the development of associative activism surrounding these changes. Two associations in particular – the *Association des paralysés de France* (APF[3]), and the *Groupement des intellectuels handicapés physiques* (GIHP) – were particularly influential in these developments. Beginning in the early 1980s, the APF brought disability issues to national attention, following a number of local initiatives.[4] The 1983 convention of the APF proclaimed 'freedom of mobility' as the association's first objective, and in 1985 the association newsletter, *Faire face*, created a column entitled 'Accessibility of individual and collective transportation'. APF headquarters also established a 'national accessibility service' in 1987.

The association initially adopted a classically confrontational approach, organizing street protests such as a 1982 protest by 4,000 individuals in wheelchairs in Paris to express their collective demand for 'autonomous individual and collective mobility'. These early tactics were followed by a more professional, technicist strategy intended to generate influence by focusing on expertise rather than confrontation. As part of this new direction, the APF began to offer training to agencies such as the departmental equipment services and transportation agencies. While benefiting from a greater number of consultations with government agencies, the APF also trained local activists to participate at the departmental level in safety and accessibility commissions that had been established in 1978. Developing 'a professional image as a specialist in accessibility' (Larrouy 2011: 107) positioned the APF as a 'partner' with the government.[5] To this technicist orientation, the organization added a strategy of 'frame extension' to reach out to a nondisabled public by demonstrating that accessibility benefits the general population. In 1988, *Faire face* described accessibility as 'a gift to nondisabled people' (Larrouy 2011: 107).

This mobilization favoured greater legal recognition of the notion of accessibility, initially confirmed in a 1991 law covering accessibility in places of residence, workplaces, and public facilities.[6] A 1999 ministerial delegation was established by the Ministry of Transportation, Housing, and Tourism and, more importantly, accessibility became a central pillar of the Law of 11 February 2005. Unlike the Law of 1975, which had promoted highly general objectives, unenforced by penalties or sanctions, the 2005 law included specific objectives, as well as how and when to attain them, and significantly, sanctions and penalties for enforcing their application.

The obligation to implement accessibility applied to 'residential locations, whether private or public property, establishments that receive the public, installations open to the public, and workplaces' (Article 41). Facilities open to the public were required to implement the accessibility requirement within ten years of the promulgation of the law, and exemptions would be granted only on an 'exceptional' basis 'after demonstration of the technical impossibility of making the site accessible or due to constraints related to the preservation of the architectural heritage, or in the event of a clearly disproportion between the modifications to be made and their consequences'. The granting of a subsidy by a public authority for work on the construction or conversion of a facility was subject to the production of an accessibility file by the project supervisor. Accessibility training became mandatory in education programmes for architects and construction professionals.

Regarding transportation, the requirement to conform with accessibility norms encompassed the entire 'chain of mobility, including the built environment, public spaces and their design, and transportation systems and their interconnections' (Article 45). The ten-year deadline for making public transportation services accessible (with the notable exception of underground rail transportation networks) was imposed based on a system of accessibility guidelines. When they were judged technically impossible, transportation agencies were required to provide disabled people with alternative adapted transportation whose cost was not to exceed that of standard forms of public transportation. Implementing accessibility in public spaces was a mandatory component of communal and inter-communal planning processes. Finally, Article 46 provides for the creation of a 'municipal commission for accessibility for disabled people' in municipalities of over 5,000 inhabitants. Including association representatives, these commissions were responsible for generating annual reports regarding the state of accessibility of the built environment, facilities open to the public, and transportation, and to make 'any useful proposals to improve the accessibility conformity of the existing infrastructure', as well as to keep a record of available accessible housing.

The law required that all places of residence, facilities open to the public, and the complete transportation network, be made accessible by 2015, a deadline after which penalties would be imposed on non-conforming sites and institutions. Implementation lagged behind, however. In the autumn of 2011, several inspection services reported delays to the government, particularly involving facilities open to the public, and suggested changes in the legally mandated accessibility specifications (CGEDD et al 2011). Initially confidential, this report was made public by the new socialist government in September 2012. Senator Claire-Lise Campion was appointed to manage discussions and consultations surrounding the proposed changes. In a report in March 2013, the senator proposed adjusting the 2015 deadline by means of '*agendas d'accessibilité programmée* (Ad'AP)' (programmed accessibility agendas) (Campion 2013) that would commit facilities open to the public to planning and financing accessibility infrastructure beyond 2015. In return for signing an Ad'AP, facilities would be exempted from the penalties included in the 2005 Law. Following a new round of consultations that included associations, ordinances adopted in September 2014 allowed the postponement of accessibility accommodations through the Ad'AP programme for periods of three, six, or nine years. In August 2015, parliament ratified these ordinances. Ironically, this postponement, which temporarily erased a recognized right, was adopted in the name of making this right more effective through a better monitoring of its implementation.

This postponement was a blatant reversal of CDPH requirements, which recognized accessibility as a fundamental right in Article 9. How did the APF – which had promoted accessibility since the 1980s – respond to these changes? First, by calling on presidential candidates in January 2012 to support the key demand of the APF: 'An accessible France in 2015' (Baudot and Revillard 2016: 96). As part of a consultation organized by the government between September 2013 and February 2014, however, and despite publicly affirming its commitment on several occasions, the APF finally offered its support to the Ad'AP programme. The organization simply issued a reminder of the need to remain vigilant regarding effective and rapid implementation.[7] The APF was widely criticized by other opponents of the postponement for its conciliatory position and its excessive proximity to the administration. Indeed, the *Non au report* (No to Postponement) collective was organized to oppose the AFP's conciliatory approach. The postponement of accessibility requirements received little coverage in the mainstream French press, but the alarm was resonated throughout the specialized disability press. Nearly every participant in this study had learned about the postponement through this press or through their social or associative networks, and the postponement was spontaneously referred to by several participants during the interviews.

Progress … but also persistent obstacles

The evolution and current status of accessibility, as retraced through participant interviews, can be characterized in terms of urban mobility within public spaces and public transportation, as well as the built environment, including housing and facilities open to the public.

The majority of the participants, particularly the elder ones among them, reported advances in the accessibility of public transportation and public spaces. Alluding to a number of improvements for visually impaired people, for example, Marie Germain (60) reported feeling "soothed" by the increased security ("[tactile strips] really do make you feel safer"), facilitation in locating oneself ("Thanks to [tactile strips], you're at least sure you cross at the right spot"), and greater comfort (due to audible announcements in public transit stations), because it was no longer necessary to "pay attention to your path" and remain "perpetually vigilant".

Interviewees also described limitations in these advances, however. First, far from 'generalized accessibility' specified by the Law of 2005, accessibility measures were only partially implemented at best. Beyond structural differences between different modes of transportation, the same accessibility provision was implemented incompletely and unevenly installed across similar sites and transportation systems. For example, only certain traffic signals and subway lines are equipped with audible announcements. The lack of uniformity in the installations fuelled frustration and a sense of randomness among users, while also contributing to an impression that the urban environment remained hostile and that public spaces and transportation require a specific type of personal caution:

> 'In public transportation, there's still some progress to be made because half of the Metro lines are not yet equipped with audible signals. And when I was on Line 6, it was tough because to know where I was, I had to count stations or pay attention to the curves – "OK, now I know we're at Bercy station." So, after that, when I took the RER B [suburban train], I was more comfortable. … I felt like I weighed less when I got out.' (Chloé Lamarche, visual impairment, 23, April 2015)

Accessibility provisions do not always address user needs appropriately. The presence of a chime (instead of an audible announcement of the street name) at pedestrian crossings, for example, creates potentially dangerous confusion at intersections because visually impaired individuals have no way of knowing which street they are crossing. Some accessibility needs also continue to be completely unaddressed or are inadequately accommodated. Lucien Rémo, for example, described himself as "unable to use the RER [light rail] and suburban trains" due to a lack of toilets on board. Julie Ferandi was forced to sit on the floor of the Metro platform because there were no seats. A further complicating factor, beyond partial, ineffective, and non-existent accessibility provisions, are frequent technical problems, the most frequently cited of which involve Metro elevators and bus access ramps, as Leila Saddi discussed: "Buses are more or less OK. I've noticed for the past two years that there are fewer failures with the ramps, when the drivers agree to let them down, that is. Because that's a whole different problem. But on Line 14, the elevators are horrible."

In addition to these persistent problems, participants often complained about the lack of follow-up or maintenance of accessibility equipment. The accumulation of these difficulties explains some participants' preference for being accompanied when they venture into public urban spaces. The availability of friends, family members, or association volunteers then is an additional factor in determining mobility. For more isolated participants, services for accompanying disabled people provided by associations provide a crucial solution to mobility. Claudine Durand (56) and Lydie Sonnet (73), for example, live alone and refuse to go out without being accompanied. Because they have no nearby family or friends, they use services provided by an association and a foundation for their outings.

The lack of accessibility of public transportation and public spaces leads some disabled individuals to resort to specialized transportation. The functioning and availability of these services vary from city to city. The most popular is the closest to the standard transportation system, with buses that stop on demand. Systems that require advanced reservations such as the Parisian 'PAM' (*Pour aider à la mobilité* [Helping with Mobility]), however, are frequent targets of criticism among participants. The need to reserve up to two or even three weeks in advance precludes spontaneous outings and is perceived as an obvious obstacle to mobility. These services are also described as lacking in punctuality and costing considerably more than standard public transportation – although being less expensive than taxis. Specialized transportation services, on the other hand, were not mentioned as discriminatory because they separate disabled people from the rest of the population. Indeed, complaints tended to focus on questions of inefficiency rather than segregation. This does not necessarily suggest that users are insensitive to being segregated from the general population, but instead suggests that pragmatic issues are perceived as more important to achieving mobility, independently of the specific mode of transportation.

From this perspective, participants do not generally consider the two transportation systems – specialized and standard – as being opposed to each other. Indeed, they often referred to several modes of transportation simultaneously, whether standard or specialized, as among an array of mobility options, while also citing their respective defects. For example, when asked about the city's accessibility, Lydie Sonnet jointly refers to provisions pertaining to universal design (dropped sidewalk curbs and improvements in standard public transportation) and to specialized transportation:

AR: In terms of the city's accessibility, have you observed any changes over the years?

LS: Yes. The sidewalks have gotten lower, a lot lower. With transportation for disabled people, there's nevertheless more. ... How should I say it? More autonomy. Even if you are being helped, somehow, there is some autonomy. [...] Buses are alright too. But sometimes there are. ... But they're good! Trams – it's already done [accessibility] because they're more recent. (Lydie Sonnet, mobility impairment, 73, November 2014)

While different modes of transportation are mentioned here, using specialized transportation is experienced as asking for 'help'. Echoing this impression, Marie Germain (visual impairment, 60) reported that she and her partner occasionally used specialized transportation, but she also pointedly clarified that "we only ask for it every now and then". As in the case of social policies, this perception that a service puts users in the position of 'asking for help' functions as a disincentive. The very name of the service ('Helping Mobility') encourages this perception.

In practice, most participants reported alternating between standard public transportation and specialized transport. Among visually impaired people, the decision is based primarily on their previous familiarity with the destination: "In my case, I walk a good bit. I still take the bus to places I know, but if the destination is a place where I won't know where I am when I get out, I prefer to take specialized transportation" (Élise Bastien, visual impairment, 47, January 2015). The variety of available modes of public transportation does not necessarily translate into ease of mobility, however. In the context of a sequence of displacements in which accessibility is only partial, specialized transport represents an inadequate alternative. Such gaps occasionally force users to resort to more expensive individual transportation, particularly taxis. This is true of Léa Martin, whose testimony plainly illustrates the low level of adaptation of the various modes of transportation available to her in Paris:

> 'Today, I'm in a wheelchair and I have to take a taxi at my own cost. Because the Metro – there's only one line, the 14, that's adapted – and where are you supposed to go after Line 14? You have to get around. So, the Metro is basically impossible, even risky, because I know plenty of people who take the escalators in their wheelchairs, but I don't take that risk. [...] It's really pretty tough. I just don't have the musculature, and I don't have the courage. I don't have. ... I mean, I'm just scared. So anyway, the Metro is not the ideal solution for me. After that, there's the bus. But between buses, which are supposedly accessible, and the ones where that doesn't work. [...] I'm still in a manual [non-motorized] wheelchair, so you have to have the strength to go up the little ramp. There have to be people there, too, if I can't get up the

> ramp, who can tell [the bus driver] "Hey Sir!" so he doesn't just close the door on me, "Sir, there's someone trying to get in, but they can't manage." Because if they don't say it, the driver just closes the door and takes off. So that's not an ideal solution, either. [...] Then you have the PAM system. Which is a good system because it's at reduced cost and it's paid for by the municipality, but it has a lot of inconvenient aspects. Because now there are way too many requests for the available spaces. You also have to notify PAM two weeks or even a month ahead of time if you want to go out. You have to say that it's for professional reasons in order to get priority, and you have to justify that. ... So it's not really all that flexible. ... And I just don't know what I'm doing in two weeks or a month. So it's a bit complicated. So you end up calling too late, there's no room. If there's no room, you can't go out. So otherwise you have taxis, but at a cost. So what does it all mean? It means saving up money, it means not going on vacation, almost never going to the theatre anymore. ... Why? Because we have to move around, because we have lives and we're socially integrated like anybody else.' (Léa Martin, mobility impairment, 28, January 2015)

Léa describes a universe of possibilities that is also bounded by a host of limitations.[8] Using a manual wheelchair, access to public transportation is not perceived as a mundane activity, but described as an enterprise requiring specific physical strength, courage and luck: "musculature" to descend escalators in a wheelchair, "strength" to propel the wheelchair up the bus ramp, "courage" of risking one's life in an escalator or of calling out to other bus passengers to alert bus drivers. The PAM system, a "good system" in theory, is in fact poorly adapted to Léa's lifestyle due to unpredictable professional requirements as well as her desire to go out socially whenever she chooses, without having to plan her outings two weeks in advance. Therefore, Léa is often compelled to utilize taxis, a financial drain on other expenses that reduces her overall mobility and activities. As a young woman, she calls attention to the gap between the social status to which she aspires – "we're socially integrated like anybody else" – and the inferior status assigned to her by the partial realization of accessibility.

This mixed report also applies to the built environment. This study has revealed signs of progress in accessibility, particularly in housing. The three quadriplegic participants we met who live in autonomous public housing reported benefiting from complete accessibility, with apartments often on the ground floor and, in one case, with a system of caregivers shared between several disabled individuals housed in the same public housing facility. This positive evaluation should be viewed with a measure of caution, however. These situations demonstrate the emergence of the possibility of autonomous living for quadriplegic individuals due to a combination of accessible housing and compensation benefits that compensate for the cost of personal assistants. However, these three cases are far from representing the norm: institutionalized housing, or living with family members, remain very frequent (Rapegno 2014).

Among the many facilities referred to during participant interviews, the advances in the accessibility of museums are much appreciated: "In terms of museums, there has been a great effort and I have to emphasize that things are great with museums. There's no problem with that."[9] Nadine Trappier also reports "great progress" in the hotel industry: "There are an increasing number of rooms adapted to accommodate disabled people." This progress nevertheless has limits and depends on the type and severity of the impairment. Laëtitia Roger has trouble in finding vacation housing in hotels or rental housing that permits her to install her adapted bed, despite her commitment to supervising the installation, removal, and re-arrangement of the room:

> 'I have had to return to the same housing three different times, because other places refused to allow my medical bed in their hotels. Even in rental housing, when I tell them that the medical equipment rental company will do the set-up and re-arrange the furniture on my departure day, they don't want to hear about it.' (Laëtitia Roger, mobility impairment, 40, November 2014)

In most other public spaces mentioned by participants, accessibility is more the exception than the rule. Laëtitia Roger, for example, observes that "few [concert] halls are accessible". When asked about she thinks about the 2005 law's promotion of rights, citizenship, and autonomy, she points out that even doctor's offices are not adapted for disabled people: "Autonomy is a really big word. It wouldn't be bad to make places accessible to us and to allow doctors to have patient lift systems to help place us on their examining tables and render medical infrastructure accessible, with trained staff." She was forced to abandon her physical therapy sessions because there was no accessible practitioner near her place of residence. The distance she needed to travel to reach her previous physical therapist was so exhausting that it cancelled out any benefits of the session. She also reported fearing the moment when she would have to begin to undergo regular mammogram tests, which require patients to remain in a standing position. Individuals with mobility impairments also pointed out that shops and restaurants are rarely accessible:

> 'There are always large steps whenever I want to take my scooter inside a shop. And even when you're not in a wheelchair and you can walk, the stairs to enter certain stores are very tall. … Even to go to the physical therapist, there's a heck of a step.' (Nadine Trappier, mobility impairment, 61, January 2015)

Léa Martin was particularly critical of the lack of respect of accessibility regulations in newer buildings:

> 'When I see so many new buildings without elevators or with a small entry step, I tell myself "It's inexcusable." I accept it with older establishments, but new ones like [two retail clothing chains] with an elevator to the second floor but not the third, or a small step in the entryway – all it takes is a small step [to make it inaccessible].' (Léa Martin, mobility impairment, 28, January 2015)

Far from the norm, what is expected, accessibility is the exception, and continues to be viewed as such by the establishments mentioned by participants. For example, accessible seats are restricted to the first row in cinemas, whereas, as Nadine Trappier notes, "I don't feel like watching a movie with my nose glued to the screen. I want a good seat." Marie Germain complains that audio-description is unavailable in cinemas except for during an annual film festival organized by an association: "That's just one time, one place, one moment."[10] Only partially present in public transportation, accessibility is thus an exception within the built environment.

From inaccessibility to its contestation

How do participants react to this very partial accessibility?[11] The existence of an 'injurious experience', to use Felstiner, Abel and Sarat's terms, does not mechanically induce claiming (Felstiner et al 1980). First, the situation must be identified as such ('naming'), and responsibility assigned ('blaming') – two processes that tend to be confused with each other in the case of accessibility, the very notion of which conveys the role of the environment in creating conditions that enable individual mobility. The question is then to what extent and in what ways study participants responded to this perceived lack of accessibility.

Policy feedback and the production of discontent

Participants' expressions of discontent with a lack of accessibility does not result from the influence of activist groups, but from the interaction between two factors: the physical, daily experience of different levels of accessibility, and expectations in terms of social participation and inclusion. These two factors are shaped by public policies (see Figure 5.1 later in this chapter).

In order to observe and characterize a lack of accessibility, one must first have imagined alternative situations that differ from one's own everyday lived experience. For participants, developing this awareness and vision of possible alternatives is not of a theoretical character. Nor is it overtly influenced by cultural media. It is not generally accompanied by participation in activist circles. Instead, this awareness tends to arise from the concrete, physical, day-to-day experience of different levels of accessibility. For some participants, travel is the factor that opens their eyes to other possibilities:

> '[Discussing a trip to the United States in the 1960s] That's where I saw the gap, where they were over there. Not all that far from where we are now, you see. […] It had already happened over there. Ramps, wheelchairs everywhere. People didn't look at you like … that's how it was. Yes, I saw that. I saw that it was possible.' (Maryse Cloutier, mobility impairment, 72, November 2014)

This remark – "I saw that it was possible" – quite literally translates how the concrete experience of a more accessible environment opens up possibilities. Experiencing various levels of accessibility also results from the contemporary context of partly achieved accessibility, such as the installation of audible traffic signals in some places and not others, bus access ramps that sometimes function and sometimes do not, elevators in only a few Metro stations. Indeed, as Marie Germain observed, "once you get used to comfort, when it's no longer there, it's even harder."

> '[Referring to audible announcements of Metro stations] There are lines that aren't planned before at least 2020, so ouch. … You tell yourself, wow, they're totally dragging things out. Whereas abroad, they've been doing that for a long time, a very long time. And once you get used to comfort, when it's no longer there, it's even harder. You just say, darn it!' (Marie Germain, visual impairment, 60, November 2014)

According to a policy feedback mechanism (Pierson 1993), public policy, through its partial implementation, produces the discontent of which it is itself the target. Increased awareness of accessibility issues is also nourished, however, by the effects of other policies, notably the promotion of inclusive education, and disability compensation, which favours independent living rather than institutionalization. Indeed, specialized institutions are more accessible than standard public spaces because they target a disabled public. For those who leave institutions, moving into autonomous housing corresponds to quitting a relatively accessible environment[12] in favour of a far less accessible daily life. Laëtitia Roger refers to accessibility in answer to a question concerning her schooling in a specialized institution:

LR: When you're inside the institution, you don't realize what kinds of problems people can have since we're always with educators. … Now, I've become aware of the real problems in the past 12 years, since I've been here [designating her apartment].

AR: And what sort of problems have you experienced?
LR: Inaccessibility. ... The buses are OK. They're accessible, but the Metro – you just can't take it, except for Line 14, which is totally accessible. The more time passes, the more marginalized we are. (Laëtitia Roger, mobility impairment, 40, November 2014)

Therefore, travelling abroad, the partial and sometimes seemingly random accessibility of public transportation, and exiting a specialized institution, all provide hands-on experience with contrasting levels of accessibility. This initial factor in generating discontent interacts with a second, more subjective factor: individual expectations concerning social participation and inclusion, when confronted with the reality of the lack of accessibility, foster relative deprivation (Gurr 1970). These expectations are partially fuelled by concrete experience with different levels of accessibility, but the link is not remotely mechanistic: not all individuals who experience the uneven accessibility of the Paris Metro develop the same level of discontent.

This variable response can be explained by differences in individual aspirations in terms of social participation. Unlike Léa Martin (28), who wants to be able to go out alone whenever she wishes, Lydie Sonnet (73) goes out only when accompanied by a volunteer and does not complain that these accompanied outings are sometimes cancelled at the last minute. In general, she is not highly mobile, and she plans her outings in advance. But these aspirations also reflect certain expectations about the social status assigned to disabled people. While several participants notably among the elder ones described flawed or partial accessibility as a simple fact with few additional remarks, others, particularly younger participants, experienced low-level accessibility as a denial of citizenship and a devaluation of their social status. This is what Laëtitia Roger meant when she observed that "the more things go, the more they marginalize us". Her perception was echoed by Chloé Lamarche (23) when, with reference to the postponement of the 2015 deadline, she contended that "it's frustrating. It's really as if they take people for idiots". Victor Jaucourt (30), a lawyer, approaches the question from a more legal perspective, remarking that "What other minority could they do that to these days, just getting rid of a right? Maybe foreigners?"

As these last two reactions in response to the postponement of the 2015 deadline illustrate, expectations are to some extent shaped by public policy. Rights discourse plays a crucial role, as does the experience of mainstream schooling, which contributes to the expectation of equal treatment (thus partially explaining the pattern of generational differences). The effect of discontent produced by the gap between a policy discourse based on rights and the reality of the lack of accessibility is amply illustrated by Chloé Lamarche's remarks, quoted in the introduction of this book, criticizing this discourse as just "a lot of blather". Policy feedback mechanisms are at play in expectations raised by public policy at both the symbolic level (through discourses centred on rights) and physical level (through the experiences of partial accessibility and mainstream schooling notably). Ultimately, discontent with a lack of accessibility results from the interaction between two factors: the concrete experience of different levels of accessibility and expectations regarding social participation and inclusion, both of which are fuelled by policy feedbacks (see Figure 5.1). The present situation in France thus offers an opportunity to analyse relative deprivation in real time as it develops, and despite the fact that it has not fuelled mass protest (unlike the findings of many other sociological studies of social movements pointing to relative deprivation after a political crisis has arisen).[13]

Collective and individual action for accessibility

Feeling discontent does not necessarily result in expressing it. What forms does this expression take?

Several participants reported participating in the few actions (petitions, demonstrations) that attracted limited media visibility – on the part of APF or the *Non au report* collective. Marie Germain, for example, reported "signing petitions on the Internet". In Michel Simon's opinion, it is "sad to see the government is questioning it in some ways [the Law of 2005] in the September decrees". Faced with what he described as a "renunciation", he affirmed "I've signed petitions, I've been to protests, sure, yeah, yeah. … The associations are reacting for good reasons."

Beyond the initiatives of these national associations, several participants emphasized the importance of municipal-level collective mobilizations in support of accessibility. Several participants reported being involved in local associations that were active in their municipal accessibility commissions. Their narratives differed from others in attributing less weight to the postponement of the accessibility mandate. Instead, they perceive the bulk of accessibility debates and improvements as occurring at the municipal rather than the national level, thus being more subject to local influence than to legal documents or regulations. Louis Resnais referred to a "relation of trust" between the association in which he participated and local authorities:

> 'You must have a relationship based on trust between us and local authorities, so you don't just ask for whatever you feel like. You need to know how to work on public spaces with urbanists to make things accessible. We worked a lot with the city. We earned their confidence. […] There's a real democracy of usage.' (Louis Resnais, visual impairment, 59, February 2015)

Figure 5.1: From inaccessibility to its contestation

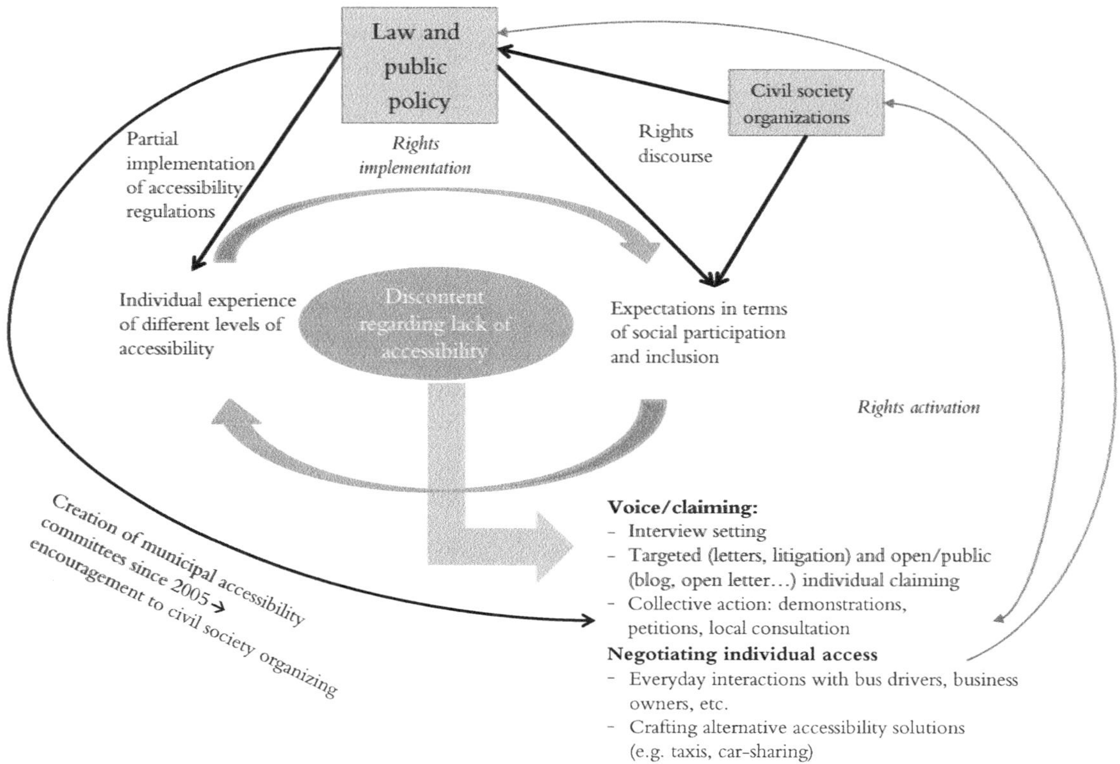

Source: Reproduced from Revillard, 2019c

Influence is acquired through moderation, which in turn builds credibility ("you don't ask for whatever you feel like"), and by promoting the association's technical contributions through experience-based expertise ("a democracy of usage"). Jeannette Houde also reported belonging to a local association that was created in the aftermath of the Law of 11 February 2005 and that participates in her municipal accessibility commission:

> 'They listen to us a lot, and we're lucky compared to other cities. There are a lot of crosswalks equipped with audible crossing lights. … There's an annual budget to expand it. […] The engineers call to ask us what's better, what's less good, about this or that. Yeah, [here] we are recognized.' (Jeannette Houde, visual impairment, 75, March 2015)

According to Jeannette, at the local level, the delay of the 2015 deadline seems less significant than was suggested by national mobilizations: "We follow the flock, nevertheless, you might say out of solidarity, I guess. For example, we participated in the protest with the APF on February 11, things like that. [But] our goal is to be effective on the local level." Younger people, among whom discontent is highest, tend to be less involved in either the larger national associations or the smaller ones that participate in local consultations regarding accessibility. They tend to engage in more individual forms of protest. These tend to be more targeted, including verbal or written complaints to specific establishments or institutions. Following a refusal by the PAM to finances travel from his residence, Kader Zyeb was forced to remain as a boarder at the site of his training programme. He described having "harassed the PAM", without any result:

> 'I fight with them. I show the problems. I harassed the PAM. […] After that, it's always complicated because either they don't pay attention to you, because, well, "Who's this punk who comes up here …", or when they do listen to you … they hear you, but nothing changes. I can tell you that I really gave the PAM a hard time! I called the PAM departmental director – I got his direct number! And I called him for a week, every day. "Yeah, so what's the status? What are we doing?" And all he did was ask me "How'd you get my number?" And did things change after that? No!' (Kader Zyeb, visual impairment, 24, March 2015)

After failing in his claim, Kader envisaged publicizing and collectivizing his complaint by creating a blog to inventory all the difficulties encountered by "an entire series of individuals who have had problems" with this specialized transportation service. Chloé Lamarche describes how she responded after a bank refused to install an accessible cash distributor:

> 'I had a conflict with a bank that didn't want to install this type of software. I went to see them and explained what I needed and that it was causing me problems. [...] It limits my personal freedom. It's unacceptable in this century. The employee replied, "Just take your precautions." [I answered] "Yeah but that's not what I'm asking you. It's not up to me to take my precautions. I just want to dispose of my personal money how I see fit and when I see fit." He said "You're just going to have to make do. And in any case, it's not provided for in our budget." [...] I told them that if I had to, I would press charges. But pressing charges costs money and takes time and energy, and what will I get out of it? I have no idea, because in any case, the laws have been postponed. ... In the end, we learned to memorize the gestures required to withdraw money. And I guess that's how it ended.' (Chloé Lamarche, visual impairment, 23, April 2015)

While illustrating the existence of individual protest towards specific institutions, this example also highlights obstacles to filing a more institutional, formal complaint (pressing charges). Indeed, Chloé used the threat of a lawsuit against the bank, although without true conviction. The legal process demands investments of time, money, and energy. Her account also conveys the loss of confidence in the protective value of the law caused by the postponement of the 2015 deadline ("anyway, the laws have been delayed"). After evoking the prospect of a formal complaint, she decided that she was ultimately unlikely to press charges, choosing instead to compensate for the lack of accessibility by individual effort (that is, by learning how to "memorize the gestures required to withdraw money").

In addition to approaches that target specific establishments, individuals also resort to more public methods to express their complaints. Several participants wrote blog posts and open letters or communicated on accessibility issues on social networks. The interview context is part of these modes of expression, because of the hope that research will help disseminate participants' critical views. Indeed, referring to administrative difficulties encountered in requesting a free transportation pass from her municipality,[14] Maryse Cloutier remarked that "Yes, well, there's something I would really like to communicate to them." This effect was also clear from exchanges with Laëtitia Roger, who used the interview context to indirectly address members of parliament when she returned to the matter of the postponement of the accessibility deadline at the end of the interview ("I have this to say to them ..."):

AR: In the course of your life, do you have the impression that there have been changes in terms of how others see you as a disabled individual?

LR: No. On the contrary. I have the impression that we've gone back to the 1970s. From the point of view of rejection, the way you're looked on, and accessibility. Especially since the ruling was …
AR: The postponement was passed …
LR That's right.
AR: How did you take that episode?
LR: Badly.
AR […] What did you think about all the debates?
LR: The people who pass them [these laws], are not in our shoes. I have this to say to them: "Put yourself in my wheelchair and I'll take your place for a day. And in addition, I'm going to tie your legs together, and when you have to go to the toilet, you'll see what it's like." (Laëtitia Roger, mobility impairment, 40, November 2014)

Finally, in conjunction with individual and collective forms of protest, disabled people cobble together solutions to accessibility that are independent of institutional initiatives. Their improvised solutions are often individual, but they can also reflect broader ambitions. Kader Zyeb, a participant who was furious about the inefficiency of the PAM transportation system in Paris, decided to launch his own ridesharing app to organize mobility solutions for blind and visually impaired people: "[These transportation problems] make it necessary to make things get better, and for that, we have to create a company. I'm in the process of forming my own transportation firm. I'm a web developer, so I am working on creating an app."

From the collective actions of the 1980s to today's individual initiatives, from the creation of a ridesharing app to taking part in municipal consultations, and even including filing formal complaints against a bank, disabled people contribute to the improvement of accessibility on a daily basis. Far from being granted to them, this right is to a great extent their own collective and individual conquest, through a combination of initiatives that lead to actions ranging from negotiation to confrontation. In the process, they help forge their own freedom of movement, despite the inadequacies of public policies. The constraints on this freedom are not exclusively concrete, however.

From accessibility to mobility

Accessibility is a necessary but not sufficient condition for mobility, whose practices differ for the same functional limitations, even in the same urban space (Dejoux 2010). In addition to the variation in individual aspirations, two complementary factors open possibilities for public intervention: the articulation between generalized accessibility and individual compensation devices, and the apprehensions that mark the investment of public space. The analysis of the social factors at the origin of these apprehensions will be deepened by a case study on the uses of the priority card.

Accessibility and individual compensation devices

Mobility does not only depend on the accessibility parameters of the environment; it is made possible by their combination with individual compensatory devices, such as the wheelchair, the white cane, the guide dog, the orthopaedic device, or personal assistance. For the same functional limitation, mobility varies according to the type of device, but also according to the way in which it is used by the individual. Chloé Lamarche thus describes the difference in mobility experiences between travelling with a cane and with a guide dog:

> 'The cane really requires you to be very focused all the time and to analyse the environment all the time. You must be on guard. On known routes, it's fine, but on unknown routes you still must be very vigilant. The cane will come into contact with the obstacle, whereas the dog will anticipate it visually and bypass it. [...] So from that point of view, [with the dog] it's more freedom, it's more fluidity, it's much more comfortable.' (Chloé Lamarche, visual impairment, 23, April 2015)

Similarly, different types of wheelchairs lead to different possibilities of mobility. Pierre Béraud described how he was 'very happy' when he acquired his first electric wheelchair at the age of 12, unlike one of his peers who remained in a manual wheelchair all his teenage years and could not move it by himself: "I have had an [electric] wheelchair since I was in fifth grade. When you're 12 years old in a small car like this, you're very happy. And [this classmate], his parents were. ... He never had an [electric] wheelchair. He was dependent. He was pushed in a wheelchair." He also tells how he has gained mobility with his current wheelchair, which he was slow to acquire. Indeed, the old wheelchair restricted his mobility, but allowed him to write, which he can no longer do with the new one. Pierre therefore made a trade-off between his career progression as a researcher, which he initially prioritized, and his mobility: "[With the new wheelchair] I don't write anymore but I move."

The devices are therefore subject to varying degrees of appropriation, depending on the actions that they make possible in various ways and that one wishes to prioritize, but also for what they symbolize. Indeed, for many people, the individual compensation device, whatever it may be, is what makes the disability visible. A visual impairment, for example, can remain unnoticed until it is accompanied by the use of a white cane. The equipment signals the disability to others and thus is subject to ambivalent perceptions. At first it may be rejected as a stigma (Goffman 1963):

> 'When you go from a world where you can see clearly to a world where you can no longer see, the hardest thing is to accept the cane.' (Daniel Morand, visual impairment, 58, November 2014)

> '[My eyesight] had gone down, it had dropped … That's when I started to take on the status of a disabled person, with very hard sides, if only the white cane.' (Michel Simon, visual impairment, 57, February 2015)

It is common for people with vision impairments to postpone the use of the cane for as long as possible, by developing alternative compensation strategies or by using it selectively or partially. This includes the tactic of walking with a folded cane, or folding the cane when approaching a destination to avoid arriving with a white cane:

> 'Very quickly I realized that [the white cane] gave me security. No more dread of bumping into other bystanders, no more fear of crossing streets. I knew that motorists would in principle pay a little more attention to me. Well, I accepted the white cane in perhaps less than a year. At first, I carried it in a closed segment. … Then I folded it up completely when I got to my house, then finally I unfolded it completely until I got home, and both day and night. … I really realized that the white cane was a plus.' (Michel Simon, visual impairment, 57, February 2015)

Technical devices can be difficult to accept, but they also need to be learned to become effective mobility resources (Blatgé 2012). The white cane, to continue this example, is of limited use if one has not learned to handle it correctly. This is the purpose of locomotion courses:

> 'When I was still at the INJA, I took locomotion classes – from the 5th year onwards, I think – I took locomotion classes and little by little I was taught to find my way around the area around the INJA. So, they gave me what they called tests, they made me take tests to see if I was capable of finding my way around the neighbourhood and then they taught me – the first important journey I made was to the train station. […] So, it happened quite quickly, quite early on.' (Alain Caron, visual impairment, 48, January 2016)

The apprehension associated with moving around in public space is generally higher among people who became blind as adults than among people who were blind from birth or who became blind as children (Dejoux 2010). In addition to the length of time people have been blind, an important factor in the varying degrees of apprehension experienced by people is their more or less great ease in asking passers-by for help if they need it. This can be learned in the same way as the more technical dimensions of equipped locomotion:

AR: And is it difficult for you to ask people [to find your way in the street]?
CL: No, but before, I would completely block myself.
AR: Do you remember when you started doing this?
CL: In Paris, I think.
AR: Yes, that's when you started to move [independently] …
CL: Actually, my instructor urged me to do it and I really hated it, I hated it because I couldn't. … I could hardly feel when people were coming, when to ask them for help. … Whereas now it has become commonplace. (Chloé Lamarche, visual impairment, 23, April 2015)

Thus, the moment of identification of the disability, but also the more or less early learning of the locomotion and the modalities of this learning, contribute to explain the more or less important apprehension linked to autonomous mobility in the public space, and the modalities of this mobility (more or less limited or accompanied outings). This observation invites us to take a closer look at this fear of going into public space. Indeed, the reasons for this obstacle to mobility are not only material (fear of falling, of bumping into others) but also social: apprehension of one's own behaviour in relation to others (ability to ask for help), and of their reactions (including the possibility of stigmatization, or even violence).

Understanding the fears of disabled people in public spaces

Important research in the sociology of gender has focused on women's fears in public space, which fuel structural gender inequality in the use of this space, particularly at night (Condon et al 2005; Lieber 2008). These fears, the authors insist, should not be naturalized or reduced to a psychological manifestation, but it is important to understand their social determinants. This fear can be difficult to verbalize, appearing to be 'so obvious, intrinsically linked to being a woman, that it does not seem necessary to say it' (Condon et al 2005). Similarly, the deeply internalized fear of disabled people to go into public space is partly based on social mechanisms. It is reflected, for example, in Léa Martin's comment that "we *dare to* go out":

> '[Referring to people of her generation] Now, we dare, we dare to speak – because before I felt like disabled people were pushed

aside. … Now we dare, we dare to advocate, we dare to speak, we dare to communicate, we dare to go out. You see many more disabled people outside than even five or six years ago.' (Léa Martin, mobility impairment, 28, January 2015)

Beyond the observation of an increase in mobility, the idea of 'daring' to go out implies overcoming apprehensions. And indeed, fear is an emotion that is often present when people talk about going out. It has an impact on practices, that is mainly noticeable through restricting travel (and, like women, through being vigilant about times and routes), through planning it and by asking for support. Routine is particularly protective. For example, for Leila Saddi, the daily bus journey was no longer a cause of apprehension as it had become "a habit"; travelling at the same times on the same routes meant that "the drivers knew [her]".

However, if the use of public space is subject to such apprehensions, it is not only because of the material obstacles, lack of accessibility, or the risk of accidents. It is also because it is one of the first places where social representations of disability are faced. The Goffmanian analysis of stigmatization processes (Goffman 1963) sheds useful light on this social dimension of the constraints that weigh on disabled people when entering the public sphere, alongside material obstacles. This stigmatization takes various forms. The examples given in the interviews allow us to list four main forms: avoidance; violation of 'territories of the self'; objectification; and expression of resentment (see Table 5.1).

Table 5.1: Stigmatization mechanisms in the public space

Type of stigmatization	Typical event/ case	Illustrations
Avoidance/taboo	Averting the gaze/ looking away	"There are people who don't feel at ease, who have a shifty look" (Nadine Trappier)
	Instructing children not to ask questions/not to look	"A child who asks a question is told to 'shush'. No, not 'shh'! Explain it! […] But there are still many people who say 'No, shut up, shh, don't ask a question'" (Marie Germain) "I once had a gentleman who walked by with his child and said, 'Don't look at her, you'll turn out like that'" (Leila Saddi)
	Ostracization (not sitting/standing next to the person)	"[In all-inclusive resorts] people don't come and eat next to us" (Dora Moleiro)

Table 5.1: Stigmatization mechanisms in the public space (continued)

Type of stigmatization	Typical event/ case	Illustrations
Violation of the person's 'territories of the self'	Staring	"When I go out and that they make me eat [...] all the tables around me look at me. [...] I don't think it's right" (Leila Saddi)
	Inappropriate verbal address (expression of pity, judgement on lifestyle)	"In the street [a man said to me]: 'What an idea to have three children when you are blind.' [...] I also had the kind of answer: "My poor little girl, I will pray for you'" (Geneviève Bertaux)
	Taking the arm of a blind person without talking to them	"Before, one would come up to you and just grab your arm to guide you, but without telling you anything, you see" (Marie Germain)
	Shoving/impacting equipment	"How many times, my joystick that I use to move around, to drive, to move my wheelchair, has been bumped into?" (Leila Saddi)
Objectification/ denial of existence	Interpellation of the accompanying person to address the person/ reference in the third person	"In a street, if I want to buy something, no one is going to see me, and no one is going to talk to me" (Pierre Béraud)
	Comment on the guide dog without addressing the owner	"[Referring to a blind friend] One day we were walking in the Metro, with her and her dog. People started saying, 'Oh, what a beautiful dog!' She [replied]: 'And the mistress too!', and I said: 'And the lover too!' [Laughs]" (Louis Resnais)
Expression of resentment	Comments on lifestyle and resources perceived as undue privileges	"People in the street, it's incredible, because they have the impression that everything is given to me! That the person who comes [to assist me] it's free, that the wheelchair is fully paid for, it's not true." (Maryse Cloutier)
	Refusal of priority	"Every day when I take [the line 14 lift], I need to fight. I need to fight with people to take it. Recently I was insulted by a young person because I wanted to take it. He didn't want to get off, a 14- or 15-year-old youngster. ... He said to me 'Get out, don't tell me your life story'" (Leila Saddi)

The first two modalities manifest themselves in two sets of opposing behaviours: distancing, which gives disabled people a kind of taboo status, and conversely, violating their 'territories of the self'. The first, avoidance, the turning of the gaze, is a very common form of stigmatization. Several interviewees mentioned these 'shifty looks',[15] a sign that nondisabled people feel 'uncomfortable'.[16] This distancing is not restricted to the gaze but can be embodied in the positioning of the body, in the fact of physically keeping one's distance from a disabled person. Dora Moleiro regretted that when she goes on holiday in an all-inclusive resort with her blind partner, this discomfort felt by other people 'put them a bit at a distance' – a distance that is manifested, for example, in the fact that 'people don't come and eat next to [them]'.

This distancing goes hand in hand with the maintenance of a taboo around disability (one does not look at it, but one does not talk about it either), which is sometimes made explicit by the children's questions. Leila Saddi recounts how she scolded a man who told his son while pointing at her: "Don't look at her, you'll turn out like that," thus expressing a fear of contagion through the gaze that very literally confirms the taboo status assigned to disability (Douglas 1966). Marie Germain deplores that adults often respond to children's questions about her by telling them to be silent. The children's questions about her blindness break the otherwise common strategy of 'normals' dealing with the 'stigmatized', which is going on as if nothing had happened (Goffman 1963). But by refusing to answer them and by silencing them, the adults give disability a taboo status, present it as an unspeakable subject, which, she believes, goes against the interests of disabled people.

In a symmetrical excess of this avoidance, stigmatization can be embodied in violations of the 'territories of the self'. Developing in *Relations in Public* the concept of 'territories of the self' (that over which the individual claims a right of territoriality[17]) which includes, among others, personal space, stall, the Sheath, possessional territory, and conversational preserve,[18] Goffman notes the 'socially determined variability' of these forms of territoriality: 'In general, the higher the rank, the greater the size of all territories of the self, and the greater the control across the boundaries' (Goffman 1971: 40–41). From this perspective, the frequency of violation of various territories of the selves of disabled people signals the dominated social status assigned to them. These violations include different dimensions. First, it can be a visual intrusion, a staring that is just as unwelcome as the reciprocal ignorance mentioned earlier. The intensity of the intrusion is then much stronger than Goffman's reference to the 'glance, look, penetration of the eyes' among the modes of violation of the territories of the self (Goffman 1971: 44). Far from the sociologist's idea of a glance that is displaced and quickly disciplined by its target, the visual intrusion, in the case of disability, can be persistent. It is a 'staring', to use the verb used by Leila Saddi evoking such a scene:

> 'When I go out and that they make me eat, because I don't eat by myself, they put the fork in my mouth, so. ... There too, the reaction of people is incredible. All the tables around me look at me. It's ... you can have a look, because I also look when I see ... someone, in quotes, "a bit different", with red hair or whatever, I look, but I'm not like that [she mimics staring] ... staring. I look very quickly because it's surprising but. ... Staring is different ... I don't think it's right. So ... that's the mentality of the people.' (Leila Saddi, mobility impairment, 31, March 2015)

The intensity of the scrutiny here reveals the objectification of its target (Garland-Thomson 2009). It is because the person is seen as an object, as 'not quite human' (Goffman 1963: 3), to use Goffman's terms, that one allows oneself to stare them with such intensity.

But the violation can also be in the 'conversational preserve', referring to the 'The right of an individual to exert some control over who can summon him into talk and when he can be summoned' (Goffman 1971: 40), with unsolicited and inappropriate 'addressing of words' (Goffman 1971: 46), similar to the forms of verbal harassment women suffer in the public space. The intrusive and offensive nature of these addresses can be linked to the expression of pity and the use of diminutive terms of address, as in the "My poor little one, I'll pray for you" that a passer-by addresses to Geneviève Bertaux. But it also stems from the expression of judgements about people's lifestyles and abilities:

> 'I remember when I was – I think I was in high school then – I arrived on a Metro platform one morning, and a lady said to me "But what are you doing here?" I said "I think I'm doing the same as you, I'm taking the Metro." She said: "But you're going to kill yourself! – No, no, it's OK." It was funny.' (Alain Caron, visual impairment, 48, January 2016)

Geneviève Bertaux, on the other hand, was subjected to comments in the public arena about both her motherhood and her profession:

> 'In the street [a man said to me]: "What an idea to have three children when you are blind." The guy was called a fascist that day. I told him to go away. ... [Another time] a guy came and asked me: "Do you need help?" I told him no. It was on [this street], I'll always remember it. He said: "What are you doing in the street at 7am?" "I'm going to work." "What do you do?" "I'm a teacher." "It's not possible, you're illiterate!".' (Geneviève Bertaux, visual impairment, 62, December 2014)

Narrating these episodes, Geneviève insists on their exceptional character. She does not receive such comments every time she walks down the street. They were nonetheless significant for her ("I will always remember it"), illustrating how the experiences of stigmatization (particularly violent in this case) can structure the relationship to public space. Finally, the violation of the territories of the self can also take the form of an unsolicited intrusion on the body or on equipment (chair, cane, and so on). Marie Germain recounts how, in the past, people who wanted to help her in the street could take her arm and guide her without asking her opinion or even speaking to her. This, she believes, has changed, as people now greet her:

> 'People come to you now, they say hello. That's because there were TV shows and so on that explained all that. Whereas before, one would come up to you and just grab your arm to guide you, but without telling you anything, you see. So, it could be helping sometimes but I mean ...' (Marie Germain, visual impairment, 60, November 2014)

Leila Saddi describes how her wheelchair (especially the joystick) can be bumped in dense spaces – a violation of the technical equipment that she likens to a violation of the body ("when you are hit") as she is ' "one" with her wheelchair' (Winance 2007):

LS: In the street you are not seen. ... In short, it is not ... people are not ...

AR: People don't see you, you mean, people look away, or don't pay attention to you?

LS: No, but ... when you're bumped. ... How many times, my joystick that I use to move, to drive, to move my wheelchair, has been bumped into? So when there are too many people, no, I. ... I don't go to places where there are too many people. All the bars, all the places where people meet, I don't go there because ... especially people of my age, it's not even worth it. Because when you complain, you look like a killjoy. (Leila Saddi, mobility impairment, 31, March 2015)

Alongside avoidance and its symmetrical counterpart, the violation of territories of the self, a third classic form of stigmatization is objectification, the denial of existence. This refers to one of the possibilities of behaviour on the part of the 'normals' evoked by Goffman, which consists in 'try[ing] to act as if he were a "non-person," and not present at all as someone of whom ritual notice is to be taken' (Goffman 1963: 18). For accompanied people, this typically translates into an interpellation of the personal assistant when the discussion concerns the disabled person, who is then ignored and referred to in the third person. Dora Moleiro, whose severe visual impairment is not identifiable at first glance (she moves around without a cane), experienced this when accompanying her blind husband, who uses a cane: "They say hello to me and not to my husband because he cannot see the person, they say 'Hello Mrs!' while I am with him. We still experience this today." Pierre Béraud, a quadriplegic man, describes this feeling of invisibility as a daily experience: "In the street, if I want to buy something, no one is going to see me, and no one is going to talk to me." A variant of this denial of existence, frequently experienced by blind people who travel with a guide dog, consists in addressing the dog rather than its owner: "[Referring to a blind friend] One day we were walking in the Metro, with her and her dog. People started saying: 'Oh, what a beautiful dog!' She [replied]: 'And the mistress too!' And I said: 'And the lover too!'" (Louis Resnais, visual impairment, 59, February 2015). Avoidance, intrusion into the territories of the self, and objectification are three classic primary mechanisms of stigmatization of disabled people in the public space. A number of the episodes described earlier date from relatively long ago, and several people insist on the fact that the most violent stigmatizing behaviours have reduced over time:

> 'If I compare how things were in the 1960s and then now, I say to myself that I no longer live in the same France. … The way people see disability, frankly, is very different. Because, before, if we were blind, practically, the word "blind" corresponded more or less to "mental deficiency". […] Doctors used to talk to the person accompanying you and not to you, and that's a bit complicated. It still happens, but it no longer happens in medical circles, etc. […] It happens less and less often. But it used to happen to me all the time.' (Jeannette Houde, visual impairment, 75, March 2015)

This positive assessment of the evolution of the social treatment of blindness has only a little echo in the field of mobility impairment, where testimonies describe more systematic stigmatization practices. While some of these classic reactions seem to be on the decline, new forms of stigmatization are emerging, no longer based directly on subordination (assignment, through various methods, to a sub-human or non-human status), but on a perception that disabled people enjoy undue privileges. This idea is based on a misunderstanding of the accommodation logic as a support for equity, combined with a lack of information about the resources available to disabled people. It sheds light on the perception of disability policies by nondisabled people, as policies that err on the side of generosity. The public space is also the place where these representations confront the reality: "People in the street, it's incredible, because they have the impression that everything is given to me!

That the person who comes [to assist me], it's free, that the wheelchair is fully paid for, it's not true." Maryse Cloutier thus perceives a form of resentment on the part of "people in the street". Similarly, Leila Saddi struggles to establish the legitimacy of her priority right in public transportation. She recounts how "when there are too many people [in the bus], they don't even let me pass", with parents with strollers retorting: "You're sitting down, you have time to wait for the bus" ("You don't believe it when you hear it. People dare"). She also has to "fight" daily to get access to the elevator on line 14:

> 'Every day when I take [the line 14 lift], I need to fight. I need to fight with people to take it. Recently I was insulted by a young person because I wanted to take it. He didn't want to get off, a 14- or 15-year-old youngster. [...] He said to me, "Get out, don't tell me your life story".' (Leila Saddi, mobility impairment, 31, March 2015)

These various acts of stigmatization vary in frequency, and all the interviewees emphasize the diversity of attitudes they encounter. Moreover, the victims are not passive in the face of stigmatization (Lamont et al 2016): they respond ("fascist", "go your own way"), explain (for example, that they are safe on the Metro platform), make complaints to third parties (Leila Saddi complained to the Metro agents), or deflect the stigma with a humorous line. While these reactions are susceptible, by their accumulation, to contribute to a shift in social representations of disability, they do not take away the violence of the initial stigma and the equally structural effect of its recurrence. The existence of such behaviours helps to understand how challenging public space investment is, for reasons that are not only related to material barriers. As Jenny Morris pointed out in 1991, '[it] is not only the physical limitations that assign us to home and the perimeter of our loved ones. It is the fact to know that every entry into public space will be dominated by scrutiny, condescension, pity and hostility' (Morris 1991: 25). Accessibility in the material sense is a fundamental issue and a necessary condition for mobility, but it is not a sufficient condition.

Negotiating priority right with an invisible disability

The situations of stigmatization described so far correspond, by definition, to cases where the disability is visible (it is because it is visible that it is stigmatized). But the mobility of people with invisible disabilities also deserves attention. We will approach it from the question of the uses of the priority card, which provides a paradigmatic case for studying rights consciousness. The purpose of the priority card (formerly known as the *station debout pénible*, or painful standing card) is to allow its holder priority access to public administration counters and public transport. It concerns people for whom standing is difficult, but whose level of disability recognized by the MDPH is less than 80 per cent. People who exceed this level are eligible for the disability card, which also gives them this priority right.[19]

There is nothing obvious about asserting a priority right. Indeed, the exercise of this right constitutes, to use Goffmanian terms, a 'territorial offense' on one of the 'territories of the self', 'the turn'. This corresponds to 'the order in which a claimant receives a good of some kind relative to other claimants in the situation' (Goffman 1971: 35). Goffman points out that 'In our Western society, perhaps the most important principle in turn organisation is "first come, first served," establishing the claim of an individual to come right after the person "ahead" and right before the person "behind"' (Goffman 1971: 36). The priority right claim, which overturns this principle, therefore constitutes a 'territorial offense' (Goffman 1971: 49), on the part of the person claiming it, on the 'turn' of other users. The mobilization of the priority (or disability) card is one way of gaining acceptance for this 'offense', but it is not the only one, and it is not always effective. Priority right as defined by the law can be contrasted with priority right as it is constructed in social interactions, and the priority card is only one of the possible supports.

Only people with an invisible disability referred, during the interviews, to their use or non-use of the priority card. Among them, several who had previously been visibly disabled (using a cane or crutches) indicated that priority was then given to them more easily, without them having to use their card:

> 'Between the time when you don't have a cane and when you have a cane, you have a completely different relationship [with other passengers]. People pay attention. ... [Without a cane] I used to get into the Metro, they wouldn't make room for me; with a cane they do, for example.' (Nadine Trappier, mobility impairment, 61, January 2015)

> 'When I had my crutches I didn't need it [the card] because you could see it, people would stand up.' (Julie Ferandi, mobility impairment, 39, March 2015)

As we have seen from the case of Leila Saddi, negotiating a right of priority when using a wheelchair can be complex ("You are sitting down, you have time," say the bus passengers). However, we will focus here on cases or invisible disabilities, where the claim to priority involves the recognition of the existence of a disability. As priority is not offered by other users, disabled people have to take action themselves. This is experienced as difficult, for several reasons: the desire not to show one's vulnerability, not to place oneself in a position to ask for help from others, concern about the inconvenience caused to other people, fear of a refusal. All these reasons are mentioned, for example, in the testimony of Carole Perret:

CP: When I'm really exhausted in the Metro, then I take out my card. I try not to take it out, but when I'm really exhausted in the Metro, I take out my card, and there are people there, they look at me from head to toe like: but you're not sick.
AR: Why are you trying not to take it out?
CP: Out of pride. [Silence.] Out of pride because it's difficult. ... When I have to do it, I say very kindly, 'Good morning, Madam, good morning, Sir' – I try to get the gentlemen to stand up – 'Good morning, Sir, I'm sorry, I can't stand for long. Could you give me your seat?' And it's energetically exhausting. Because everyone is looking at you. (Carole Perret, mobility impairment, 53, February 2015)

The 'energetic' expenditure involved in claiming a right of priority explains why Carole makes selective use of this claim, only resigning herself to it when she is "really exhausted" and trying as much as possible "not to ... take out" her card. The precision with which she refers to her interaction with passengers ("Good morning, Sir ...") suggests that the wording has been thought out, rehearsed to optimize the chances of success. There is nothing natural or automatic about the use of the card. Similarly, Nadine Trappier only uses her card when visiting museums, and not systematically ("I've often queued up, so as not to disturb. ... I had it [the card], I didn't use it"). She does not use it in other places where she could use it, such as the post office: "the queue at the post office is not going to be a huge one, so I think 'Oh, well, that's fine, I can ...'."

The priority card is therefore selectively used, and often as a last resort. Claiming a right of priority is a matter of need, not of right: one does not mobilize one's right of priority because one is entitled to it, but because one needs it. However, the scope of situations in which one needs to have priority goes beyond the jurisdiction of the priority card (limited to public transport and public service counters). The supermarket is thus often mentioned as a place where it is necessary to assert one's right of priority, with an unequal awareness, depending on people, of the gap between the right of priority thus understood and the scope of application of the priority card 'in the texts'. While Lucien Rémo spontaneously mentions the supermarket as the ideal place where he learnt to make good use of his priority card, Julie Ferandi, who was refused priority by her local supermarket, knows that the priority card is not intended to apply in this context: "The trade legislation says that only wide passages are mandatory, it does not say at any time that they are obliged to give priority to priority cards. [...] It is up to the goodwill of those who do not know the law, in the end." The priority card can therefore be used beyond its legal jurisdiction. Moreover, the effective use of the card is the result of a learning process:

> 'I learnt. At first, I asked the person in front of me, then the other person. … And as I asked people, I started to break down, I wouldn't feel well, I had a big trolley, maybe they were with children. … And as time went by. … And then people grumbled, because my disability is not visible. […] At one point I said to myself: "I need to find another solution." So, I tried it out. The trial-and-error game, and I found the trick that made me feel comfortable: I go to the very end, I arrive next to the first person, I ask: "Do you have a priority card?" I show mine. If the person doesn't have a priority card, I ask: "Do you mind?" I show it to the cashier and pass. It's not easy. It's a learning process.' (Lucien Rémo, mobility impairment, 56, January 2015)

Through "trial-and-error", Lucien has found a routine that allows him to negotiate his right of priority without excessive personal cost, 'in comfort',[20] by asking directly to the first person in the queue without questioning each previous user. This same process of trial and error led him to abandon the use of the priority card in a context that falls within its legal scope of application, namely public transport. Facing too many refusals of priority despite the presentation of his card, he found the 'ultimate solution' by taking the Metro with a walking stick. Although he has no functional need for it (he walks perfectly well without a cane), he uses it as a means of negotiating a right of priority:

LR: [Pointing at his cane] This is for the Metro. [Pointing at his priority card] This is for the supermarket. The cane is useless to you [in the supermarket]. The cane is useful from time to time [in the Metro]. When I get into the Metro, I have my cane, I directly get a seat.

AR: Then you don't need to show your card?

LR: If I show my card, I have to argue for three hours: 'What do you have?' 'What proves me that it's not a fake?' […] 'But why me?' 'Why don't you ask the other guy for a seat?' This is madness. So, I found the solution. This is the ultimate trick. The underground parade. So, you'll notice that I'm an organized guy! [He shows the cane folding.]

AR: Is it foldable?!

LR: It's foldable, so I can wear it on my motorbike. But I teach people that too. 'You want to be safe in the Metro? Come on, take a cane'. Tricks of disabled people. … I tell you: to me,

> the disability is the others. It's management. Of course, I didn't do this directly. First, I broke my nose, then I learnt. (Lucien Rémo, mobility impairment, 56, January 2015)

As he could not efficiently claim a right of priority on legal grounds (showing his card), Lucien developed a strategy of negotiating this right alongside the law, using the cane to portray a disability more commonly recognized than his own.

Conclusion: The multiple supports of the right to mobility

Beyond the observation of the current limits in the accessibility of the built environment and transport, the collected accounts have made it possible to explore the ways in which discontent emerges and is expressed, in particular from a mechanism of relative deprivation fuelled by the policy feedbacks. The individual and collective local actions highlighted offer an insight into the conflicts, but also the negotiation processes that are currently at play around this issue, often away from the main national associations. The anger expressed, particularly among the youngest, does not meet a satisfactory vector of expression in the perceived associative offer. This helps to explain the importance of individual initiatives, whether they are targeted (complaints to a transport company or a given commercial establishment) or open (blog posts, use of social networks, and so on). The role of these individual initiatives in the difficult progress in accessibility should not be neglected, as well as the work of associations that participate in communal and inter-communal commissions. Far from being granted a right to accessibility, individuals create it daily, sometimes using the law as a resource, and sometimes despite or alongside it.

Accessibility (considered here mainly from the point of view of the built environment and transport) is a necessary condition for mobility, but not a sufficient one. In addition to the material obstacles to mobility, there are also social hurdles, which are highlighted by an analysis of the many forms of stigmatization in public space. This confirms the interest of a micro-sociological approach to reception processes. This approach to rights realization at the individual level is likely to enrich policy reflections, by inviting us to think about accessibility beyond its material dimension. The social obstacles to the mobility of disabled people are based on mechanisms on which public policies have levers for intervention, in particular through information and training for both disabled and nondisabled people: systematizing learning about locomotion and mobility by integrating techniques for asking for help from passers-by, 'instructions for use' of the priority card and support in its use, raising public awareness and knowledge about disability, and sanctioning hateful behaviour. Finally, the material and social obstacles that hinder the right to mobility of disabled people give an essential role to human support. Whether because of a physical environment that is insufficiently and randomly accessible, or because of fears that are not always easy to name, many people only go out accompanied or express a preference for this type of outing, *at least* for certain journeys. While specialized transport offers (often under restrictive conditions) this accompaniment on finalized journeys, the available accompaniment for more leisurely outings is much more uncertain. Apart from the cases of people who already have permanent personal assistance, this accompaniment depends on the availability of relatives, friends, or associative services. In addition to the necessary legal guarantee of physical accessibility, the combination of these different levers of intervention will be crucial to the realization of the 'sweet dream' of mobility.

6

Conclusion

Why talk about 'fragile' rights? In the field of disability, the idea of fragility is more commonly associated with people themselves than with their rights. In contrast to the classic image of fragile disabled people as passive objects of protection, the experiences described in this book show active subjects, endowed with reflexivity, critical capacity, and a potential for innovation.

Their rights, on the other hand, deserve to be described as 'fragile': often imprecise from the moment they are legally enshrined, they suffer from major shortcomings in terms of effectiveness in all the studied areas (education, employment, social policy, accessibility). Faced with these imperfectly realized rights, many individuals protest (at least in the interview situation) and take action, negotiate, tinker, adapt, to make their rights more concrete, and in the same movement, to assert themselves as subjects of rights. This everyday politics takes place at a distance from the collectives involved in the politicization of disability, whether they be associations or, *a fortiori*, public officials, towards whom several people make a demand for descriptive representation.

Fragile rights

While disability rights are often reduced to anti-discriminatory civil rights (Heyer 2005), we insisted on the need to understand them in a broader way, including social rights. Taken as a whole, disability rights in France present vulnerabilities as of their legal inscription, and even more so in their implementation.

The limits of rights in the texts

There are several limitations to the enactment of these rights. Despite the rise of a rhetoric of individual rights, the explicit reference to rights struggles to make it past the explanatory memorandum and into the legal texts themselves. The Law of 11 February 2005 is a good illustration of this. Rights are more likely to be included in the law in the form of a reference to collective obligations (for example in the fields of education or accessibility) than in the form of an explicit statement of individual rights (right to schooling in a mainstream environment, right to accessibility). Although individual rights and collective obligations can be considered as two sides of the same coin, we note here the limits of the acclimatation of the rights register in the field of disability in France.

Secondly, several texts suffer from imprecise wording. The case of the right to education in the Law of 11 February 2005 is a good example. Commonly interpreted as instituting a right to schooling in a mainstream environment, the law is in fact vague on this point, instituting the sole principle of enrolment in a mainstream 'reference' establishment while leaving open the possibility of schooling in a specialized establishment. The reforms relating to accessibility have also been marked by a step backwards in relation to an acquired right. The postponement by ordinance of the obligation to provide access indicates a fragility of the legal registration of rights.

Finally, one may be tempted to take a critical look at the coexistence of theoretically contradictory orientations in disability rights: school inclusion and special education, non-discrimination in employment and sheltered work, work integration and welfare assistance based on an assumption of unfitness for work. As we have developed in relation to employment (see Chapter 2), this wobbly nature of rights is not necessarily a sign of fragility, but can be interpreted as a strength, allowing for a better adjustment to the diversity of aspirations and capacities, and ultimately to the vulnerability of individuals. To the functional basis of this vulnerability, one can add a social source of vulnerability, linked to structural discrimination. This is, for example, what the people we met refer to when, not considering themselves 'unfit' for work for a moment, they point to the structural obstacles to their professional integration (discrimination, economic crisis, and so on). Although the vulnerability they face is more social than physiological, it is nonetheless real and deserves legal recognition.

Major shortcomings in effectiveness

Despite their imprecision and fragility in some cases, these rights, which have been enshrined in law since 1975 and more clearly since 2005, have nonetheless provided an ambitious perspective of social change: inclusion in education and employment, equal participation in the labour market, full accessibility of the built environment and transport, which frees up mobility, and the introduction of a principle of universal compensation which can be read as compensation for structural discrimination. Yet in all these areas, the realization of rights is not up to their ambitions.

In educational terms, mainstream schooling does appear as a strong symbolic norm today, and seems to have become a more common practice, at least in the case of visual impairment, for which there was a strong pre-existing tradition of schooling in specialized institutions. But access to mainstream institutions is not synonymous with inclusion. Facilities and support are still lacking, and we are also a long way from the idea, conveyed by the Salamanca declaration, of a school that would rethink itself from an inclusive perspective rather than concede integration on the margins. In higher education, access to universities, in the literal sense, still faces major constraints (lack of physical accessibility). Accommodation and support are less institutionalized and even more random than in primary and secondary education. However, as has been the case for other social minorities (women, ethnic minorities), more widespread access to higher education is likely to be a decisive lever for destabilizing inequalities. The right to education still not completely achieved, from kindergarten to higher education, is therefore a major challenge for the years to come.

In the field of employment, the qualitative perspective of this research offers a complementary and convergent viewpoint in relation to the statistics that highlight the still marginal place of disabled people in the labour market (Barhoumi and Chabanon 2015; Bouchet 2019; Revillard 2019a). The diagnosis regarding rights' effectiveness in this field must, however, take into consideration the limits of what rights can do in a capitalist market economy. The effects of public policies are modulated by the economic situation, but also by other structural inequalities that mark access to and progression in the labour market, primarily social class and gender.[1] The labour market is also an area (together with social policies) where the constraining dimension of certain rights is particularly apparent, especially when they involve labelling people as 'disabled workers'. In this respect, the RQTH is the subject of ambivalent accounts, between a constraint and a vector of access to resources.

What about the effectiveness of social rights? Among the people we met, the use of disability-related social benefits (AAH, ACTP, PCH) is frequent, and makes an objective difference in the lives of most of them. On the other hand, the way they are allocated and the very process of making them effective make them fragile rights. Labelling, a feeling of strong social control, forms deemed unsuitable, excessive delays, lack of information, all contribute to the overall distance felt towards an administration which claimed to place 'the disabled person at the heart of the systems that concern them'.[2]

Finally, the lack of effectiveness in making the built environment and transport accessible is so obvious that it has led public authorities to temporarily remove this right from the law. The people we met experience this daily. Limited in their movements, forced to use specialized transport that is sometimes excessively expensive and of uncertain availability, many of them feel this lack of accessibility as a lack of consideration, a status issue. The case of accessibility also shows how the partial implementation of rights fuels relative deprivation. Faced with these imperfectly effective rights, most research participants are very active.

Co-producing one's rights, becoming a subject of rights: the politics of everyday life

To our initial questioning about the consequences of the different forms of mobilization of rights within public policy, inviting an investigation of how rights are realized in disabled people's everyday lives, this research provides two essential answers. People play an active role in the realization of their rights, and they struggle to be considered as subjects of rights as much as to obtain rights.

Co-producing one's rights: an active reception

At the beginning of this book, we raised the question of the ways in which the rights of disabled people can be realized from a micro-sociological point of view, by proposing a theoretical distinction between rights that are realized without necessarily going through a conscious mediation (constitutive dimension), and rights that people have to fight for, that they have to mobilize, and that require specific steps to be taken in order to be realized (instrumental dimension) (Stryker 2003).

In a context where the effectiveness of rights is not automatic, the dominant image that emerges from this research is that of particularly active individuals. Policy uses and the instrumental dimension of rights are at the heart of the accounts. To use a recurring expression in the interviews, the people we met 'fight' to obtain recognition of their rights to accommodation, social benefits, and accessibility.

Litigation is not central for research participants, who use a wide range of tactics including explanation, negotiation, or threats of legal action, to have their rights recognized. Beyond these given situations in which they fight to obtain a specific right (access to an establishment, the implementation of an accommodation), many people express themselves publicly on the denial of rights they face, particularly through digital media (blogs, social networks).

The processes involved do not only involve representatives of the public authorities. Rights are negotiated with schools and the MDPH, for example, but also with a private employer, the manager of a shop or other passengers on the Metro. This diffuse nature of rights makes their (non-)realization a process by which political stakes are translated into everyday life, into a 'politics of everyday life' (Hunt 1993). While one might be tempted to make this individual propensity for anger and action an anthropological hypothesis,[3] one must also recognize what it owes to the effects of public policies themselves. In contemporary France, the gap between the statement of rights and their ineffectiveness is a powerful driving force of individual reflexivity. Public policy thus produces some of its effects, not directly but through the reactions it provokes in its target audience, through a mechanism of policy feedback (Pierson 1993).

Becoming a subject of rights: the centrality of a statutory claim

The second key finding of this research relates to the close articulation between the 'having' and 'being' of rights: having rights, being a subject of rights. Reflection on rights and the study of their implementation generally focus on the first dimension: for example, are the right to education and the right to income security legally recognized, and to what extent are they effective: are people enrolled at school? Do people receive a minimum income? But rights also include a processual dimension, which involves the consideration due to a subject of rights (how is the individual treated in the process of realizing their rights?). This question of the 'being' of rights refers to the statutory dimension of social inequalities, corresponding to the consideration that individuals feel entitled to expect from others (Ridgeway 2014).

This concern is omnipresent among the people we met, and has a strong impact on the way they experience the (non-)realization of their rights in their more substantial dimensions. It is visible both in the way individuals experience their treatment by institutions and by nondisabled people in general, and in their reactions to this treatment.

For example, what makes the right to education a fragile right is not only the fact that the access to mainstream institutions and accommodation is not guaranteed. It is also, and perhaps more importantly, that when they are granted, they are still often granted as favours (Buton 2009), in a way that constructs people as lucky recipients of an individual's or organization's indulgence rather than as subjects of rights. Similarly, the distant relationship that disabled people have with social rights (AAH, PCH) that make a difference in their lives is the result of a process of attribution of these rights that is perceived as marked by suspicion, social control, and in some cases pity, rather than by the simple recognition of eligibility. In other words, there is a sense of recognition, sometimes difficult and random, as having a right to, but not a real recognition as a subject of, rights.

A third example, that of access to public space, will show how this process not only involves the relationship to institutions and their representatives, but also the more general relationship to the nondisabled world. The lack of accessibility experienced by disabled people is not only material. It is not just a matter of elevators that do not exist or constantly break down, or traffic lights without sound. It also appears in the reflections of passengers who refuse to give up their seats on the grounds that a person in a wheelchair can wait, or through the intrusive and violent comments of a passer-by who questions your choice to have children or your ability to work as a blind person. In all these situations, the experience of the denial of rights, or of fragile rights, coincides with a lack of consideration for disabled people, who do not feel treated as subjects of rights.

Faced with these situations, however, these people are not passive. Their struggles to realize their rights are, inseparably, demands to be recognized as subjects of rights and worthy of respect (Honneth 1995). For example, when Chloé Lamarche replies to the bank officer that she does not have to "take [her] precautions" and that she simply wants to "dispose of [her] personal money as [she] sees fit and when [she] sees fit", she is not only claiming a right to use a material device (accessible ATM). She is also contesting unequal treatment, and thus asserting herself as a subject of rights, on an equal footing with nondisabled people.

But this relationship between the 'having' and the 'being' rights is not always mutually reinforcing. In some cases, the desire to assert oneself as a subject of equal rights also leads to distancing oneself from certain rights perceived as stigmatizing: distancing oneself from social assistance, non-take-up of the PCH, perception of the RQTH as a constraint, etc. The assertion of oneself as a subject of rights is therefore linked in a complex way with legally enshrined rights, sometimes drawing on them, sometimes distancing from them. In all cases, the centrality of this claim reveals the importance of the statutory dimension of disability-related inequalities: both the centrality of this symbolic dimension in the subordination of disabled people, and the subjective attachment of people themselves to this issue.

A modality of social change

By fighting for their rights, individuals participate in a dynamic of social change: not only by potentially changing in the immediate future what they have access to (whether it be a high school or an ATM), but also by paving the way for others, and potentially destabilizing the usual course of disregard for disabled people. All the micro-subversions, which can take the form of insults ("Fascist, get out of the way!"), humour ("What about the lover?") or polite negotiation ("I understand but ..."), are all modalities through which social change is produced daily.

However, the scope of these actions should not be overestimated either. On the one hand, they are partly conditioned by a certain state of implementation of public policies (partial effectiveness of rights, which fuels relative deprivation). On the other hand, their effectiveness is limited in comparison with the effects that can be achieved through proactive public policy or collective action in this area. Based on proven mechanisms for making rights effective in other areas (Stryker 2007; Haglund and Stryker

2015), it can be hypothesized that legal constraint, combined with its mobilization by collective actors, is a more effective lever for making rights real than individual negotiation. This raises the question of the possible more collective outlets for this discontent facing the ineffectiveness of rights.

What political representation?

Associations are omnipresent in the disability sector and intervene in various ways in the lives of research participants, but relatively little as driving forces of politicization or places of activist commitment. People nevertheless express strong expectations in terms of political representation.

A distanced relationship with associations

In the course of individual narratives, associations are first of all mentioned as managers of the structures that provide schooling for some (INJA, ERDV) or accompany the schooling of others (S3AIS), but also provide accessibility services, from the most professional (specialized transport) to the most voluntary (local associations providing voluntary services for accompanied outings). They also appear as more or less institutionalized employment intermediaries, from continuous training offered by a large national association to informal support services provided by small associations. In these different areas, associations can also function as places of work or volunteering. Several research participants work or have worked in specialized structures with associative status, and nine people have a significant investment as volunteers in associations in the disability sector. The associations are also mentioned in their functions of disseminating information, socialization, and mutual aid. They therefore make a difference in people's lives primarily through the services they offer (and in some cases, the establishments they manage), and indeed, it is often around this idea of service provision that comments are made in response to the more direct questions about their role asked in the interviews.

Associations are therefore very present in everyday life. However, they are very rarely mentioned as vehicles for politicization. None of the people we met told us that they had radically changed their view of disability, or made disability a political issue, through contact with an association in the sector. This does not mean that such conversions are not possible. We simply see that there is a production of discontent that is relatively disconnected from existing structures of collective mobilization. As analysed in the case of accessibility, this discontent can be linked to a mechanism of relative deprivation fuelled by policy feedbacks. The few associations mentioned that have a more explicitly political activity are the local associations involved in the negotiation of accessibility at the municipal level, whose creation or re-foundation was triggered by the creation of the communal accessibility commissions in 2005.

Not only can the emergence of discontent not be clearly linked to the effect of collective mobilization by one or more associations, but the latter function sparsely or not at all as outlets for this anger. The discontent barely translates into membership, particularly in the large associations of the sector. To explain this relative disconnection between politicization at the individual level and associative action, an important clue lies in the difficult articulation between the activist logic and the service provision logic. Indeed, the perception of associations as service providers (because they objectively intervene in people's lives in this way) hinders their investment in an activist sense in several ways. Firstly, many people are aware of the potential conflict of interest between the different audiences of associations that manage services while promoting users' rights: according to Maryse Cloutier, "[associations] sometimes tend ... to favour the fate of the personal assistant, rather than that of the people they are targeting". Distrust can also be linked to an experience of being assigned to an inferior status by a nondisabled associative leadership: Chloé Lamarche notes that in some associations, "there is a tendency towards pity, to have volunteers who either feel a little more powerful, or who overprotect people. There is a very infantilizing dimension". Similarly, Leila Saddi deplores the fact that "the people in charge of us are not disabled". This comment reveals, beyond the associations, a concern about the lack of political representation.

A demand for descriptive representation

The stories make visible a critique of the lack of descriptive representation of disabled people, *a fortiori* in associations but also in policymaking in general. By descriptive representation, the philosopher Hanna Pitkin means an evaluation of the quality of political representation based on the correspondence of the characteristics of the representatives with those of the represented (Pitkin 1967). The point is to deplore the absence or low presence of disabled people among the elected officials or political actors who define and implement disability policies. Such a criticism is surprising both in relation to the universalist French political culture and to the claims made by the major associations in the sector: unlike, for example, the women's organizations mobilized as part of the campaign for parity (Bereni 2015), these associations were not, at the time of the survey, making strong claims for improving the descriptive representation of disabled people. For some of them, this is due to the fact that the descriptive representation of disabled people within their own ranks is also an issue.

Yet this issue emerges from the interviews with surprising salience. Referring to the postponement of accessibility, Laëtitia Roger comments: "The people who vote [these laws], they are not in our place. … The nondisabled people who decide for us, I don't see how they can decide since they are not in the situation." When asked about changes or improvements to be made to public policies, Pierre Béraud answers: "Disabled people in charge [of policies], I would like that." But this question of representation also often comes up when evoking the difficulties encountered in the implementation of rights: when Kader Zyeb describes the maladjustment of traffic lights, he comments: "But why? Because it is made by people who are not visually impaired." Recounting the difficulties in obtaining a response from the MDPH on her file after waiting a year, Lydie Sonnet concludes: "There should be disabled people working in this field." Surprising in the French context, not echoing an associative agenda, this demand for descriptive political representation expresses a sensitivity to the issue of access to power as a lever for transforming disability-related inequalities. It raises the question of political rights, in addition to the other types of rights studied in this book.

The imperfect implementation of public policies thus favours not only an active role for individuals in the realization of their rights, but also the emergence of a political questioning. The politics of everyday life thus bears the seeds of a more extensive politicization of the issue, calling into question not only public policy but also political representation.

APPENDIX 1

Methodology

This book builds upon the research project 'the reception of disability policy', funded by LIEPP as part of its 2013 call for projects. The project aimed at providing an overview of how the changing context of disability policy in France (notably since the adoption of the 2005 law) had impacted disabled people's lives and how they reacted to it.

This appendix provides complementary elements on methodology, beyond what is presented in the introduction.

The study draws on 30 biographical interviews with people with either visual (N=15) or mobility (N=15) impairments, conducted between November 2014 and January 2016.

Because of my interest in the consequences of long-term legal and policy change, I chose to focus on two types of impairments, visual and mobility impairments, which have been legally recognized for a long time (as opposed to more 'recent' ones in French disability policy, such as mental health conditions or learning disabilities, which have only been recognized as disabilities since the 2005 law). In the post I disseminated to find research participants, I also limited the perimeter to people who had lived with an impairment for more than 15 years. This followed the same idea of tracking the effects of policy and legal changes in individual lives; I also sought to meet people whose relation to their impairment was rather stabilized, who were not in the middle of a major biographical disruption.

The goal of studying policy reception poses a challenge regarding how the object of research is to be presented to participants. Indeed, in a similar way to the approach promoted by legal consciousness studies, the aim is to include in the perimeter of inquiry (although not exclusively of course) people who have a very distant relationship to law and policy. This, concretely, raised the question of how the research would be presented in the call to potential participants. Being too explicit about the policy focus of the research in the call risked inducing a selection bias against people who would not feel competent to answer questions about policy. Conversely, not mentioning it raised ethical issues. The compromise adopted as a solution consisted in just referring to possible policy implications of the research on the post, and then explaining more clearly to people the type of research at hand in the conversation prior to setting up the interview:

> As part of a sociological study on disability, I am seeking to meet people who have had a mobility or visual impairment for more than 15 years, in order to exchange on their experience.
>
> These interviews follow a very open format. You will be invited to talk about your personal trajectory (in terms of family, schooling, etc.) and your experience of disability in everyday life. These interviews take place face-to-face. They generally last about one hour and a half. They are recorded and used anonymously in the research. [...]
>
> This work should result in academic publications. One of the aims is to feed into a reflection on disability policy.

When participants called me back, I explained to them the context of my research and the goal of examining the effects of policy and legal change, while insisting on my indirect way of proceeding (asking questions about the person's past and everyday life, rather than explicitly policy-related questions). I made sure they agreed with the general framework of the research before going on to plan the interview.

I tried multiple approaches and types of intermediaries to get in touch with potential research participants (for example, a job fair, the disability unit of a large company, an occupational therapist, a personal support worker, numerous non-profit service providers, and so on). Two types of intermediaries proved most effective: first, two non-profit service providers (mobility support and career advice) that gave me access to their users and, second, an advert placed on the website of a specialized magazine (*Handirect*), which was reposted on several forums and social networks. Service-providing NGOs proved the most efficient in order to reach out to more isolated people. I also took advantage of the snowball effect from the first responses, and made sure to obtain a diverse sample in terms of gender, social origins, education, and current occupation.

Participants include 17 women and 13 men, aged 23 to 75 years. Fifteen have a visual impairment (from very poor vision to total blindness) and 15 have a mobility impairment, which can take various forms: para-, hemi-, or tetraplegia, chronic pain, or neurological or digestive problems affecting mobility, with progressive or stable situations. Two-thirds of the interviewees had their disability diagnosed in childhood (before 16 years of age), whether it was pathological (for example, poliomyelitis, myopathy, congenital cataract) or accidental in origin. The diagnoses in adulthood could either be the result of an accident or disease (for example, retinitis pigmentosa, ruptured aneurysm, cancer), or correspond to the identification of a pre-existing but previously undiagnosed condition (for example, undetected visual impairment, fibromyalgia). Four of the interviewees have combined disabilities (for example, blindness and digestive disease, hemiplegia and hearing loss).

The participants are from diverse social backgrounds and age groups, and their levels of education range from no diploma with schooling interrupted at the end of junior high school, to a doctorate. Eleven of the interviewees have a level of education lower than or equal to the high school diploma (*baccalauréat*), and 19 hold higher education qualifications. Their occupational situations are more difficult to categorize because of the instability of many careers. A third of the interviewees live solely on the disabled adult benefit and are far removed from the labour market. The others have jobs of varying degrees of stability and prestige, from sheltered employment to university professor. Twenty-one participants were living in the Paris region at the time of the study (but the majority had also lived in other cities), and nine in other medium or large French cities or their outskirts. Almost all currently live in independent housing or with their parents (with two exceptions, one person in a hotel and one in a residential institution), but many have had experiences of living in an institution, either during their schooling (boarding school) or as adults (rehabilitation centre).

The interview outline (see Box A1.1) included elements on: the family context; the outset of the impairment, its diagnosis and its impact on everyday life; modes of schooling; housing and personal life; occupational trajectory (when applicable); other activities (such as leisure or political participation); everyday life and mobility; administrative tasks in relation to disability. Broader questions on perceptions of disability policy and the evolution of social attitudes towards disability were included at the end of the interviews. This interview grid was partially used in every interview and generally very loosely used, giving priority to each person's focus and own way of telling their story. In the conduct of the interviews, an effort was made to avoid asking policy questions before the corresponding interventions or policy tools were mentioned by the interviewee, in order not to bias their accounts. The majority of the interviews took place at the respondent's home, and they lasted one hour and 35 minutes on average.

The interviews were transcribed in full[1] and analysed using three methods that correspond to an inductive approach (Strauss and Corbin 2003): the drafting of individual portraits; thematic content analysis (using Atlas. Ti); and in-depth analysis of excerpts (Revillard 2017a). In the excerpts cited throughout the book, the individuals' first and last names have been modified, as have the cities outside Paris. When I cite an interviewee (under a pseudonym), I indicate the type of impairment (mobility impairment or visual impairment) and his or her age in brackets. These characteristics are compiled in Table A2.1.

Box A1.1: Interview grid

[Reminder of the conditions of the interview: I'm looking to see the effect of public policies, but I'm interested in how all this fits into the whole of a life story; so I'm going to ask you much broader questions, about your childhood, your schooling, your trajectory in general, and then I have more specific questions about public policy. It's a very open interview; don't hesitate to tell me if you don't want to answer certain questions, so we can move on.]

Family background:
To situate myself: year of birth? Originally from the Paris region or ...?
Parents' professions. Place of residence during childhood.
Age, education and professions of brothers and sisters.

Onset of disability (if during childhood), medical diagnosis and hospitalizations:
Diagnosis, prognosis, equipment.
Reaction of parents (father/mother) and siblings; what involvement of both parents?
Were there any other disabilities in the family?
Dates and frequency of hospitalizations. Status of the institutions in which one stayed. Account of the experience in the institution (Attitude of carers and educators? Memories of violence?). What kind of education during hospitalizations?
Frequency of visits from parents; explore the reasons (willingness, authorization, distance, transport). Other means of communication: correspondence, telephone ...

Schooling:
Type of schooling; how was it decided? Role of doctors or parents? Were you asked for your opinion?
How was the disability perceived at school?
Time missed at school due to hospitalizations? Difficulties encountered at school? For what reasons?
If mainstream schooling: do you feel that your experience was different from that of other children? In what way? Explore extra-curricular activities, friendships, emotional relationships.
How far did you go to school? Would you have liked to continue? How did you envisage your orientation?
Assessment of childhood: general memory of childhood (happy, unhappy ...).

Housing and personal life:
As an adult, where did you live? Parents, institutions, or access to independent housing?
At what age did you leave your parents' home?

Living alone or in a couple? Do you feel that the disability may have affected your emotional life (reaction of others, access to outlets, etc.)?
If children: what were the reactions of those around you, of the institutions, at the time of the birth and education of the children?

Professional trajectory:
After your studies, did you work professionally?
If no professional activity, try to find out the reasons. For women: without the disability, do you think you would have been active (what type of activity?)
Sheltered or ordinary environment? Part-time or full-time? Account of working conditions.
If mainstream: how was the disability perceived? Reaction of colleagues?
Did you take steps to obtain the RQTH? How did the idea come about? Perception of this system (effective or not, perception of quotas).
Career progression: are you satisfied with it? Do you think it would have been different if nondisabled?

Other activities:
Electoral participation and possible difficulties to access the vote.
Participation in associations: disability and others.
Hobbies, possible substitutes to professional activity; travel.

Administrative procedures related to disability:
Have you taken any administrative steps in relation to your disability? Who gave you the idea to take them the first time? Did you do it yourself? Or when did you start doing them yourself? (Transition from parents to personal steps.)
What were the first steps you took? Do you remember going to the COTOREP/MDPH? For which benefits? How did it go? Did you get help to submit your file?
How did it go the first time you went through these procedures?
What did it change for you to receive these benefits (financially, in terms of status (positive or negative), etc.)?
How did you experience the change from COTOREP to MDPH? In terms of benefits? In terms of the accessibility of the institution? Were you informed of the possibility of being heard by the CDAPH?
Since 2005, associations have been represented on the CDAPH: Did you know? What do you think about it? In your opinion, does this change anything?

Description of daily life today:
Housing.
What help is needed?
Description of a typical day or week.

What outings? What obstacles? When you travel, what means of transport do you use? Have you ever given up going somewhere because of your disability?

General questions about disability:
When you were a child, was the term disability used? What other terms were used? Do you remember when the term disability became popular? Is it a term you identified with?
Over the years, do you feel that the way others look at your disability has changed? In what way? Have you heard of a disability rights movement, and when?
What do you think would have changed in your experience if you had been born later? What helped you? What was difficult? Where did the obstacles come from?
Have you ever experienced discrimination because of your disability?
Have you read any books related to disability? Have you seen any films? Which ones?

Questions related to the relationship with public policies and their perceived evolution:
Do you remember particular moments when the issue of disability was debated in the public space?
Perception of the role of associations?
The 2005 law has put a lot of emphasis on the rights of disabled people: What does this mean to you?

APPENDIX 2

List of Participants

Table A2.1 shows, for each person interviewed, the pseudonym used (first and last name), the age at the time of the study and the type of disability (broadly characterized).

Table A2.1: Interviewees

Surname	First name	Age	Type of disability
Barut	Nicolas	40	visual
Bastien	Elise	47	visual
Béraud	Pierre	44	mobility
Bertaux	Geneviève	62	visual
Caron	Alain	48	visual
Cloutier	Maryse	72	mobility
Durand	Claudine	56	mobility
Ferandi	Julie	39	mobility
Germain	Marie	60	visual
Houde	Jeannette	75	visual
Jaucourt	Victor	30	mobility
Lamarche	Chloe	23	visual
Martin	Léa	28	mobility
Moleiro	Dora	47	visual
Morand	Daniel	58	visual
Perret	Carole	53	mobility
Perrin	Alice	40	mobility
Rémo	Lucien	56	mobility
Resnais	Louis	59	visual

(continued)

Table A2.1: Interviewees (continued)

Surname	First name	Age	Type of disability
Ricordeau	Jérôme	28	visual
Roger	Laëtitia	40	mobility
Saddi	Leila	31	mobility
Sernin	Jean-Marc	61	visual
Simon	Michel	57	visual
Sonnet	Lydie	73	mobility
Tain	Philippe	47	visual
Tournut	Joséphine	44	mobility
Trappier	Nadine	61	mobility
Vallat	Luc	46	mobility
Zyeb	Kader	24	visual

APPENDIX 3

Main Disability-related Social Statuses and Benefits Mentioned in the Interviews

As these statuses are frequently changing, they are described here as they were in effect (particularly in terms of amounts) at the time the survey was conducted (2014–2016). The source, unless otherwise specified, is service-public.fr.

- Disabled child education allowance (*Allocation d'éducation de l'enfant handicapé* [AEEH]): Paid to the parents of a disabled child, the benefit aims at compensating the costs of education and care. It was previously called the special education allowance (*Allocation d'éducation spéciale* [AES]). It is made up of a basic benefit (awarded based on a disability rate of 50 per cent or more) and possibly a 'complement', the amount of which depends on the administrative classification of the child's 'level of disability' (on a scale from 1 to 6). The amount of the basic AEEH is €130.12. Supplements range from €227.71 (level 1) to €1,234.30 (level 6). There is a 'single parent supplement' for single parents who raise their child alone.
- Disabled adult benefit (*Allocation aux adultes handicapés* [AAH]): Created in 1975 (following the *allocation aux handicapés adultes* created in 1971), this benefit is designed as a minimum subsistence income (Ville et al 2014). It is part of the minimum social benefits and is means-tested. It is awarded based on an administrative determination of the person's 'disability rate', which must be greater than 80 per cent, or between 50 per cent and 79 per cent but accompanied by a 'substantial and lasting restriction on access to employment'. The monthly amount of the AAH for a single person without children is thus €808.46. In addition to the AAH, a 'supplement for independent living' of €104.77 per month may be paid to people with a recognized disability of more than 80 per cent

who live in independent accommodation. After notification from the MDPH, the CAF is the paying agency for this benefit.

- Third-party compensation benefit (*Allocation compensatrice pour tierce personne* [ACTP]): Created in 1975, the ACTP, which is means-tested and paid in cash, is intended to finance human assistance for people with a recognized level of disability of more than 80 per cent, generally for no more than three hours a day (Beyrie 2015). Blindness is covered by a flat-rate ACTP: the 'blindness flat-rate' ACTP amounts to €880 per month. After notification from the MDPH, the departmental council is the paying body for this benefit.
- Disability compensation benefit (*Prestation de compensation du handicap* [PCH]): Created in 2005 and intended, in the long term, to replace the ACTP (from which recipients may, however, continue to benefit), the PCH is a more ambitious compensation benefit in its scope: it is based on the idea of a universal right to compensation, and is therefore allocated without means testing, and is intended to meet individual compensation needs in a personalized manner (through a 'personalized compensation plan' [PPC] based on the person's 'life project'), including up to 24-hour human assistance if necessary. This benefit is intended to finance technical, human, animal, home improvement, or transport assistance, as well as 'specific or exceptional assistance' (one-off needs). Generally paid based on invoices for specific expenses, the PCH is paid as a lump sum in the case of blindness. The 'blindness package' of the PCH amounts to €620 per month. After notification from the MDPH, the departmental council is the paying agency for this benefit.
- Recognition of the status of disabled worker (*Reconnaissance de la qualité de travailleur handicapé* [RQTH]): This status is the heir to an initial classification of disabled workers introduced by the Law of 23 November 1957 on the 'professional reclassification of disabled workers'. The RQTH allows its beneficiary to be counted as part of the 6 per cent disability quota, and opens the right to training and rehabilitation measures, and to the adaptation of workstations and working hours.
- Disability card (*carte d'invalidité*): The purpose of the disability card is to certify the existence of a disability. It is awarded to people whose disability rate is administratively recognized as being greater than 80 per cent and to the recipients of a category 3 disability pension. It gives priority access to a seat on public transport, waiting rooms, and facilities open to the public, as well as priority in queues in public places.
- Priority card (*Carte de priorité d'accès aux lieux publics*): Formerly known as the 'painful standing card' (*station debout pénible),* this card allows priority access to the counters of public administrations and public transport for people whose degree of disability is less than 80 per cent (people above this level are eligible for the disability card) and for whom standing up is painful.

- European parking card (*carte européenne de stationnement*): This card allows the disabled person or their carer to park free of charge in public spaces (whether or not reserved for disabled people). It is issued to people whose disability reduces their ability to walk or requires the presence of a third party to help them get around.

[Note that as of January 2017 these three cards (disability, priority, and parking) have been replaced by a single 'Mobility Inclusion' card.]

Notes

Chapter 1

1 Introduction translated by Jessica Edwards, revised by Anne Revillard. The names of research participants have been modified.

2 This characterization draws on interactive approaches to disability, which incorporate the medical and social dimensions of the phenomenon (Ravaud and Fougeyrollas 2005; WHO 2011; Shakespeare 2013).

3 Assemblée nationale, *Projet de loi d'orientation en faveur des personnes handicapées*, 10 May 1974, p 3.

4 In the French civil law system, *droit commun* is the law that applies in general, as opposed to law covering specific circumstances.

5 The French *départements* are the 94 French administrative territorial units. Policy prerogatives at this level notably include the implementation of social policies.

6 For more details on this modelling of the social experience of disability, see Revillard (2019b). On the link between disability and social stratification, see also Jenkins (1991) and Shandra (2018).

7 Fabrizio Cantelli approaches this question similarly, in terms of patients' 'comfort' or 'discomfort' over the course of experiences where the realization of their rights is at stake (Cantelli 2015).

8 My analysis here reflects the work of Nancy Fraser and Axel Honneth on recognition policies (Fraser 1995; Honneth 1995).

9 These are presented in Appendix 3.

10 Note, in particular, the work of Philippe Warin and Nicolas Duvoux (Warin 1998; Duvoux 2015).

11 We will see in Chapter 5 how Goffman's analysis of face-to-face interaction and stigmatization processes can enrich the micro-sociological analysis of rights claims and realization (Goffman 1971).

Chapter 2

1 Chapter translated by Jennifer Higgins, revised by Anne Revillard.

2 Assemblée nationale, *Projet de loi d'orientation en faveur des personnes handicapées*, 10 May 1974, p 6.

3 Source: French Ministry for Education, https://www.gouvernement.fr/sites/default/files/action/piece-jointe/2016/05/lecole_inclusive_une_dynamique_qui_samplifie_en_faveur_des_eleves_et_des_etudiants_en_situation_de_handica.pdf (accessed 24 April 2020).

4 Unless otherwise indicated, all of the sections within quotation marks come from the interview with the person in question.

5 This chimes in with Joël Zaffran's study of school integration (Zaffran 2007, 2015).

6 On this movement of student activism, see Jérôme Bas (Bas 2017).
7 This assessment needs to be nuanced, however, especially among different types of disabilities. Some deaf people, for example, remain very attached to special schooling.

Chapter 3

1 Chapter translated by Jennifer Higgins and Aline Tertre, revised by Anne Revillard
2 Law of 14 July 1905 organizing assistance to the elderly, the infirm and the incurable deprived of resources.
3 Law No 75-535 of 30 June 1975 on social and medico-social institutions.
4 The directive also recalls the existing provisions against discrimination based on sex, but also on race or ethnic origin – the latter having just been covered by the 'race' directive adopted six months earlier (Guiraudon 2003).
5 Law No 90-602 of 12 July 1990 on the protection of persons against discrimination on the grounds of health or disability.
6 This result for our sample should not be subject to hasty generalizations: disability may in other cases limit a priori the capacity to work, and other studies show a diversity of aspirations in the relationship to employment (Ville and Winance 2006).
7 For a quantitative approach aimed at identifying the specific effects of disabilities on occupational trajectories, see Bouchet (2019).
8 This includes his wife, who is also visually impaired.
9 There is nothing obvious about this conditionality in the letter of the 2005 law, which does not formally make the RQTH a prerequisite for obtaining 'appropriate measures' (reasonable accommodation). This conditionality has, however, tended to impose itself in administrative practices, reflecting a particular acclimatization of anti-discrimination law in a policy context where a binding quota system already exists. This helps to explain why it is found in the representations of the participants in the research. See Lejeune (2017).

Chapter 4

1 Chapter translated by John Angell, revised by Anne Revillard
2 See Appendix 3 for a general description of these programmes.
3 In order to increase the AAH's potential of de-familialization, French disability organizations have recently campaigned to make eligibility based solely on individual income, instead of also considering the partner's income when the person is part of a couple.
4 Source: amounts in November 2016, service-public.fr.
5 This is less often the case when a disability results from an accident.
6 Regarding the social control of disabled mothers, see Malacrida (2007) and Frederick (2017).
7 "I idealized the MDPH. It means the Departmental House for Disabled People, so I said to myself, 'They'll be able to solve a lot of problems.' But that wasn't the case at all. They just shuffle paperwork" (Laëtitia Roger, mobility impairment, 40).
8 Although not explicitly mentioned in the decree, this appears indirectly through a reference to the possibility 'of being assisted or represented by the person of one's choice' (Decree no 2005-1589 of 19 December 2005 relative to the CDAPH, art. R. 241-30).
9 Michel Simon used similar terms to describe his non-recourse to the benefit when he stated, "either you have a right or you don't have a right".
10 This situation has changed since: a 'parenting' disability compensation benefit was created in 2020, effective as of January 2021.

11 The Social Action and Families Code stipulates in Article R. 241-33 that 'A non-response from the Disabled People's Rights and Autonomy Committee of more than four months following the submission of an application to an MDPH as specified in Article R. 146-25 is the equivalent of a rejection.'

12 The mechanisms for assigning these benefits were modified (after this study) by a decree on 24 December 2018 that adopted an unlimited length of time for individuals with severe or irreversible disabilities.

13 Geneviève Bertaux (visual impairment, 62).

14 An old notion in welfare policy, the 'assistance residence' (*domicile de secours*) corresponds to the address that determines which department is responsible for providing 'assistance' to those in need.

Chapter 5

1 Chapter translated by John Angell and Aline Tertre, revised by Anne Revillard.

2 The recent experience of confinement in the context of the COVID-19 epidemic has nevertheless disturbed this obviousness.

3 The association was renamed 'APF France Handicap' in 2018.

4 In Grenoble, Régis Herbin identified an APF protest on 11 March 1972 as the beginning of local accessibility claims, centred on the slogan 'Charity, pity, we've had enough!' ('*Quête, pitié, ras l'obole!*') (Herbin 2014: 24).

5 During the same period, the right to accessibility in the United States was achieved by the disability rights movement using a far more confrontational approach (Shapiro 1993; Fleischer and Zames 2011).

6 Law no 91-663 13 July 1991 contained measures to promote accessibility for disabled persons within places of residence, workplaces, and locations receiving the public. The law specifically subordinates 'grants of assistance from the State in favour of living spaces ... consistent with respect for the rules of accessibility'.

7 As evidenced by the intervention of the APF president during the closing session of the meeting on 26 February 2014: Alain Rochon 'salutes the consultation which took place' and positioned the APF as a partner with the government ('Together we must change how French people look at disability'). Regarding the Ad'AP, he observed that 'We expect the three-year rule to be the general rule, and beyond that, six years, or maybe less, to be an exception; and nine years should constitutes a strictly limited exemption' (source: *Réflexe-handicap*, 'Accessibilité: le Premier ministre conclut la concertation', 26 February 2014).

8 This finding echoes the results of quantitative studies. Based on data obtained during the *Handicap Santé* study 2008, Virginie Dejoux showed that 37 per cent of officially recognized 15- to-24-year-old disabled individuals asserted that the range of accessible locations for social outings was limited (compared to 8.5 per cent of non-disabled youth), and 41 per cent reported that times for social outings were also limited (they were unable to go out when they wished, as opposed to 16 per cent of the general youth population) (Dejoux 2015).

9 Léa Martin, mobility impairment, 28.

10 Marie Germain indicated several months later that since our interview this state of affairs had changed, with a greater number of cinemas offering films with audio-descriptions and lending the necessary equipment.

11 This section is based on findings developed in Revillard (2019c).

12 Accessibility is nevertheless far from perfect, including in specialized institutions. In 2002, 387,600 people residing in institutions declared difficulties of accessibility in their housing (Roussel 2002: 23).

13 See Michel Dobry's criticisms of the findings of James Davies (Davies 1962; Dobry 2009).
14 When she filed her request, the city hall employee responded that she did not have the right because, since she was provided with a remote alarm, she was assumed not to use public transportation.
15 Nadine Trappier, mobility impairment, 61.
16 Dora Moleiro, visual impairment, 47.
17 This concept of 'territories of the self' in Goffman's work can be related to our perspective inspired by legal consciousness studies. Indeed, Goffman's reflection takes as a starting point the concept of claim, which can be likened to how rights are defined in legal consciousness studies, as what one claims to be entitled to: 'At the centre of social organisation is the concept of claims, and around this centre, properly, the student must consider the vicissitudes of maintaining them' (Goffman 1971: 28).
18 Goffman lists a total of eight territories of the self, of which we only include here those whose violations were reported in the interviews (Goffman 1971).
19 These cards have been replaced by a 'mobility inclusion' card since the time of this fieldwork.
20 The expression is reminiscent of Fabrizio Cantelli's analysis in terms of the comfort or discomfort of patients in the realization of their rights (Cantelli 2015).

Chapter 6

1 The profile of the people we met did not allow us to document the equally essential link with ethno-racial inequalities.
2 Explanatory memorandum to the Law of 11 February 2005.
3 According to the way Erving Goffman (Goffman 1971: 40–41) or James Scott (Scott 1991), for example, analyse individual capacities for 'secondary adaptations' (according to Goffman) or 'resistance' (according to Scott) in constrained environments.

Appendix 1

1 Nicolas Berthelot, Hugues Bonnefon, Pauline Detuncq, Marion Goffart, Sonia Planson, Jean-Simon Salvage, and Vincent Tomas transcribed the interviews, funded by LIEPP. I performed the analyses alone.

References

Abberley, Paul. 1987. 'The Concept of Oppression and the Development of a Social Theory of Disability'. *Disability, Handicap and Society* 2 (1): 5–19.

Abberley, Paul. 2002. 'Work, Disability, Disabled People and European Social Theory'. In *Disability Studies Today*, edited by Colin Barnes, Mike Oliver, and Len Barton, 120–138. Cambridge: Polity Press.

Abdelnour, Sarah, and Anne Lambert. 2014. '"L'entreprise de Soi", Un Nouveau Mode de Gestion Politique Des Classes Populaires? Analyse Croisée de l'accession à La Propriété et de l'auto-Emploi (1977–2012)'. *Genèses* 95: 27–48.

Ameri, Mason, Lisa Schur, Meera Adya, F. Scott Bentley, Patrick McKay, and Douglas Kruse. 2018. 'The Disability Employment Puzzle: A Field Experiment on Employer Hiring Behavior'. *ILR Review* 71 (2): 329–364.

Barhoumi, Mériam, and Léa Chabanon. 2015. *Emploi et Chômage Des Personnes Handicapées*. Paris: DARES Synthèse Stat.

Barral, Catherine. 2007. 'Disabled Persons' Associations in France'. *Scandinavian Journal of Disability Research* 9 (3–4): 214–236.

Barrault, Lorenzo. 2014. 'Jouer Avec l'instrument. Les Usages Institutionnels et Sociaux de La Carte Scolaire'. In *L'instrumentation de l'action Publique*, edited by Charlotte Halpern, Pierre Lascoumes, and Patrick Le Galès, 397–416. Paris: Presses de Sciences Po.

Bas, Jérôme. 2017. 'Des Paralysés Étudiants Aux Handicapés Méchants. La Contribution Des Mouvements Contestataires à l'unité de La Catégorie de Handicap'. *Genèses* 107: 56–81.

Baudot, Pierre-Yves. 2015. 'La Donnée et Le Système. Comment Socialiser Un Instrument d'action Publique? Le Cas Du Système d'information Partagé-Personnes Handicapées (2006–2014)'. *Gouvernement et Action Publique* 4 (2): 25–56.

Baudot, Pierre-Yves. 2018. 'Layering Rights: The Case of Disability Policies in France (2006–2016)'. *Social Policy and Society* 17 (1): 117–131.

Baudot, Pierre-Yves, and Anne Revillard. 2014. 'L'autonomie de l'équilibriste. Contribution à Une Sociologie de La Production Institutionnelle Des Droits'. *Gouvernement et Action Publique* 3 (4): 83–113.

Baudot, Pierre-Yves, and Anne Revillard. 2015. 'Une Sociologie de l'Etat Par Les Droits'. In *L'Etat Des Droits. Politique Des Droits et Pratiques Des Institutions*, edited by Pierre-Yves Baudot and Anne Revillard, 11–58. Paris: Presses de Sciences Po/Gouvernances.

Baudot, Pierre-Yves, and Anne Revillard. 2016. 'Faire Campagne sans Prendre Parti: Opportunités et Contraintes Des Campagnes Électorales Pour Les Associations de Personnes Handicapées'. In *Le Lobbying Électoral. Groupes En Campagne Dans l'élection Présidentielle de 2012*, edited by Guillaume Courty and Julie Gervais, 77–102. Lille: Presses du Septentrion/ 'Espaces politiques'.

Baudot, Pierre-Yves, Nicolas Duvoux, Aude Lejeune, Gwenaëlle Perrier, and Anne Revillard. 2013. *Les MDPH: Un Guichet Unique à Entrées Multiples*. Paris: MiRe-DREES/CNSA.

Beadle Brown, Julie, Mario Biggeri, Rune Halvorsen, Bjorn Hvinden, Jan Tossebro, and Anne Waldschmidt, eds. 2018. *Lived Experiences of Persons with Disabilities: Active Citizenship and Disability in Europe Volume 2*. London: Routledge.

Becker, Howard S. 1977. 'The Life History and the Scientific Mosaic'. In *Sociological Work*, edited by Howard S. Becker, 63–73. New Brunswick: Transaction.

Bellemare, Charles, Marion Goussé, Guy Lacroix, and Steeve Marchand. 2017. 'Physical Disability and Labor Market Discrimination: Evidence from a Field Experiment'. *Cahier de Recherche de La Chaire de Recherche Industrielle Alliance Sur Les Enjeux Économiques Des Changements Démographiques* 17 (3): 1–23.

Bereni, Laure. 2009. '"Faire de La Diversité Une Richesse Pour l'entreprise". La Transformation d'une Contrainte Juridique En Catégorie Managériale'. *Raisons Politiques* 35: 87–106.

Bereni, Laure. 2015. *La Bataille de La Parité. Mobilisations Pour La Féminisation Du Pouvoir*. Paris: Economica/Etudes politiques.

Bereni, Laure. 2018. *Aux Frontières de La Raison Des Affaires. Le Management de La Diversité à New York et à Paris*. Original manuscript prepared for the accreditation to supervise research, Université Paris Nanterre.

Bertaux, Daniel. 2016. *Les Récits de Vie*. Paris: Nathan - 128.

Bertrand, Louis, Vincent Caradec, and Jean-Sébastien Eideliman. 2014. 'Devenir Travailleur Handicapé. Enjeux Individuels, Frontières Institutionnelles'. *Sociologie* 5 (2): 121–138.

Bette, Peggy. 2006. 'Reclasser Les Victimes de La Première Guerre Mondiale: Le Cas de La Loi Du 30 Janvier 1923 Sur Les Emplois Réservés En France (1923–1939)'. *AMNIS* 6: 1–10.

Beyrie, Adeline. 2015. *Vivre Avec Le Handicap. L'expérience de l'incapacité Motrice Majeure*. Rennes: Presses Universitaires de Rennes/Le Sens social.

Bezès, Philippe. 2009. *Réinventer l'Etat. Les Réformes de l'administration Française (1962–2008)*. Paris: PUF/Le lien social.

Blanc, Alain. 1999. *Les Handicapés Au Travail: Analyse Sociologique d'un Dispositif d'insertion Professionnelle*. Paris: Dunod.

Blatgé, Marion. 2012. *Apprendre La Déficience Visuelle*. Grenoble: Presses universitaires de Grenoble.

Borelle, Céline. 2015. 'Qualifier Des Cas, Produire Concrètement Des Droits. Le Cas Du Handicap'. In *L'Etat Des Droits. Politique Des Droits et Pratiques Des Institutions*, edited by Pierre-Yves Baudot and Anne Revillard, 211–244. Paris: Presses de Sciences Po/Gouvernances.

Bouchet, Célia. 2019. 'Handicaps et Inégalités Professionnelles En France: Des Disparités Qui Se Creusent Au Fil Des Parcours de Vie'. *LIEPP Working Paper No 84*. https://hal-sciencespo.archives-ouvertes.fr/hal-03457316

Boudinet, Mathéa. 2019. *Intégrer Par Le Travail: Les ESAT Dans Les Politiques de l'emploi Des Personnes Handicapées*. Paris: Mémoire de Master 2 en sociologie, Sciences Po.

Bureau, Marie-Christine, and Barbara Rist. 2011. 'Professionnels, Associatifs et Personnes Handicapées Réunis Autour de La Table: Un Droit En Train de Se Faire?' In *Reconfigurations de l'Etat Social En Pratique*, edited by Marie-Christine Bureau and Ivan Sainsaulieu, 119–132. Villeneuve d'Ascq: Presses Universitaire du Septentrion.

Burke, Thomas F. 2002. *Lawyers, Lawsuits, and Legal Rights. The Battle over Litigation in American Society*. Berkeley: University of California Press.

Buton, François. 2009. *L'administration Des Faveurs: L'État, Les Sourds et Les Aveugles (1789–1885)*. Rennes: Presses universitaires de Rennes.

Campion, Claire-Lise. 2013. *Réussir 2015: Accessibilité Des Personnes Handicapées Aux Logements, Aux Établissements Recevant Du Public, Aux Transports, à La Voirie et Aux Espaces Publics*. Paris: Sénat.

Cantelli, Fabrizio. 2015. 'Comment Faire Exister Les Droits Du Patient?' In *L'Etat Des Droits. Politique Des Droits et Pratiques Des Institutions*, edited by Pierre-Yves Baudot and Anne Revillard, 149–175. Paris: Presses de Sciences Po/Gouvernances.

Castel, Robert. 1995. *Les Métamorphoses de La Question Sociale. Une Chronique Du Salariat*. Paris: Fayard.

CGEDD, IGAS, and CGEFi. 2011. *Rapport Sur Les Modalités d'application Des Règles d'accessibilité Du Cadre Bâti Pour Les Personnes Handicapées*. Paris: IGAS.

Chappe, Vincent-Arnaud. 2011. 'Le Cadrage Juridique, Une Ressource Politique? La Création de La HALDE Comme Solution Au Problème de l'effectivité Des Normes Anti-Discrimination. (1998–2005)'. *Politix* 94: 107–130.

Chauvière, Michel. 2009. *Enfance Inadaptée. L'héritage de Vichy*. Paris: L'Harmattan.

Chevallier, Jacques. 2011. 'De l'administration Démocratique à La Démocratie Administrative'. *Revue Française d'administration Publique* 137–138: 217–227.

CNSA. 2014. *Document de Restitution 2014 Des Données d'activité et de Fonctionnement Validées Des Départements. Mise En Perspective Des Données Départementales Avec Le Niveau National.* Paris: CNSA.

Condon, Stéphanie, Marylène Lieber, and Florence Maillochon. 2005. 'Insécurité Dans Les Espaces Publics: Comprendre Les Peurs Féminines'. *Revue Française de Sociologie* 46 (2): 265–294.

Coutu, Michel. 1995. *Max Weber et Les Rationalités Du Droit.* Paris: LGDJ-Droit et société.

Cret, Benoît, Magali Robelet, and Guillaume Jaubert. 2013. 'La (Dé) Construction Politique Des Associations Gestionnaires d'établissements'. *Terrains & Travaux* 23: 39–58.

Davies, James C. 1962. 'Toward a Theory of Revolution'. *American Sociological Review* 27 (1): 5–19.

Dayan, Daniel. 1992. 'Les Mystères de La Réception'. *Le Débat* 71: 141–157.

Défenseur des droits. 2015. *2005–2015: Dix Ans d'actions Pour La Défense Des Droits Des Personnes Handicapées.* Paris: Défenseur des droits.

DeJong, Gerben. 1979. 'Independent Living: From Social Movement to Analytic Paradigm'. *Archives of Physical Medicine and Rehabilitation* 60: 435–446.

Dejoux, Virginie. 2010. *Situations de Handicap Lors de Déplacements: Caractéristiques Individuelles, Pratiques de Mobilité, Environnement Physique et Social.* Université Paris 1: Thèse de doctorat en démographie.

Dejoux, Virginie. 2015. 'Les Difficultés d'accès à l'environnement. Un Frein Lors de La Transition Vers l'âge Adulte Des Jeunes Reconnus "handicapés"'. *Agora Débats/Jeunesses* 71: 69–82.

Delphy, Christine. 1998. *L'ennemi Principal. t.1: Economie Politique Du Patriarcat.* Paris: Syllepse, coll. Nouvelles questions féministes.

Diatkine, Daniel. 2016. 'Les Ambiguïtés Du Droit Au Travail: Les Débats de 1848'. *L'Economie Politique* 71: 56–64.

Dobry, Michel. 2009. *Sociologie Des Crises Politiques. La Dynamique Des Mobilisations Multisectorielles.* Paris: Presses de Sciences Po.

Douglas, Mary. 1966. *Purity and Danger: An Analysis of Concepts of Pollution and Taboo.* London: Routledge.

Doytcheva, Milena. 2009. 'Réinterprétations et Usages Sélectifs de La Diversité Dans Les Politiques Des Entreprises'. *Raisons Politiques* 35: 107–124.

Dubois, Vincent. 2009. 'Le Paradoxe Du Contrôleur. Incertitude et Contrainte Institutionnelle Dans Le Contrôle Des Assistés Sociaux'. *Actes de La Recherche En Sciences Sociales* 178: 28–49.

Dubois, Vincent. 2010. *The Bureaucrat and the Poor: Encounters in French Welfare Offices*. Farnham: Ashgate.

Dupont, Hugo. 2015. 'La Loi de 2005 et l'accessibilité Scolaire: Une Certaine Ambiguïté'. In *Accessibilité et Handicap*, edited by Joël Zaffran, 235–250. Grenoble: PUG/Coll. Handicap vieillissement société.

Dupont, Hugo. 2016. *Ni Fou, Ni Gogol! Orientation et Vie En ITEP*. Grenoble: PUG/Coll. Handicap vieillissement société.

Duran, Patrice. 2009. *Penser l'action Publique*. Paris: LGDJ-Droit et société.

Duvoux, Nicolas. 2015. *Les Oubliés Du Rêve Américain: Philanthropie, Etat et Pauvreté Urbaine Aux Etats-Unis*. Paris: PUF/Le lien social.

Ebersold, Serge. 2014. 'Orchestration de l'accessibilité, Handicap et Enseignement Supérieur'. In *Les Processus Discriminatoires Des Politiques Du Handicap*, edited by Patrick Legros, 147–166. Grenoble: Presses universitaires de Grenoble.

Ebersold, Serge, and Philippe Cordazzo. 2015. 'Passage à l'âge Adulte, Handicap et Configurations Inclusives'. *Agora Débats/Jeunesses* 71: 55–67.

Engel, David M., and Frank W. Munger. 2003. *Rights of Inclusion: Law and Identity in the Life Stories of Americans with Disabilities*. Chicago: University of Chicago Press.

Esping-Andersen, Gøsta. 1990. *The Three Worlds of Welfare Capitalism*. Princeton: Princeton University Press.

Ewald, François. 1986. *L'Etat Providence*. Paris: Grasset.

Ewick, Patricia, and Susan Silbey. 1995. 'Subversive Stories and Hegemonic Tales: Toward a Sociology of Narrative'. *Law and Society Review* 29 (2): 197–226.

Ewick, Patricia, and Susan S. Silbey. 1998. *The Common Place of Law: Stories from Everyday Life*. Chicago: University of Chicago Press.

Felstiner, William, Richard L. Abel, and Austin Sarat. 1980. 'The Emergence and Transformation of Disputes: Naming, Blaming, Claiming'. *Law and Society Review* 15 (3/4): 631–654.

Fine, Michael, and Caroline Glendinning. 2005. 'Dependence, Independence or Inter-Dependence? Revisiting the Concepts of "Care" and "Dependency"'. *Ageing and Society* 25 (4): 601–621.

Fleischer, Doris Z., and Frieda Zames. 2011. *The Disability Rights Movement: From Charity to Confrontation*. Philadelphia: Temple University Press.

Fleury-Steiner, Benjamin, and Laura Beth Nielsen, eds. 2006. *The New Civil Rights Research: A Constitutive Approach*. Aldershot: Ashgate.

Flynn, Eilionóir. 2011. *From Rhetoric to Action: Implementing the UN Convention on the Rights of Persons with Disabilities*. Cambridge: Cambridge University Press.

Fraser, Nancy. 1995. 'From Redistribution to Recognition? Dilemmas of Justice in a "post-Socialist" Age'. *New Left Review* 212: 68–93.

Frederick, Angela. 2017. 'Risky Mothers and the Normalcy Project: Women with Disabilities Negotiate Scientific Motherhood'. *Gender and Society* 31 (1): 74–95.

Garland-Thomson, Rosemarie. 2009. *Staring: How We Look*. Oxford: Oxford University Press.

Glaser, Barney G., and Anselm L. Strauss. 1967. *The Discovery of Grounded Theory: Strategies for Qualitative Research*. Chicago: Aldine.

Goffman, Erving. 1961. *Asylums: Essays on the Social Situation of Mental Patients and Other Inmates*. New York: Anchor Books.

Goffman, Erving. 1963. *Stigma: Notes on the Management of Spoiled Identity*. New York: Simon & Schuster.

Goffman, Erving. 1971. *Relations in Public: Micro Studies of the Public Order*. London: Penguin.

Guiraudon, Virginie. 2003. 'Construire Une Politique Européenne de Lutte Contre Les Discriminations: L'histoire de La Directive "Race"'. *Sociétés Contemporaines* 53 (1): 11–32.

Gurr, Ted. 1970. *Why Men Rebel*. Princeton: Princeton University Press.

Hafner-Burton, Emilie M. 2005. 'Human Rights in a Globalizing World: The Paradox of Empty Promises'. *American Journal of Sociology* 110 (5): 1373–1411.

Haglund, LaDawn, and Robin Stryker, eds. 2015. *Closing the Rights Gap: From Human Rights to Social Transformation*. Oakland: University of California Press.

Hall, Stuart. 1973. *Encoding and Decoding in the Television Discourse*. Birmingham: Discussion paper, University of Birmingham.

Halvorsen, Rune, Bjorn Hvinden, Jerome Bichenbach, Delia Ferri, and Ana Marta Guillén Rodriguez, eds. 2017. *The Changing Disability Policy System: Active Citizenship and Disability in Europe Volume 1*. London: Routledge.

Herbin, Régis. 2014. 'Les Savoirs de l'aménagement et de l'urbanisme'. In *Handicap, Une Encyclopédie Des Savoirs. Des Obscurantismes à de Nouvelles Lumières*, edited by Carles Gardou, 23–41. Toulouse: Erès.

Heyer, Katharina. 2005. 'Rights or Quotas? The ADA as a Model for Disability Rights'. In *Handbook of Employment Discrimination Research*, edited by Laura Beth Nielsen and Robert L. Nelson, 237–257. Dordrecht: Springer.

Heyer, Katharina. 2015. *Rights Enabled: The Disability Revolution, from the US, to Germany and Japan, to the United Nations*. Ann Arbor: University of Michigan Press.

Honneth, Axel. 1995. *The Struggle for Recognition: The Moral Grammar of Social Conflicts*. Cambridge, MA: MIT Press.

Hunt, Alan. 1993. *Explorations in Law and Society: Towards a Constitutive Theory of Law*. New York: Routledge.

Jenkins, Richard. 1991. 'Disability and Social Stratification'. *British Journal of Sociology* 42 (4): 557–580.

Joly, Laurène. 2015. *L'emploi Des Personnes Handicapées Entre Discrimination et Égalité*. Paris: Dalloz/Nouvelle bibliothèque des thèses.

Kergoat, Danièle. 2000. 'Division Sexuelle Du Travail et Rapports Sociaux de Sexe'. In *Dictionnaire Critique Du Féminisme*, edited by Helena Hirata, Françoise Laborie, Hélène Le Doaré, and Danièle Senotier, 35–44. Paris: PUF.

Lamont, Michèle, Graziella Moraes Silva, Jessica Welburn, Joshua Guetzkow, Nissim Mizrachi, Hanna Herzog, and Elisa Reis. 2016. *Getting Respect: Responding to Stigma and Discrimination in the United States, Brazil, and Israel*. Princeton: Princeton University Press.

Larrouy, Muriel. 2011. *L'invention de l'accessibilité. Des Politiques de Transports Des Personnes Handicapées Aux Politiques d'accessibilité de 1975 à 2005*. Grenoble: PUG/Coll. Handicap vieillissement société.

Lascoumes, Pierre, and Patrick Le Galès, eds. 2005. *Gouverner Par Les Instruments*. Paris: Presses de la FNSP.

Lawson, Anna, and Mark Priestley. 2013. 'Potential, Principle and Pragmatism in Concurrent Multinational Monitoring: Disability Rights in the European Union'. *The International Journal of Human Rights* 17 (7–8): 739–757.

Lebeer, Guy, and Jacques Moriau, eds. 2010. *(Se) Gouverner. Entre Souci de Soi et Action Publique*. Brussels: PIE Peter Lang.

Lejeune, Aude, ed. 2017. *Handicap et Aménagements Raisonnables Au Travail. Importation et Usages d'une Catégorie Juridique En France et En Belgique*. Paris: Rapport de recherche pour la Mission de recherche Droit et Justice.

Le Laidier, Sylvie, and Patricia Prouchandy. 2016. 'Pour La Première Fois, Un Regard Sur Les Parcours à l'école Primaire Des Élèves En Situation de Handicap'. *Note d'information (DEPP)* 26: 1–8.

Lieber, Marylène. 2008. *Genre, Violences et Espaces Publics. La Vulnérabilité Des Femmes En Question*. Paris: Presses de Sciences Po.

Lipsky, Michael. 1980. *Street-Level Bureaucracy: Dilemmas of the Individual in Public Services*. New York: Russell Sage Foundation.

Lister, Ruth. 1997. *Citizenship: Feminist Perspectives*. Basingstoke: Macmillan.

Lovell, George. 2012. *This Is Not Civil Rights: Discovering Rights Talk in 1939 America*. Chicago: University of Chicago Press.

Malacrida, Claudia. 2007. 'Negotiating the Dependency/Nurturance Tightrope: Dilemmas of Motherhood and Disability'. *Canadian Review of Sociology* 44 (4): 469–493.

Malhotra, Ravi, and Morgan Rowe. 2014. *Exploring Disability Identity and Disability Rights through Narratives: Finding a Voice of Their Own*. London: Routledge.

Marshall, Thomas H. 1950. *Citizenship and Social Class*. Cambridge: Cambridge University Press.

Mazereau, Philippe. 2015. 'Inclusion Scolaire et Action Publique, Entre Contradictions et Inachèvement'. *Vie Sociale* 3 (11): 113–125.

McCann, Michael. 2006. *Law and Social Movements*. Aldershot: Ashgate.

Méda, Dominique. 2010. *Le Travail. Une Valeur En Voie de Disparition?* Paris: Flammarion / Champs.

Mesnel, Blandine. 2017. 'Les Agriculteurs Face à La Paperasse. Policy Feedbacks et Bureaucratisation de La Politique Agricole'. *Gouvernement et Action Publique* 1 (1): 33–60.

Minow, Martha. 1987. 'Interpreting Rights: An Essay for Robert Cover'. *The Yale Law Journal* 96 (8): 1860–1915.

Minow, Martha. 1990. *Making All the Difference: Inclusion, Exclusion, and American Law*. Ithaca, NY: Cornell University Press.

Mor, Sagit. 2018. 'With Access and Justice for All'. *Cardozo Law Review* 39: 611–647.

Morris, Jenny. 1991. *Pride against Prejudice: A Personal Politics of Disability*. London: The Women's Press Ltd.

Morris, Jenny. 1993. 'Feminism and Disability'. *Feminist Review* 43: 57–70.

Naples, Nancy A. 1998. 'Bringing Everyday Life to Policy Analysis: The Case of White Rural Women Negotiating College and Welfare'. *Journal of Poverty* 2 (1): 23–53.

Oliver, Michael. 1990. *The Politics of Disablement*. Basingstoke: Macmillan.

Oliver, Michael, and Colin Barnes. 2012. *The New Politics of Disablement*. London: Palgrave Macmillan.

Omnès, Catherine. 2015. 'La Réinsertion Professionnelle Des Pensionnés de Guerre En France: La Loi Du 26 Avril 1924. Un Legs de La Première Guerre Mondiale?' *Revue d'histoire de La Protection Sociale* 8: 167–181.

Orloff, Ann Shola. 1993. 'Gender and the Social Rights of Citizenship: The Comparative Analysis of Gender Relations and Welfare States'. *American Sociological Review* 58 (3): 303–328.

Perrier, Gwenaëlle. 2013. '"Mettre l'usager Au Cœur Du Dispositif"? Regards Croisés Sur Quatre Maisons Départementales Des Personnes Handicapées'. *Terrains & Travaux* 23: 93–112.

Peters, Susan J. 2007. '"Education for All?": A Historical Analysis of International Inclusive Education Policy and Individuals with Disabilities'. *Journal of Disability Policy Studies* 18 (2): 98–108.

Pierson, Paul. 1993. 'When Effect Becomes Cause: Policy Feedback and Political Change'. *World Politics* 45 (4): 595–628.

Pinto, Paula Campos. 2011. 'Monitoring Human Rights: A Holistic Approach'. In *Critical Perspectives on Human Rights and Disability Law*, edited by Lee Ann Basser, Marcia Rioux, and Melinda Jones, 451–478. Leiden: Brill.

Pitkin, Hanna Fenichel. 1967. *The Concept of Representation*. Berkeley: University of California Press.

Plaisance, Eric. 2009. *Autrement Capables. École, Emploi, Société: Pour l'inclusion Des Personnes Handicapées*. Paris: Autrement.

Priestley, Mark. 2003. *Disability: A Life Course Approach*. Cambridge: Polity Press.

Rapegno, Noémie. 2014. *Etablissements d'hébergement Pour Adultes Handicapés En France: Enjeux Territoriaux et Impacts Sur La Participation Sociale Des Usagers*. Paris: Thèse de doctorat en géographie, EHESS.

Ravaud, Jean-François. 1995. 'La Scolarisation Des Enfants Handicapés'. In *Les Personnes Handicapées En France: Données Sociales*, edited by Annie Triomphe, 81–126. Paris: Editions du CTNERHI.

Ravaud, Jean-François, and Patrick Fougeyrollas. 2005. 'Le Concept de Handicap et Les Classifications Internationales: La Convergence Progressive Des Positions Franco-Québécoises'. *Santé, Société et Solidarité* 2: 13–27.

Ravaud, Jean-François, Béatrice Madiot, and Isabelle Ville. 1992. 'Discrimination towards Disabled People Seeking Employment'. *Social Science & Medicine* 35 (8): 951–958.

Revillard, Anne. 2017a. 'Analyzing the Reception of Disability Policies: The Contribution of Biographical Interviews'. *Revue Francaise de Sociologie* 58 (1): 71–95.

Revillard, Anne. 2017b. 'Social Movements and the Politics of Bureaucratic Rights Enforcement: Insights from the Allocation of Disability Rights in France'. *Law and Social Inquiry* 42: 450–478.

Revillard, Anne. 2018. 'Saisir Les Conséquences d'une Politique à Partir de Ses Ressortissants: La Réception de l'action Publique'. *Revue Francaise de Science Politique* 68 (3): 469–492.

Revillard, Anne. 2019a. *Handicap et Travail*. Paris: Presses de Sciences Po/ Sécuriser l'Emploi.

Revillard, Anne. 2019b. 'L'expérience Sociale Du Handicap'. *OSC Papers* 2. https://sciencespo.hal.science/view/index/identifiant/hal-03456065

Revillard, Anne. 2019c. 'Realizing the Right to Access in France: Between Implementation and Activation'. *Law and Society Review* 53 (4): 950–982.

Revillard, Anne. 2022. 'Disabled People Working in the Disability Sector: Occupational Segregation or Personal Fulfilment?' *Work, Employment & Society* 36 (5): 875–892.

Ridgeway, Cecilia. 2014. 'Why Status Matters for Inequality'. *American Sociological Review* 79 (1): 1–16.

Romien, Pierre. 2005. 'À l'origine de La Réinsertion Professionnelle Des Personnes Handicapées: La Prise En Charge Des Invalides de Guerre'. *Revue Française Des Affaires Sociales* 2: 229–247.

Roulstone, Alan. 2012. 'Disabled People, Work and Employment: A Global Perspective'. In *Routledge Handbook of Disability Studies*, edited by Nick Watson, Alan Roulstone, and Carol Thomas, 211–224. New York: Routledge.

Roussel, Pascale. 2002. *La Compensation Des Incapacités Au Travers de l'enquête Handicap-Incapacités-Dépendance de l'INSEE*. Paris: CTNERHI.

Rustin, Michael. 2006. 'Réflexions Sur Le Tournant Biographique Dans Les Sciences Sociales'. In *La Société Biographique: Une Injonction à Vivre Dignement*, edited by Isabelle Astier and Nicolas Duvoux, 33–53. Paris: L'Harmattan/Logiques sociales.

Sarat, Austin. 1990. ' "The Law Is All Over": Power, Resistance and the Legal Consciousness of the Welfare Poor'. *Yale Journal of Law & the Humanities* 2 (2): 343–379.

Scheingold, Stuart A. 1974. *The Politics of Rights: Lawyers, Public Policy, and Political Change*. New Haven: Yale University Press.

Schneider, Anne L., and Helen M. Ingram. 1997. *Policy Design for Democracy*. Lawrence: University Press of Kansas.

Scott, James. 1991. *Domination and the Arts of Resistance: Hidden Transcripts*. New Haven: Yale University Press.

Segon, Michaël, and Nathalie Le Roux. 2013. 'Parcours de Formation et d'accès à l'emploi Des Anciens Étudiants Handicapés: Recours Aux Dispositifs et Dynamiques Identitaires'. *Agora Débats/Jeunesses* 65: 77–92.

Sen, Amartya. 2004. 'Elements of a Theory of Human Rights'. *Philosophy and Public Affairs* 32 (4): 315–356.

Shah, Sonali. 2007. 'Special or Mainstream? The Views of Disabled Students'. *Research Papers in Education* 22 (4): 425–442.

Shah, Sonali, and Mark Priestley. 2011. *Disability and Social Change: Private Lives and Public Policies*. Bristol: Policy Press.

Shakespeare, Tom. 2013. *Disability Rights and Wrongs Revisited*. London: Routledge.

Shandra, Carrie L. 2018. 'Disability as Inequality: Social Disparities, Health Disparities, and Participation in Daily Activities'. *Social Forces* 97 (1): 157–192.

Shapiro, Joseph. 1993. *No Pity: People with Disabilities Forging a New Civil Rights Movement*. New York: Times Books.

Spire, Alexis. 2011. 'La Domestication de l'impôt Par Les Classes Dominantes'. *Actes de La Recherche En Sciences Sociales* 190: 58–71.

Stiker, Henri-Jacques. 2013. *Corps Infirmes et Sociétés*. Paris: Dunod.

Strauss, Anselm, and Juliet Corbin. 2003. 'L'analyse de Données Selon La Grounded Theory. Procédures de Codage et Critères d'évaluation'. In *L'enquête de Terrain*, edited by Daniel Cefaï, 363–379. Paris: La Découverte.

Stryker, Robin. 2003. 'Mind the Gap: Law, Institutional Analysis and Socioeconomics'. *Socio-Economic Review* 1: 335–367.

Stryker, Robin. 2007. 'Half Empty, Half Full or Neither? Law, Inequality and Social Change'. *Annual Review of Law & Social Science* 3: 69–97.

UNESCO. 1994. *Déclaration de Salamanque et Cadre d'action Pour l'éducation et Les Besoins Spéciaux*. Salamanca: UNESCO.

Vanhala, Lisa. 2011. *Making Rights a Reality? Disability Rights Activists and Legal Mobilization*. New York: Cambridge University Press.

Vanhala, Lisa. 2015. 'The Diffusion of Disability Rights in Europe'. *Human Rights Quarterly* 37 (4): 831–853.

Velche, Dominique. 2009. 'Les Lois de 1987 et 2005: Une Chance Pour Le Travail Protégé?' In *L'insertion Professionnelle Des Travailleurs Handicapés*, edited by Alain Blanc, 231–281. Grenoble: PUG/Handicap vieillissement société.

Vérétout, Antoine. 2015. 'Etre En Situation de Handicap et Diplômé de l'enseignement Supérieur'. In *Accessibilité et Handicap*, edited by Joël Zaffran, 249–273. Grenoble: PUG/Coll. Handicap vieillissement société.

Ville, Isabelle. 2008. *Le Handicap Comme Épreuve de Soi. Politiques Sociales, Pratiques Institutionnelles et Expérience*. Original manuscript prepared for the accreditation to supervise research, Université de Rennes 2.

Ville, Isabelle. 2010. 'From Inaptitude for Work to Trial of the Self: The Vicissitudes of Meanings of Disability'. *ALTER: European Journal of Disability Research* 4 (1): 59–71.

Ville, Isabelle, and Myriam Winance. 2006. 'To Work or Not to Work? The Occupational Trajectories of Wheelchair Users'. *Disability and Rehabilitation* 28 (7): 423–436.

Ville, Isabelle, Jean-François Ravaud, and Emmanuelle Fillion. 2014. *Introduction à La Sociologie Du Handicap*. Louvain-la-Neuve: De Boeck Supérieur/Ouvertures politiques.

Waddington, Lisa. 1994. 'Legislating to Employ People with Disabilities: The European and American Way'. *Maastricht Journal of European and Comparative Law* 1 (4): 367–395.

Waddington, Lisa, and Andrea Broderick. 2020. *The Post-2020 European Disability Strategy*. Brussels: European Parliament.

Wajcman, Judy. 1996. 'The Domestic Basis for the Managerial Career'. *Sociological Review* 44 (4): 609–629.

Waldschmidt, Anne. 2009. 'Disability Policy of the European Union: The Supranational Level'. *ALTER: European Journal of Disability Research* 3 (1): 8–23.

Wang, Simeng. 2013. '"Handicapé? C'est Insulter Ma Descendance et Aussi Mes Ancêtres!". Négociations Autour de l'inscription de l'enfant d'origine Chinoise à La MDPH'. *Terrains & Travaux* 23: 77–92.

Warin, Philippe. 1998. *La Réception Des Politiques Par Les Destinataires. Esquisse d'une Approche Des Relations Entre Action Publique et Lien Politique.* Grenoble: Note de synthèse pour l'Habilitation à diriger des recherches en science politique.

Warin, Philippe. 1999. 'Les "Ressortissants" Dans Les Analyses Des Politiques Publiques'. *Revue Française de Science Politique* 49 (1): 103–121.

Warin, Philippe. 2016. *Le Non-Recours Aux Politiques Sociales.* Grenoble: PUG/Libre Cours Politiques.

Weygand, Zina. 2003. *Vivre sans Voir. Les Aveugles Dans La Société Française Du Moyen-Age Au Siècle de Louis Braille.* Paris: Créaphis.

WHO. 2011. *World Report on Disability.* Malta: World Health Organization and World Bank.

Winance, Myriam. 2007. 'Du Malaise Au "faire Corps": Le Processus d'ajustement'. *Communications* 81 (1): 31–45.

Zaffran, Joël. 2007. *L'intégration Scolaire Des Handicapés.* Paris: L'Harmattan/Technologie de l'action sociale.

Zaffran, Joël. 2015. 'Être Élève Handicapé à l'école Ordinaire: L'épreuve Biographique de l'inclusion Scolaire'. *Le Sujet Dans La Cité* 2 (6): 71–80.

Index

References to figures appear in *italic* type; those in **bold** type refer to tables.

Printed and bound by CPI Group (UK) Ltd, Croydon, CR0 4YY

15/09/2026

14962385-0004